D0651732

Objection

Disgust, Morality, and the Law

DEBRA LIEBERMAN

AND

CARLTON PATRICK

OXFORD
UNIVERSITY PRESS

Oxford University Press is a department of the University of Oxford. It furthers
the University's objective of excellence in research, scholarship, and education
by publishing worldwide. Oxford is a registered trade mark of Oxford University
Press in the UK and certain other countries.

Published in the United States of America by Oxford University Press
198 Madison Avenue, New York, NY 10016, United States of America.

© Oxford University Press 2018

Library of Congress Cataloging-in-Publication Data
Names: Lieberman, Debra (Professor of psychology), author. | Patrick, Carlton, author.
Title: Objection : disgust, morality, and the law / Debra Lieberman and Carlton Patrick.
Description: New York, NY : Oxford University Press, 2018.
Identifiers: LCCN 2018008292 | ISBN 9780190491291 (hardback) |
ISBN 9780190491314 (epub)
Subjects: LCSH: Aversion. | Ethics. | Law and ethics. | Criminal behavior. |
Law—Psychological aspects. | BISAC: PSYCHOLOGY / Forensic Psychology. |
PSYCHOLOGY / Social Psychology. | LAW / Ethics & Professional Responsibility.
Classification: LCC BF575.A886 L54 2018 | DDC 150—dc23
LC record available at https://lccn.loc.gov/2018008292

9 8 7 6 5 4 3 2 1

Printed by Sheridan Books, Inc., United States of America

For William & West
—D. L.

For Jenny & Remy
—C. P.

CONTENTS

What's captivating about disgust is its power. Like lust, jealousy, or anger, it rises up, takes the reins, and takes over. Then we—of a species that prides itself on its capacity for reason—are for a time fully ruled by an emotion so wide, so muscular, and so futile to resist that it leaves reason little room.

Disgust, having risen, defines and narrows our reactions. So we shun or condemn what we find disgusting. And, more than we might care to catalog, disgust then insinuates into our legal system. What is gross to me becomes wrong for you.

This book asks a profound question: How legitimate is that legal logic, that leap from gross to bad? It answers that question with a compelling new tour of disgust's origins, patterns, and implications. The authors—with expertise between them in psychology, evolutionary biology, neuroscience, and law—provide a rich, vivid, and eminently readable theory that is simultaneously sweeping in scope, detailed in particulars, and well grounded in research. I found it a fascinating read—and not just because, after reading the chapter on obscenity, I now know some colorful (and singularly disgusting) insults tossed by Thais, Nigerians, Finns, and the Dutch.

I particularly enjoyed learning how disgust came to have the features it does, why that matters, and why understanding all that can be useful. And it turns out that this book comes just when needed most. For disgust has lately generated significant interest and a thriving scholarly literature from social historians, psychologists, anthropologists, sociologists, neuroscientists, evolutionary biologists, legal scholars, philosophers, moral theorists, ethicists, art theorists, and scholars of comparative literature. Some document and describe. Some characterize and categorize. Others seek to explain, defend, or reject disgust as a basis for "ought" (or "ought not") propositions.

But what's interesting about the study of disgust at this particular moment—across countries, cultures, and eras—is what we can learn from interdisciplinary approaches that simultaneously embrace both the commonalities and the differences in what evokes the disgust response. As one might expect, there are—*naturally*—some important variations among groups in what tangible things and intangible concepts inspire revulsion and social taboos. Yet, at the same time, there are core commonalities so persistent and so pervasive that—coupled with the survival and health advantages provided by the behaviors that tend to follow initial disgust reactions—they suggest that evolutionary processes have been subtly and steadily at work in humans, shaping the patterns in which this exquisite emotion not only reveals itself, but also functions.

Of course, we know of no natural pathway by which humans could instead have been categorically exempt from the evolutionary processes that shape all living organisms, both in their various shapes and forms and in some of their core (and often conditional, algorithmically complex) behavioral predispositions. For this reason, while it was once possible and respectable to study psychology independent of evolutionary biology and neuroscience, those days are past—as is evident from tracing the trajectories, extending from current curricula to research publications, within the major universities. There is no psychology without the brain; there is no brain divorced of biology; and there is no biology divorced of evolution and its processes.

Still, and perhaps most interestingly, our evolved brain tends us toward intensely social societies that amply demonstrate flexibility, sensitivity to social norms, and our extraordinary capacity for self-reflection. For this reason, Lieberman and Patrick, the book's authors, carefully develop and explain a compelling interdisciplinary psychological model of the underlying cognitive architecture and mechanisms of disgust. The model ties together, as complementary and reciprocal, two key components:

1. The evolved superstructure, by which the emotion of disgust provides a shortcut to adaptive actions (such as avoiding pathogens, parasites, and toxins); and
2. The cultural contexts, which can coopt disgust reactions, and even extend them into social, moral, political, and legal domains.

By doing this, Lieberman and Patrick avoid and then transcend the musty, tired, and false dichotomies that would situate emotions and behavioral predispositions within either nature or nurture, each exclusive of the other. For as psychologist Donald O. Hebb famously observed, just as it takes both length and width to create the area of a rectangle, it takes both genes and environment—both nature and nurture—to generate anything interesting in human capabilities.

And it's when attending to these subtleties of interactions that these authors really shine. They systematically raise hypotheses, examine the evidence, and integrate the resulting interdisciplinary insights in a comprehensive way that reaches all the way to the role of disgust in law. What they find is a shared psychological architecture that is well tailored to solving avoidance problems of deep ancestral environments, but that has also been conscripted into service far from its ancestral, individual-protecting home psychological turf. Viewed in this light, that shared psychological history explains many of the dominant patterns by which laypeople, legislators, judges, and others—often across international cultures, and within widespread legal systems—reflect strongly overlapping intuitions about, and proscriptions against, what is disgusting. In a career spanning more than 20 years working at the intersection of law and behavioral sciences, I've rarely encountered a work that bridges these two distinct fields so well.

You'll likely be inspired to wonder, as I did: Just how far should we trust disgust? How comfortable should we be with disgust playing, as it does, an important role in the regulation of sex, pornography, obscenity, and even zoning?

Perhaps you come to that question from the starting position that disgust is indispensable to law, to be harnessed in the pursuit of valuable social ends. Or perhaps you instead see disgust as an irrational influence, more likely to lead to unsupportable and socially harmful outcomes. Either way, you will find within these pages a great deal to learn from, reflect upon, chew over, and debate. For the authors very engagingly argue that despite the psychological architecture of disgust—or perhaps especially because of it—the biasing role disgust plays in legal and political affairs should be critically reexamined and challenged. The natural origins and neurobiological mechanics of this emotion should not be automatically privileged, merely by virtue of its strength and (often) near-ubiquity.

The book makes four major contributions. The first is to a deeper, interdisciplinary understanding of disgust. The second is to further contextualizing—historically and biologically—the variety of core emotions (which are as much a part of our distinctive human brain and evolutionary history as are our thumbs) as these core emotions go about orchestrating and prioritizing our behavioral inclinations. The third contribution is to furthering and sharpening debates over what constitutes the proper relationship between disgust (and other emotions) on one hand, and morality and law, on the other. And the fourth, revealing something even broader and deeper at work in all this, is to demonstrating the extent to which this method of analysis, which I've previously called "evolutionary analysis in law," can not only trace common features among legal systems to common psychological roots, planted in the deep structures of the human brain, but can also add value to our efforts to guide and regulate behaviors, consistent with whatever democratically percolated goals society asks law to further.

Any one of these contributions, alone, provides a landmark. Together they interact and reinforce one another, providing a powerful new view.

Owen D. Jones
New York Alumni Chancellor's Professor of Law &
Professor of Biological Studies, Vanderbilt University
Director, MacArthur Foundation Research
Network on Law and Neuroscience
Nashville, Tennessee

ACKNOWLEDGMENTS

Thank you, first and foremost, to our editor Sarah Harrington and her team at Oxford University Press for taking this project on. We'd also like to pay a special thank you to Wendy Walker for her meticulous copyedits.

We owe a great debt of gratitude to the great many people who made intellectual contributions to this book, but we owe a particular debt, which we would like to recognize upfront, to the folks who took the time to read the manuscript in its entirety and to give us invaluable feedback, including two anonymous reviewers solicited by Oxford, Owen D. Jones (who also provided buoying encouragement and involvement at every stage in the process), and, especially, Joseph Billingsley, who provided numerous read-throughs of the manuscript and countless discussions of the ideas that would eventually become this book. Thank you!

Deb would also like to thank her undergraduate advisors David Sloan Wilson and Eric Dietrich; graduate advisors Leda Cosmides and John Tooby; and the many supportive friends and colleagues, including Howard Benson, Paul Bloom, Jim Davies, Peter DeScioli, Alice Dreger, Elaine Hatfield, Martie Haselton, Steve Gangestad, Doug Kenrick, Kent Kiehl, Rob Kurzban, Mike McCullough, Geoffrey Miller, Steve Neuberg, Steve Pinker, Matt Ridley, Walter Sinnott-Armstrong, Don Symons, Josh Tybur, Richard Wrangham, and the entire UCSB Center for Evolutionary Psychology network.

Carlton would like to thank the many people who took the time to answer his calls and emails with questions, to spitball ideas over coffee or lunch, to provide feedback on presentations, and to read and comment on earlier drafts of chapters, including David Rossman, Mike Guttentag, Rob Kar, Oliver Goodenough, Keelah Williams, Paul Robinson, Martha Farah, Geoffrey Goodwin, Rob Kurzban, and a host of other folks that he will only come to remember after this book has been printed. He would also like to thank the artist Andres Serrano for generously allowing the use of his photograph *Piss Christ*, as well as the various stimulating and supportive institutions where this book was written, which include the Department of Psychology at the University of Miami, the Center for Neuroscience and Society at the University of Pennsylvania, and the best Starbucks that ever was, at 10th and West on South Beach.

We also want thank our families: for Carlton, his mom Kirsten Patrick and dad Steven Patrick, who together—in all senses of the phrase—made the whole thing possible; for Deb, the Lieberman, Charles, Futterman, Whittle, Wisneski, and Pocker clans; and for both, the members of the Evolution and Human Behavior Lab at the University of Miami, Department of Psychology.

Last, but in no way least, neither of us could have completed this project without the love and support of our mates—Jenny and William, we owe you one (OK, maybe two).

Objection

PART I

Introductions

Disgust and the Law

The central character of this book isn't a person or a historical event, but is instead a feature of human psychology. The feature itself—that humans have a tendency to equate "gross" with "wrong"—is not in and of itself news. For the past two decades, researchers have taken a keen interest in disgust and its role in moral psychology, producing scores of books with titles such as *Yuck!, The Anatomy of Disgust, That's Disgusting, The Meaning of Disgust, Savoring Disgust, From Disgust to Humanity*, and *Disgust: Theory and History of a Strong Sensation*. Indeed, in 2012 a *New York Times* commentator wrote that disgust was "having its moment" in the academic spotlight, and yet since that article was written more than 100 *additional* articles about disgust and morality have been published in scholarly journals.

What is becoming clear as of late, however, is just how significant a role disgust plays in coloring human affairs. In the 2016 US presidential election, for example, Donald Trump repeatedly evoked disgust to demonize his opponents, calling Hillary Clinton's bathroom break during a Democratic debate "too disgusting" to talk about, referring to Clinton as a "nasty woman" during a presidential debate, suggesting that Fox News host Megyn Kelly's interrogation of him was connected with "blood coming out of her wherever," displaying revulsion at primary opponent Marco Rubio's sweat, calling the United States a "dumping ground" for the world's problems, and using the word "disgusting" to describe everything from the Iran nuclear deal, to the electoral system, to the press, to windmills, to a lawyer's need to take a break from a deposition so that she could pump breast milk. Trump's deployment of disgust was so overt and so prevalent, in fact, that a number of outlets, including *CNN, The New York Times, Rolling Stone, The New Republic*, and even *Jimmy Kimmel Live!* ran pieces specifically highlighting it.

And precisely because disgust plays such an outsized role in human affairs, the explanations of *why* it does, and *how* it does, matter. This book is about those explanations—about the whys and the hows; *why* disgust has the particular psychological features that it does, *how* our brains go about executing the tasks disgust evolved to accomplish, *why* disgust ends up playing such a prominent role in our moral, political, and legal affairs, and *why* this explanation should matter for lawmakers and those tasked with shaping policy.

But before we get ahead of ourselves, let's take a moment to establish just what is at stake. Consider the following scenario, developed by the psychologist Jonathan Haidt and his colleagues to illustrate a phenomenon they termed "moral dumbfounding":[1]

> Julie and Mark are brother and sister. They are traveling together in France on summer vacation from college. One night they are staying alone in a cabin near the beach. They decide that it would be interesting and fun if they tried making love. At the very least it would be a new experience for each of them. Julie was already taking birth control pills, but Mark uses a condom too, just to be safe. They both enjoy making love, but they decide not to do it again. They keep that night as a special secret, which makes them feel even closer to each other. What do you think about that? Was it OK for them to make love?

If you are like the majority of people who participated in Haidt's study, your initial, immediate reaction was a twinge of disgust, accompanied by the intuition that it was obviously wrong for them to make love. Only after intuitively deciding *that* it was wrong, likely you then began to assemble an argument for *why* it was wrong. Perhaps you thought about the possible genetic risks of inbreeding, or maybe the idea that one party didn't consent, or that one or both people felt regret after the fact for their actions. But then you reread the prompt to realize that your objections had been preempted by the hypothetical—the use of protection nullified the genetic risks, Julie and Mark both consented to the experience, it did not lead to further episodes, and in fact Julie and Mark both felt content and even happy about it afterward. Unable to directly justify your feeling, you might begin to look for remote contingencies ("the condom could break," "the birth control pills might not work") or take issue with the format of the hypothetical ("well, this would never happen like this anyway, so it doesn't matter"). Finally, accepting the lack of any actual convincing evidence, you might resign yourself to the position: "I just know it's wrong, even though I can't explain why."

Consider another scenario:

> Claire has no family or friends and, down on her luck and needing some extra money, decides to sell the rights to her body after her death. Jake offers Claire $10,000 and informs her that he plans to do unspeakable things to her body after death. Claire, who doesn't care what happens to her body when she dies, promptly agrees and spends the remaining years of her life content in her decision. When she dies, Jake takes the body and does with it precisely what he promised: he mutilates the body, defecates on it, allows it to rot in the sun, and eventually disposes of it by throwing it into a pile of burning garbage. Nobody sees or is even aware of Jake's activities, and although Jake enjoyed defiling Claire's body, he never does anything like this again. What do you think? Was it OK for Claire to sell her body? Was it OK for Jake to treat the body the way he did?

We could repeat this exercise over and over again with other examples, and for many people the instinct would be the same: a sense of disgust mingled with disapproval, despite the fact that the actors in the hypotheticals bring no harm to their living selves, to the reader, or to anyone else.

This is not just an academic exercise: in the vast majority of countries and cultures, for most of recorded history, acts like these (consensual incest and the desecration of a corpse) have been socially taboo and likewise illegal, despite the fact that they often do no harm to either the individuals involved in the acts or, for that matter, anyone else.[2] These hypotheticals are structured to highlight the curious yet consistently observed feature of human psychology at the heart of this book: even when all other reasonable objections are removed, bare disgust is sometimes enough to drive moral judgments—moral judgments that often find their way into law.

This isn't a recent or isolated phenomenon either: it's a pattern that transcends cultures and political systems, and that stretches back deep into history. The prominent disgust researcher Valerie Curtis recently conducted a series of interviews and surveys of women from India, Europe, and Africa to compile a list of things that humans find disgusting. That list, assembled recently and across several cultures, included urine, menstrual blood, spilt blood, impurities of childbirth, open wounds, sores, clothes that have been worn, lice, rats, meat, dead rats, rotting flesh, a sick person, beggars, touching someone of a lower caste, betrayal, fat people, diarrhea, sexual relations with a woman before her child is weaned, vomit, rotten food, moldy food, foul language, and a man beating a woman.[3]

Now, compare that list with this list from the Book of Leviticus, made up of proscribed objects and practices handed down to Moses by God: bodily discharges such as semen and menstruation, blood, a woman who has recently given birth and is still bleeding, infectious skin diseases, festering sores, poor hygiene, flying insects, "any crawling thing," unclean food, clothes and pots and other objects that have touched dead animals, the carcasses of unclean wild animals, aging meat, rotten fruit, bodily mutilation, the blind, lame, disfigured, deformed, hunchbacked, dwarfed, with crippled foot or hand or eye defect or damaged testicles, underhandedness, incest, sex during menstruation, bestiality, prostitution, homosexuality, mildew, dead bodies, and murder.[4]

That the contemporary, cross-cultural list compiled by Curtis tracks the ancient list of religious taboos illustrates two points that make up central themes of this book: first, many of the things we find disgusting remain relatively consistent between cultures and over time, and second, the things we find disgusting tend to be among the things we think are wrong and, as a result, the things that we proscribe.

Here's another example. In the 2003 case *Lawrence v. Texas*, the US Supreme Court struck down a Texas statute prohibiting sodomy, ruling that "The Texas statute furthers no legitimate state interest which can justify its intrusion into the personal and private life of the individual." In so doing, the Court explicitly overruled *Bowers v. Hardwick*, a (then) 17-year-old case in which the Supreme Court had previously upheld a similar sodomy law of the State of Georgia. In his dissent in *Lawrence*, Justice Scalia mourned the blow to moral legislation, noting that the Court's decision called into question "[s]tate laws against bigamy, same-sex marriage, adult incest, prostitution, masturbation, adultery, fornication, bestiality, and obscenity," laws that were, in Scalia's view, "sustainable only in light of *Bowers'* validation of laws based on moral choices."[5] But the laws that Scalia chose to highlight—often referred to as his *parade of horribles*—also have another unifying characteristic: to their objectors, they are often elicitors of disgust.

Whether we consciously realize it or not, disgust pervades the law, sometimes obviously but often surreptitiously, in ways that are not so easily detected. The more obvious instances are those in which disgust is explicitly targeted or considered in the construction of the rule, such as nuisance and zoning laws that confine unpleasant or disgusting activities to a particular physical space, obscenity and pornography laws outlawing content that is "grossly offensive, disgusting or otherwise of an obscene character,"[6] or evidentiary rules that keep jurors from seeing gruesome photographic evidence. Less obvious are the occasions in which disgust creeps in unnoticed, or under pretense, such as when it is used as a psychological weapon in racial, ethnic, religious, and caste-based discrimination, or instances where disgust drives moral judgments relating to sex and relationships.

The goal of this book is to expose these connections, both the obvious and the less obvious, and analyze the many instances in which disgust and the law intersect. To do this, we'll put forth a psychological model that helps explain the mechanics of disgust, and, with that in hand, examine how and why disgust, morality, and the law intertwine in the ways they do. Our hope is to show how, by reverse engineering the psychological process of disgust, we can first explain how and why disgust has shaped our laws and legal process in the ways it has, and then subsequently show why it should no longer continue to do so.

Of course, this task does not come without a broad set of caveats, limitations, and challenges, beginning with the integration of the behavioral sciences and legal theory. The primary objective of the law is to move the populace toward a desired state of affairs. Generally speaking, criminal laws seek to reduce crime and increase safety, contract laws to facilitate commerce, property laws to prevent conflicts over resources, and so on. In pursuit of these ends, penalties (such as fines and prison sentences) and incentives (such as tax benefits and copyright protections) are established to encourage socially desirable behavior and discourage the alternative. The effectiveness of these measures is invariably related to the accuracy of the behavioral model on which the law relies; the better we can explain and predict what humans will do, the more insight we will have for deciding what "socially desirable" might be, and the more effectively we can structure a system to move behavior in the desired direction.

This may sound straightforward and obvious, but in practice this process can be quite cumbersome, for a number of reasons. To begin with, the law has no formal program for the investigation and assessment of human behavior outside of the incremental trial and error of the adjudicative process. Instead, to hone in on an accurate model of human behavior, the law must frequently turn to other disciplines for empirical research and behavioral theory. This, in turn, gives rise to the dilemma of *whom to believe*. Different disciplines can divide sharply over how to explain and predict behavior. If, for example, you were to ask a cultural anthropologist, a social psychologist, a neuroscientist, a behavioral economist, a sociologist, and a cognitive psychologist to each explain disgust, you could (and probably would) receive different and perhaps even mutually exclusive explanations.

Even within disciplines, researchers can argue bitterly over which behavioral theories are correct and how to interpret empirical results. It's a necessary inconvenience. Much like the adversarial nature of the legal system, the scientific enterprise depends on its members challenging one another on the merits of their theories in the hope that, through continuous critique and refinement, we arrive somewhere closer to the truth. But while this system in the long run is productive for scientific progress, in the short term it presents a thorny predicament for the law: of all the competing models of behavior, and everyone insisting that theirs is the correct one, how do policymakers decide which model to choose? And what happens if they're wrong?

The freedom to selectively pick and choose from among competing theories has its advantages—for one, the law isn't limited by the methodologies of one discipline, or by the myopia or disciplinary grandstanding that can wall researchers and disciplines off from one another. But if behavioral scientists who have been trained extensively on how to evaluate competing theories of behavior can't agree on which theories are the correct ones, how can lawmakers, who often have no formal, or for that matter informal, scientific training be expected to evaluate the different theories for their accuracy and make the right call? And if there isn't enough evidence one way or another to settle the issue, it isn't like the court can just delay the resolution of the case at hand until one theory emerges victorious. Justice Blackmun captures this tension nicely in his opinion in *Daubert v. Merrell Dow Pharmaceuticals, Inc.*, noting that there are "important differences between the quest for truth in the courtroom and the quest for truth in the laboratory. Scientific conclusions are subject to perpetual revision. Law, on the other hand, must resolve disputes finally and quickly."[7]

As Justice Blackmun observes, the "scientific project is advanced by broad and wide-ranging consideration of a multitude of hypotheses, for those that are incorrect will eventually be shown to be so, and that in itself is an advance. Conjectures that are probably wrong are of little use, however, in the project of reaching a quick, final, and binding legal judgment—often of great consequence—about a particular set of events in the past."[8]

The tension between the long-term quest for truth and the short-term need to quickly settle disputes is compounded by a second issue. Even if a scientific consensus forms with regard to a facet of human behavior, the law is now faced with the problem of how to implement that consensus in a fair and practicable fashion. In contrast to the sometimes rapid self-correction of the scientific process, changing laws often requires a gradual approach. Accuracy is necessary for an effective legal system, but so is stability. A stable and predictable legal system that changes slowly and incrementally allows people to effectively manage their affairs and gives them notice of exactly which behaviors they can expect to be punished for. Upsetting or overhauling an existent framework too quickly—even when the framework is premised on outmoded theory—can undermine the very stability that the legal system is designed to produce. As the famous jurist Benjamin Cardozo observed, "[j]ustice is not to be taken by storm. She is to be wooed by slow advances."[9]

With disgust, the attempt to incorporate behavioral science is made even more complex by the fact that disgust has been, and continues to be, a particularly vexing, if not also alluring, topic of investigation for scholars. And both its difficulty and its attractiveness can likely be attributed to the peculiar set of properties that set disgust apart from other behavioral phenomena.

DISCUSSING DISGUST

Part of the difficulty of seriously studying disgust stems from the inevitability of wading into the taboo. Because disgust traffics in the inappropriate—the gross, the obscene, the gory, the deviant—any attempt to seriously examine disgust will eventually mean discussing the disgusting. For many investigators, meditating on the taboo has a certain appeal, but it also means that investigators risk tainting their own reputation with the negative connotations and unpleasant subject matter of their scholarship. That isn't to say that these taboos hinder scholarship per se, but they do require a certain sense of awareness and tact in presentation that other objects of behavioral study do not. The law professor William Ian Miller opens his book *The Anatomy of Disgust* with a cautionary prologue dedicated to this very point. He makes his case for why disgust should be taken seriously, but self-consciously warns his readers that "descriptions of the disgusting have suggestive powers that work independently of an author's will. And so although I have no wish to disgust you, I cannot promise that you will not be at times disgusted."[10]

Compounding this sense of taboo is disgust's unique visceral power. Our emotions are often characterized by their rapidity, their automaticity, and the power they exude over conscious, rational deliberation. Perhaps no emotion is *more* of any of these things than disgust; the comparative literature scholar Winfried Menninghaus calls it "one of the most violent affections of the human perceptual system . . . It allows no reflective shock-defense: there are no mediating links between a disgusting stench and the sensation of disgust, and hardly any possibility for conditioning and intervention."[11] An object of disgust—such as the sight of a gory bodily injury, or the smell of feces—can quickly throw an irrepressible wave of aversion over us; we might scrunch our nose, turn our heads, lift our hands to shield our faces, physically recoil or move away from the source, become nauseated, or even vomit, all without the slightest conscious inclination to do so. Listen to the philosopher Julia Kristeva describe the experience of willingly drinking separated milk:

> When the eyes see or the lips touch that skin on the surface of milk— harmless, thin as a sheet of cigarette paper, pitiful as a nail paring—I experience a gagging sensation and, still farther down, spasms in the stomach, the

belly; and all the organs shrivel up the body, provoke tears and bile, increase heartbeat, cause forehead and hands to perspire. Along with sight-clouding dizziness, *nausea* makes me balk at that milk cream, separates me from the mother and father who proffer it.[12]

The sensation of disgust is so visceral that it can often be activated by simply re-membering, imagining, or reading descriptions of the objects we find disgusting.

A final noteworthy feature of disgust we'll mention at the outset is its breadth of application. The range of phenomena that activate disgust is remarkably diverse; it can include bodily fluids, diseases, animals, kinds of people, sexual acts, and even ideas or philosophies (recall the extensive lists from Valerie Curtis and the Book of Leviticus). The variety of stimuli that can elicit disgust and its attendant symptoms is extensive, and it's peculiar that the same, or at least similar, physical sensations should be felt for such a broad range of triggers. The benefits of gagging at the smell of rotten food seem obvious (don't eat that!), but why do many people experience a similar sensation (or, at the very least, use the same terms) at the thought of, for instance, making love to their sibling or to a very obese person? Why does sex with an extremely unattractive partner "gross us out," and why do acts we find immoral "make us sick"?

This assemblage of peculiar features has made disgust both an attractive and vexing object for scholars, a combination that has produced a vast, and vastly varied, literature on disgust. Fortunately for the law, the result is a substantial body of theory and research to draw on. Unfortunately for the law, the variety of these attempts is so great that policymakers will likely find it difficult to derive a consensus from the various formulations. To wit: the philosopher Immanuel Kant conceptualized disgust as "a rejection of an idea that has been offered for enjoyment,"[13] the psychologist Steven Pinker: "intuitive microbiology."[14] Darwin viewed disgust as a system for avoiding the ingestion of toxins, but limited his definition of the disgusting to "something offensive to the taste."[15] Winfried Menninghaus calls disgust "an acute crisis of self-assertion against unassimilable otherness."[16] The psychologist Paul Rozin formulates disgust as a mechanism for humanization, asserting that "[a]nything that reminds us that we are animals elicits disgust."[17] And while the legal scholar William Miller yokes disgust to ob-jects related to "the capacity for life,"[18] the philosopher Colin McGinn links it to "death presented in the form of living tissue . . . the death or dying of the living."[19]

Each of these views offers insight of value to the law, but even together they cannot account for the full range of disgust's features, and plenty of questions re-main unanswered. Many of these theories, for example, have trouble accounting for the disgust we feel at the thought of sex between siblings, or sex between an adult man and a very young girl. These acts don't involve keeping our bodies pure or free from pathogens and, for that matter, don't involve our own bodies at all. Traditionally, scholars have only fleetingly addressed the disgust we sometimes feel in sexual or moral contexts, and their treatments have often been theoretically tenuous and ultimately unsatisfying. In other words, despite the glut of research, the case on disgust is hardly closed.

OUR APPROACH

Our analysis relies heavily on an evolutionary-psychological view of disgust, an approach that rests on the assumption that disgust and other features of the human mind were, like the rest of the human body, forged incrementally over time to generate behavior that led, on average, to an increase in the chances of survival and reproduction for our ancestors. Combining our own research with the existing store, we suggest that disgust is best understood as a type of software program instantiated in our neural hardware that evolved originally to guide our ancestors when making decisions about what to eat and, more generally, what to touch, and was later co-opted to guide mate choice, specifically the avoidance of mates jeopardizing the production of healthy offspring.

By virtue of disgust's design features that enable it to carry out these functions, specifically, its role in assigning "value" to items, acts, and people in various contexts, disgust was also an opportune emotion for use by "moral" systems. As many psychologists and philosophers have noted, harm prevention is a core feature of our moral psychology.[20] Disgust is linked to morality because some acts that cause disgust are behaviors that cause physical harm (e.g., intentionally spreading HIV; a doctor not scrubbing up before surgery). But not all "moral" disgust serves the desire to *curb* harms. As we will discuss, some "moral" systems actively consult our disgust psychology to identify behaviors to proscribe and groups to condemn— morality has a dark side, where disgust, alongside anger and fear, serves to cultivate, organize, and promote an exploitative agenda.

What does this evolutionary-cognitive view add to our collective understanding of disgust? The devil is, of course, in the details, but there are three overarching features of our model that make it a valuable contribution to the literature. The first is that this approach provides a deductive blueprint for investigation: because natural selection operates slowly over enormous spans of time, and because for nearly all of human history we existed as small bands of hunter-gatherers, the key to understanding disgust and unraveling its many obscurities lies in examining the physical and social challenges of the environments of our hunter-gatherer and hominid ancestors. By identifying the ancestral problems that disgust evolved to solve, we can then begin to uncover the mechanics of the software programs within the brain that were selected to accomplish these tasks, and then, in turn, we can begin constructing a psychological schematic for how they work. To do this, we'll ask questions like: What causal forces led to the evolution of disgust? How is disgust organized in terms of its information-processing structure? What kind of information was readily available in ancestral environments that could have served as input to the disgust system? What contextual factors does the disgust system take as input to generate the range of behaviors we observe within and across cultures? And how might other psychological systems use disgust-related information to guide interpersonal and group-level behavior?

This type of thinking allows us to formulate testable hypotheses about how disgust works, and allows us to discuss the cognition of disgust in terms of information: of inputs and outputs, of algorithms and decision-rules, and eventually of thoughts and behavior.

The second feature of our model, and a consequence of the first, is that it offers a scientific explanation for disgust. It is not a complete explanation—there is much work to be done—but it is a technical explanation nonetheless. By approaching disgust in this way and anchoring it to physical systems embedded in neural circuitries, we avoid the temptation to relegate those aspects of the cognitive process that we do not yet understand to some form of a mental ether. There is no room here for traditional conceptions of a supernatural soul or psyche, or a ghost in the machine. Our explanation alleviates the need to rely on any non-physical conception of the mind in accounting for our judgments, our feelings, or our intuitions. In fact, it is meant to serve as an antidote to that sort of thinking, to provide a systematic method for decoding intuitions, like disgust, that originate outside of conscious awareness.

The last overarching strength of our model is that it provides an explanation of disgust that can reconcile many of disgust's ostensibly incongruent features. It helps explain why, for instance, a piece of fudge shaped like feces unnecessarily disgusts us when other more potentially harmful substances, like trans fats or high concentrations of fluoride, do not. Or why we feel perfectly comfortable with encountering another person's saliva when we kiss them, but would be repulsed if they were to stand over the top of us and dribble it into our mouth like a mother bird feeding her young.

As we will explain, some features of disgust are hallmarks of functional design. Contexts that activate sexual arousal and sexual attraction, for example, can dampen disgust, rendering a kiss (and what would otherwise be objectionable saliva) not disgusting. Other features can be explained by the particularities of the evolutionary process, such as the mismatch between the modern environment (e.g., where gimmicks like feces-shaped fudge exist) and the environment in which disgust evolved (e.g., where anything that looked like feces was, with near certainty, actual feces), or the fact that our system of disgust is designed to operate as best it can in a setting with imperfect information.

Together, these features—the deductive framework for investigation, the basis in natural phenomena, and the explanatory capacity of an evolutionary perspective—make for powerful inferential tools for understanding disgust, tools that are supported by a considerable body of empirical research and, we hope to show, can be of great value to the law. This book is made up of three interdependent investigations. The first explores the evolved architecture of disgust: how it works, and why it works in the way that it does. The second explores morality and how the properties of disgust made this particular emotion ripe for picking by psychological systems designed to generate and enforce cultural norms. The third examines disgust's role in the legal system, identifying the various ways in which disgust pervades the law, explaining why disgust operates as it does in each context, and eventually offering a normative recommendation about how the law should reckon with disgust going forward. The symbiotic relationship between these strands should be obvious: by explaining *how* disgust and morality operate, we are equipped with a template for exploring their interaction with the legal system in any given context. And by rooting out *why* disgust operates the way it does in the moral domain, we can begin to make normative recommendations for what the role of disgust should, or should not, be in those various contexts.

To do this, we'll work from the ground up, beginning with an explanation of why an evolutionary approach is important to psychology, generally, and to understanding our subconscious psychological systems, specifically. We'll cover the core features of this approach, and sketch an evolutionary view of one specific subset of these subconscious processes, emotions. After probing some of the universal properties of our emotions, we'll begin unraveling how disgust fits into this framework, outlining its function as a mechanism that was originally selected to help us make decisions about what to consume and touch, and then later co-opted via the evolutionary process for making decisions regarding mate choice.

With this explanation in hand, we'll then investigate how these different systems of disgust interact with our moral psychology and, as a consequence, influence the legal domain. We'll explore food taboos, the roots of our definitions of obscenity and pornography, the role of disgust in discrimination, how gruesome evidence can impact the decision-making of jurors, and all the ways in which we've historically outlawed various sexual behaviors, paying particular attention to laws prohibiting sodomy, homosexuality, pedophilia, bestiality, and incest.

Finally, we'll also weigh in on the debate concerning the role that disgust should, or should not, play in legal affairs. Generally, there are two camps. There are those who see the potential in harnessing the power of disgust for productive uses in the law. Take, for instance, the views of the bioethicist Leon Kass, who feels that we are currently in an era "in which everything is held to be permissible so long as it is freely done, and in which our bodies are regarded as mere instruments of our autonomous rational will" and sees repugnance as "the only voice left that speaks up to defend the core of our humanity." To Kass, disgust is a type of moral compass: "Shallow are the souls that have forgotten how to shudder."[21] On the opposite end of the spectrum from Kass are those who believe disgust is untrustworthy and urge for its exile from the law altogether. The philosopher and legal scholar Martha Nussbaum, for instance, believes that the "moral progress of society can be measured by the degree to which it *separates* disgust from danger and indignation, basing laws and social rules on substantive harm, rather than on the symbolic relationship an object bears to our anxieties."[22]

Any explanation of disgust, however, even if it were complete and accurate, couldn't settle the debate regarding disgust's suitability for guiding law. Our explanation is no different. Our explanation of disgust is simply that, an explanation, and it does not, on its face, mandate any normative conclusions. We do believe, however, that an evolutionary model of disgust casts serious doubt on the view that disgust should have a prominent or meaningful role in legal affairs. Though disgust is a powerful, universal experience, it isn't a mandate from the heavens, an axiomatic moral compass, or even a useful measuring stick for evaluating behavior—it is nothing more than an emotion that steered our species away from engaging in particular behaviors that jeopardized survival and the opportunity to produce healthy offspring. This, we argue, is insufficient reason to grant it privileged status in legal policy. Disgust may or may not promote socially desirable outcomes, but whether or not it does is *entirely incidental* to its form and function. Disgust wasn't designed to further the objectives of our legal system; it exists today because it helped humans survive and reproduce in the environment of our ancestors. Our hope is that by unlocking its origins and the mechanics of its operation, we can remove the aura of superstition surrounding disgust, and allow the many things that elicit disgust—whether they're objects, people, actions, or ideas—to be evaluated using more reasoned and more reliable criteria.

Tools for Excavation

The Evolutionary Framework

This chapter is about a persistent problem faced by scientists of the mind, and about a framework for how to go about attacking that problem. The problem: If you want to know why someone does something, you can't just ask them. It is perhaps the single most vexing aspect to investigating human behavior. How easy life would be for the behavioral scientist if he or she could simply sit a person down, ask them why they did this or that, and record their explanation as reliable data points. Unfortunately, though, it isn't nearly so simple. Decades of research in the social and behavioral sciences have shown, instead, that in many cases we don't actually know why we do the things we do and, adding to the confusion, we often offer up good-faith yet grossly inaccurate explanations when asked.

These phenomena stem from the fact that humans have limited conscious access to the various psychological engines driving our motivations, goals, and behavior. In their 1977 paper *Telling More Than We Can Know*—one of the most-cited papers in the history of psychology—the social psychologists Richard Nisbett and Timothy Wilson highlighted the idea that limited conscious access has made us unreliable informants of our motivations and behavior.[1] A battery of subsequent research has come to support their claims: people routinely make decisions based on their "gut," they "listen to their heart," and they act on their "feelings"—often without any ability to account for how or why those intuitions were produced (recall that many subjects in Haidt's moral dumbfounding study couldn't articulate why sibling incest was inappropriate, they just felt it was). To complicate matters, people also frequently *invent* explanations for their decisions after the fact. Rather than say "I don't know," we tend to craft narratives for our behavior, narratives that might not reflect the actual causal procedures behind those decisions.

Regrettably, this state of affairs poses a variety of challenges to those seeking to uncover how the mind works. We'll cover two such challenges in this chapter. The first is that there is a limit to what we can infer about the structure of the mind when we rely solely on verbal responses to questions regarding goals, motivations, and behaviors. Asking just isn't going to do the trick. Without a separate rubric for testing and verifying people's proffered explanations, researchers will be forced to rely on inherently unreliable information. The second challenge (and a consequence of the first) is that our limited inferential ability can lead to severely impoverished models of human cognition. If, for example, we were to rely on the explanations offered by the people who objected to the tryst between Julie and Mark (our amorous siblings from Haidt's experiment), our cognitive model for how the mind causes incest revulsion might look something like this:

Step 1: Event of incest is detected (stimulus).
Step 2: Look up how to react; derived from "social learning" (black-box operations).
Step 3: Generate disapproval (response).

Step 1 and step 3 are not (or are, at least, less) controversial—most scientists would agree on what the stimulus and the observed response are for a given event. Step 2—the nature of the internal procedure that translates stimulus to response—is the contentious step. Because we don't have access to most internal procedures that generate a response (for instance, an attitude or behavior), too many scientists explain a response as simply having been "learned," "imitated," or "culturally adopted." Yet these explanations *do no work*. And, lest you think we are staunch nativists, neither do explanations that claim a given response is "biological" or "innate." Explanations such as these do nothing to account for how, on either a functional or mechanical level, we get from stimulus to response. They are merely labels, placeholders kept until we better understand how the mind works.

Luckily, however, there is a framework for sidestepping the many problems posed by having limited conscious access to our mental machinery—a framework that shines light into the black box of cognition. Social and behavioral scientists have available to them the theoretical and conceptual toolkits offered by neighboring disciplines, particularly that of evolutionary biology—a field tasked with inferring the evolved function of living systems—and cognitive science—a discipline dedicated to mapping the algorithmic procedures instantiated in our neural circuitry. Applied jointly, evolutionary biology and cognitive science form the backbone of our home discipline, evolutionary psychology, and provide a coherent methodological approach to generating and testing models of our cognitive architecture. In the wake of both the Darwinian revolution of biology and the cognitive revolution of psychology, researchers are, for the first time in human history, equipped with a coherent framework for excavating the mind. We'll go through the particulars of this framework presently. Before we do, though, it is worth unpacking the various challenges an evolutionary-cognitive framework helps to solve.

CHALLENGE 1: TELLING MORE THAN WE KNOW

Example 1: Split-Brains

Our tendency to spin narratives for our intuitions has been documented by neuroscientists and psychologists alike, and nowhere is it more obvious than in studies on split-brain patients, individuals whose right and left brain hemispheres have been surgically disconnected to treat severe cases of epilepsy. To understand the behavior of split-brain patients, we must first consult the *brain–body opposite rule*: the right side of the brain controls the left side of the body, and the left side of the brain controls the right side of the body. In normal brains, the corpus callosum is the bundle of neurons that connects the two brain hemispheres, allowing them to share information. This is useful because some cognitive abilities are controlled via circuitry present on one side of the brain, and the corpus callosum provides access to this circuitry for information detected and processed by the other side.

In split-brain patients, the corpus callosum has been severed, leaving the two brain hemispheres without a means to communicate. Information gathered from one side is now unavailable to the other side. One result is that functions carried out by one side of the brain are not capable of receiving any inputs collected by the contralateral side. Take speech production, a function localized to the *left* brain hemisphere. A split-brain patient will have no trouble speaking a word on a screen presented to visual circuitry leading to the *left* brain hemisphere because this is where speech production is localized.[2] However, a word presented to visual circuitry leading to the *right* brain hemisphere does not gain access to the left-side-dwelling speech center because the connections have been cut. Thus, although the right brain hemisphere has detected the information, and this information is now "in there," the person will not be able to use speech to convey this.

This leads to some interesting behavior. For example, in an object identification task, if the instruction "select the office key" is presented to a split-brain patient's *left* brain hemisphere, the motor cortex in the left brain will initiate movements in the right hand to pick out the office key (remember the brain–body opposite rule). When asked why they selected the key, patients easily and perhaps with some sass might tell the experimenter "you just told me to" or "that's what the instructions said to do." This is because the left brain hemisphere, which received the instructions, governs speech production and can therefore accurately explain what the right hand is doing.

But what if the instruction "select the office key" is presented to a split-brain patient's *right* brain hemisphere, where there are no speech production centers? In this case, the motor cortex of the right hemisphere will initiate movements in the left hand (opposite rule) to pick out the key. But in this case, when asked *why* they selected the key, split-brain patients might say "I wanted to unlock the door" or "I thought you might ask me to lock up after we're done." They would *not* say, "the instructions said to select the key" because the left hemisphere, which controls speech production, did not get the memo that the right hemisphere saw those instructions. When information isn't shared across hemispheres as it typically is in healthy, uncut brains, we are prone to generating plausible, yet false, explanations for our behavior.[3]

This phenomenon isn't limited to injured or unhealthy brains, either.

Example 2: Functional Fixedness

Functional fixedness, a term coined by psychologist Norman Maier, describes our inability to naturally see the many functions for which one might use an object. Namely, we tend to be locked into or "fixed on" a particular set of functions for a given object, and our narrow focus gets in the way of seeing other potential uses. (If you've ever seen the comedy show *Whose Line Is It Anyway,* the talent for being functionally *un*fixed is often on display and is quite funny precisely because most of us are, well, fixed.) In a classic experiment on functional fixedness, Maier hung two cords from the ceiling and instructed participants to tie the two cords together while Maier walked around the room and observed. The task's difficulty stemmed from the fact that the cords were placed far enough apart that the participants could not pick up the end of one cord and walk it over to the other. In the room, there were a pair of pliers and a chair that the participants could use to aid them in the task. Most participants found this task quite difficult. The solution? Connect the pliers to the end of one rope and swing it like a pendulum over to the other. Maier explained that subjects were unable to solve this problem due to their functional fixedness—that is, the inability to use the pliers, a tool used to remove one solid object from another, for an unintended purpose, as an anchor.

Here's the important detail. If, during the experiment, the participants went 10 minutes without discovering the solution, Maier would accidentally brush past one of the ropes as he walked by, causing it to sway, and thereby subtly suggesting the solution. In an average of 45 seconds after this event, Maier's participants solved the problem. Incredibly, when Maier asked participants after the experiment whether or not the hint had helped them solve the task, the vast majority said no. In fact, when he asked where the idea for the pendulum came from, they offered answers such as "a course in physics suggested it to me" and "having exhausted everything else the next thing was to swing it. I thought of the situation of swinging across a river. I had imagery of monkeys swinging from trees. This imagery appeared simultaneously with the solution. The idea appeared complete."[4] Not only were the participants unaware of the source of their intuitive solution, but they were also prone to constructing post-hoc explanations that were not tethered to the actual source at all.

Example 3: The Bystander Effect

As a final example of how we tend not to be aware of why we act as we do, consider another classic experiment conducted by psychologists John Darley and

Bibb Latané.[5] Darley and Latané gathered groups of people in one room and had a confederate (an assistant who was actually part of the research team) fake a seizure in an adjoining room. The experiment was designed to figure out under what conditions participants would go to the other room and help the person having the seizure. In different iterations of the experiment, Darley and Latané varied the number of people in the room with the participant. They found that as the number of people in the group *decreased*, the probability that any given individual would rush to help *increased*. Said another way, the *more* people around, the *less* likely that any one person was to help—a phenomenon they termed "the bystander effect." It's an effect that has been replicated in numerous subsequent experiments.

Perhaps the most striking finding for Latané and Darley, however, was that when they asked the participants whether their behavior had been influenced by the presence of other people, they persistently denied that it had. In fact, they denied it *even when presented with the results*. And when Latané and Darley described their experiment to new individuals and asked them whether or not the presence of other people would matter to them, they uniformly agreed that it would not. In other words, despite the fact that the system (or systems) governing our motivation to help are clearly incorporating information about how many other people are nearby (and thus presumably also able to help), our illusion of conscious sovereignty is so strong that we refuse to concede that such information is being incorporated.

Our inability to directly observe unconscious cognitive processes and our stubbornness that they don't really control behavior pose special problems for researchers seeking to explain and predict behavior, and, in turn, lawmakers and policymakers seeking to regulate or influence it. If we don't understand the *actual* causes of behavior (as opposed to the often incorrectly professed causes), any attempts to move that behavior will likely be less effective or efficient than they could otherwise be. But by accurately homing in on the hidden, unconscious processes that influence decision-making, we can sharpen our ability to promote a more desirable state of affairs. One concrete example of this is how the findings of the bystander effect have influenced emergency situation policy. The standard advice often given to lifeguards and in first-aid courses is that, in an emergency, the first responder should choose a specific person from the crowd and explicitly command that person to call 911, instead of just yelling into a crowd for help. By identifying a specific person, the responder helps avoid the chance that the presence of a large crowd will reduce the likelihood of any single individual responding.

To generalize the lesson of the bystander effect, science discovered an important factor—counterintuitive and objectionable though it may be—that influences the way we behave. And the identification of this factor helped to synthesize a work-around, an alternative strategy that led to a better outcome. In the coming chapters, we will outline the factors—counterintuitive and objectionable though they may be—that contribute to the advancement of particular moral positions, many of which become institutionalized by our legal systems. We too hope that by identifying the underlying causal factors by which disgust contributes to our moral psychology, we can devise alternative paths that will lead to more preferable outcomes.

CHALLENGE 2: INSTINCT BLINDNESS

The second major challenge besetting scientists of the mind stems from the first: If we don't have conscious access to many mental processes, then we run the risk of advancing seriously impoverished models of human cognition.

We (humans) often do not appreciate the complexity of *any* information-processing device—naturally selected or artificially engineered—until it breaks down. Chances are you have no idea how your mobile phone or desktop computer works; you are just grateful they do. But when they break down (e.g., an app won't open; your voicemail won't play messages; Siri or Alexa activates without a prompt), this can lead to an acute appreciation of the many functionally specific capacities bundled into a circuit board. The same holds for the human mind/brain. It's only when a particular impairment occurs (e.g., color blindness, memory loss, the inability to recognize faces, the absence of pain, or the lack of a fear response) that we begin to have an appreciation of the many functionally specific capacities bundled into the brain. Failure to identify the complexities of cognition and failure to acknowledge the existence of functionally specialized mental programs are casualties of having a mind that (typically) operates seamlessly and efficiently.

Evolutionary psychologists John Tooby and Leda Cosmides call this failure *instinct blindness,*[6] which they note is "sanity for the individual, but . . . crippling for scientific psychology."[7] Instinct blindness is a condition created, ironically, by brains that function well and gives rise to the dual intuitions that (a) there really isn't anything "in there" to explain and (b) even if there were, then what's "in there" couldn't be all that complex. Consider vision. By and large, we take for granted much of the complicated mental process of "seeing" because it takes place outside of conscious awareness: we simply open our eyes and see. (There is an anecdote that Marvin Minsky, a pioneer of artificial intelligence who also designed the first neural network simulator, so underestimated the complexity of vision that he assigned to a graduate team as a *summer* project the task of designing a computer program that could mimic human vision. Needless to say, this was probably a rough summer for the team.)

Our perceptual systems, when they work seamlessly, generate the intuition that there's not much happening under the hood. But our experience belies a rich and complex set of processes. Hidden from view are sophisticated neural programs engaged in intricate computations, feeding information (i.e., light) gathered by two-dimensional sheets of retinal cells to the various specialized vision circuits of the brain—those inferring shape, color, distance, depth, motion—to generate the three-dimensional construction of the world that is delivered into consciousness.[8] A great deal happens, but we only perceive a little; we just *see*. And so it is with much of what transpires in our brain. The conscious thin slice of which we are aware is just a small subpart of the much larger whole. Whereas all consciously accessible activity is cognition, not all cognition is consciously accessible.

Instinct blindness applies not only to perceptual processes like vision, but also to "higher-level" cognition. Consider the following: How do you know how attractive someone is? This might sound like a silly question. After all, we just seem to *know* "who's hot" and "who's not." But much like vision, there are complex processes going on behind the scenes that deliver into consciousness the apparently simple sense that someone is physically attractive (or not). The question is, what kinds of processes are required to perform this function?

There has been a tsunami of research conducted on the factors influencing judgments of attractiveness. Much of this research points to the conclusion that physical attractiveness serves as a type of health certificate.[9] To understand why, we need to have a deep appreciation of organismic development. Development involves countless steps starting from the fusion of gametes, endless rounds of cell replication, cellular differentiation, and tissue and organ development, all leading to the three-trillion-or-so-celled reproductively capable adult. There are many errors that could occur at any step in the process. Genetic mutations, environmental irregularities, and disease-causing agents can all cause development to go awry. The ability to produce a functioning organism, let alone one with a near-perfect symmetric body plan, is quite a feat. Symmetry is thus one metric for assessing the success of development. Those body plans that tend toward greater symmetry are suggestive of developmental programs that were more or less free from harmful genetic mutations and robust against environmental threats such as pathogens. Less symmetric body plans are indicative of body plans subject to greater mutations or more sensitive to environmental perturbations.[10]

A number of studies have documented how symmetry is one factor that contributes to our sense of physical attractiveness.[11] It is, of course, not the only factor, but it is a fairly substantial one. Other factors detract from judgments of attractiveness, such as uneven skin tones, the presence of lesions, bad breath, and loss of hair (especially for women)—all factors that are intimately linked to the presence of disease-causing organisms or underlying genetic mutations.[12] Our ability to assess the cues linked to another individual's health was an important factor in mate choice. Those of our ancestors who chose to produce offspring with an individual who did not show cues to decreased health and viability would have had children who, on balance, were healthier and, in turn, had a greater chance of surviving to reproduce. Thus, our seemingly effortless and instantaneous judgments about physical attractiveness result, in part, from a complex, underlying set of information-processing procedures that evolved to guide the selection of a healthy mate. Although our explicit judgments don't typically mention symmetry (i.e., you typically never here a gaggle of women cooing, "Wow, did you see how symmetric that guy was?"), this factor does indeed play a large (albeit hidden) role guiding perceptions of attractiveness. As anthropologist Don Symons says, "beauty is in the adaptations of the beholder,"[13] and this adaptation appears to rely on nonconscious perceptions of symmetry.

Learning Matters, Learning Matters, Learning Matters

In a section entitled "Instinct Blindness" it might seem that we are implying that perceptions of attractiveness, like our vision system, are "innate," dismissing the roles that social learning and experience play. We cannot stress enough how over-simplified and underspecified labels such as "innate" and "cultural" are. Genes are just strands of chemicals. The environment—the biological, physical, and social environment—is critical in every step of the process that largely begins with rep-licators such as DNA strands and ends with the construction of a fully functional organism—visual system, attraction preferences, and all. Every feature has to be *both* a product of starter materials (e.g., DNA or RNA) and the environment that those starter materials are built to operate in. The science is in discovering what features exist and how they manifest and interact.

Unfortunately, dichotomies such as innate versus learned still seem to have a stranglehold on our intuitions regarding the origins of behavior. Take language. Some people might claim that language is learned. Some might claim that lan-guage is biological. Who's right? Of course, they both are, but labeling is not the same as explaining. Which language you speak is very much a function of the spe-cific social environment into which you are born. We *learn* our language from our social group. But the fact that everyone on Earth (save a few extreme exceptions) has a language is not the result of a global learning coincidence. It is the result of a species-universal genetic program that facilitates the acquisition of language, and allows for culture-specific tailoring.[14]

Learning—that is, the acquisition of information from the environment—is crit-ical for the functioning of many adaptations, like language. Learning is even crit-ical for functions most would dismiss as simply "innate," like vision. For instance, during development in utero, electrical signals pass across newly forming retinal cells like test patterns, enabling cells to wire up in the proper orientation. Retinal calibration to the expected electromagnetic environment is one form of system "learning." But learning is not unguided. As any artificial intelligence engineer will profess, even simple learning systems require some kind of prespecification that affords the system (individual) with the capacity to know what to learn, how to learn, the conditions under which learning should and should not occur, and which future behaviors to apply the learning to. Learning requires programming and, as we discuss next, we now have the ability to identify the variety of adapta-tions that evolved to guide human learning.

In closing, the first part of the chapter has discussed a range of challenges that beset the behavioral, social, and psychological sciences. The lack of con-scious access to our underlying mental machinery, the affliction of instinct blindness, and our intuition that only a few simple systems are responsible for generating everything from sight to behavior to beliefs all present serious stumbling blocks for even the most highly motivated scientists interested in excavating the mind.

So how do we get in?

OUR FRAMEWORK: MARRYING EVOLUTIONARY
BIOLOGY AND COGNITIVE SCIENCE

Uncovering the structure of the human mind requires a new set of tools. Self-reported explanations of behavior are not going to cut it on their own, and our intuitions can easily fool us into thinking cognition is simpler than it really is. Even worse, psychologists do not have the luxury of inferring function from structural form, a relationship used in many investigations within evolutionary biology and human physiology. A biologist studying wing design can observe the shape and composition of the wing, and can observe how wing shape changes at different speeds and angles of attack, to infer function. Likewise, a physician studying the heart can observe that the heart is composed of innervated muscle with chambers and valves; that it is connected to a system that oxygenates incoming blood; and that it is connected to a large artery that sends oxygenated blood to the rest of the body. Observing the form of the heart provided William Harvey in the 17th century with a clear idea of function.

Psychologists have been studying the brain for at least as long as biologists have been studying wings, and physicians studying hearts, and still we are far from a complete functional description. One reason is that the brain's observable physical form holds few clues to function—it all appears to be a homogeneous glob of tissue (at least from the outside). We do know, however, that the brain processes information and produces behavior. So in many respects, psychologists have been handed a very large, very complex circuit board and asked to figure out what it's for. That is, psychologists are tasked with *reverse engineering* the mind/brain. If we could understand the process by which the brain was engineered in the first place—the causal forces that led our brain to possess the features it does—then our job would be made much easier. The discipline of evolutionary psychology aims to do just this. Drawing on theory from evolutionary biology, principles from cognitive science, and evidence collected from anthropology and comparative biology, the goal of evolutionary psychology is to identify and describe the collection of mental faculties that make up our species-typical psychology by considering the forces that shaped them.[15]

The basic principles of an evolutionary approach should be familiar to anyone with a passing understanding of evolutionary biology. Sexual reproduction and genetic mutation produce random variation in offspring—here, human offspring. The presence of *random* variation is followed by the differential survival and proliferation of some of these variants. This differential proliferation is usually *not random*: the genetic variants that survive and reproduce more effectively than alternatives become more frequent in successive generations; the variants that don't disappear.

These few sentences make up the entire logic (if not all of the details) of natural selection—the only known natural explanation for the functional organization of living creatures, and, in turn, the only known natural explanation for the functional organization of the human mind. Because the mind, or if you wish the brain, is just as much a product of natural selection as our hearts or our lungs, *any attempt to understand its form and function must incorporate, at some level, the logic of the evolutionary approach.* This means that to understand how our minds work today—how social, cultural, and developmental processes operate in our current environment—we must investigate the properties of the social, biological, and physical environments of our past that led to their creation.

The process is a bit like stumbling on an incredibly complex machine where the inner workings are encased in such a way that we can't open it up to see how it works. And while we can't take the machine apart and examine its mechanics, we *are* given access to the workshop it was manufactured in, where we can observe the tools and processes that built it. For us, the machine is the human mind, and the workshop is the statistical composite of the environments of the thousands of previous generations of our hunter-gatherer ancestors. Fortunately, we can infer quite a bit about ancestral environments[16]: we lived in small nomadic groups of maybe 50 to 300; we selected mates to reproduce, often for extended periods; we encountered genetic relatives repeatedly over the course of the lifetime; females gave birth, males did not; females breastfed, males did not; we obtained food via hunting small and large game and also by gathering plants, some of which contained dangerous toxins; we got sick; we rarely had the chance to store provisions for the future; we formed friendships; we engaged in childcare; we faced a constant threat from predators; and we participated in coalitional aggression.

And so here is the key to reverse engineering the mind without having to rely on introspection: by identifying the selection pressures of our ancestral environment—the various forces or survival challenges that caused some genetic variants to be more successful than others—we can begin to deduce the functions of the systems that were selected to navigate those challenges. With the functions of these various systems in hand, we can then begin to posit and empirically test the information-processing mechanisms by which they carry out their functions.

Dissecting the information-processing systems that perform a particular function is a key component of evolutionary psychology. This is the strand of evolutionary psychology that derives from cognitive science. A particular noteworthy contribution of cognitive science is the notion that there are multiple mutually compatible explanations of any information-processing device. That is, answers to questions of why, how, what, and where are not competing explanations, but are instead unique contributions. As explained by the late vision scientist David Marr,[17] there is first the computational level of analysis, which specifies the function of the device—that is, *why* the device was designed. For an artificial intelligence engineer, a device is intentionally programmed to carry out a particular function (e.g., voice recognition, active lane assist, face identification). For an evolutionary scientist, function is defined in terms of the selection pressures that led to the creation of the device. For instance, the function (or goal) of fear is to motivate the avoidance of and escape from predators and assailants—with the threat of attack serving as the selection pressure that fashioned, over many generations, the structure of the fear program.

Marr also explains that there is an algorithmic level of analysis, which specifies *how* the device performs its function. An algorithmic level of analysis identifies the precise external and/or internal inputs accepted by the device (that is, what the device is designed to "learn"), the algorithms that operate over these inputs, and how internal states generate the output. So for fear, inputs include, among other things, visual detection of features associated with predators (e.g., large fangs, claws, sharp protrusions) and socially transmitted information regarding successful hiding places; algorithms include a signal detection analysis that assesses the probability of predator presence given the detection of these features (e.g., given that I just saw a looming shadow, what is the probability a lion is present?); and, in turn, probabilities of predator presence then activate context-sensitive motivations to freeze or flee, the output of the fear program.

The last level of analysis Marr discusses is that of physical instantiation, which specifies *what* physical machinery actually implements the algorithms and, by extension, *where* those algorithms are housed. For artificial intelligence and the computing industry, this translates into silicon chips and circuit boards; for living systems, this translates into the neurons, neurotransmitters, myelin coating, and the other physical substances that constitute our neural circuitry. Generally speaking, this is the domain of the discipline of neuroscience.

Our recipe for investigation will be based on questions of why and how (Marr's computational and algorithmic levels of analysis, respectively), questions that generate hypotheses regarding evolved function (the why) and the information-processing structure that supports that function (the how).[18] To discern the function or *goal* of any given system, we look for its role in the navigation of one or more of the many recurrent challenges of the ancestral environment—for instance, obtaining food, creating alliances, wooing mates, and avoiding incest. With respect to information-processing structure, to determine likely *inputs*, we try to identify the information that would have been available in the environment of our ancestors and could have been recruited to navigate that particular challenge. To uncover the various *algorithms,* or *decision-rules* of a system, we posit procedures that compile the available information (the inputs) and convert it into a cognitive, physiological, or behavioral *output* that would have helped navigate in a context-sensitive (flexible) manner that challenge in ancestral environments.

An Example: Kin Detection

To try to bring this blueprint into relief, let's take a look at a system that most people don't even know they have: a system for detecting genetic relatives. How do you learn which people, of all the people in the world, are your relatives? At first blush, this might seem a silly question to ask. After all, our conscious experience is that we just *know* who's related—it seems obvious. But much like vision or our assessment of attractiveness, there are complex processes going on behind the scenes that deliver into consciousness the apparently simple sense that someone is close kin: for instance, a mom, dad, brother, or sister. The question is, why do humans possess this ability, and how might "kin detection" work?

Perhaps your first thought is that a simple learning mechanism handles this function and we are just told. Throughout development other people repeatedly convey information about relatedness: "This is your sister"; "That man over there is your father." Although we are bombarded with kinship terms, there are a number of problems with language serving as the primary mechanism by which we learn about genetic relatedness. One problem is that linguistic terms can apply to genetic and non-genetic relatives alike. Take, for instance, the term "aunt." An aunt could be the sister of one's parent or the wife of a parent's brother. Likewise, in some cultures, children call all males of the older generation "Father." In English we speak of brotherhoods (e.g., band of brothers) and sisterhoods (e.g., sorority sisters), and religious groups often make use of kinship terms "father" and "mother" to denote individuals of status. Linguistic terms can thus blur genetic boundaries, making it very difficult for a general learning system that simply behaves as it is told to accurately draw the line between actual genetic kin and what anthropologists refer to as fictive kin.

But this boundary is important! There are two robust biological reasons *why* humans should be sensitive to how genetically related another person is to oneself. Said another way, accurately identifying genetic relatives solves two primary challenges, or selection pressures, of the ancestral environment. First, there are reproductive advantages to be gained by helping other individuals who share the same genes by virtue of common descent. If your genes "know" which individuals share DNA (i.e., potential copies of the genes), they can preferentially direct altruistic behavior (thus increasing the chances that those genetic copies will be passed on). This is what is known as inclusive fitness theory (developed in large part by the evolutionary biologist William Hamilton). Second, with respect to sex, there are severe reproductive costs associated with selecting a genetic relative as a mate. Children born of close genetic relatives run a greater risk of suffering from maladies and mortality. Both kin-directed altruism and inbreeding avoidance— behaviors not just theoretically predicted but commonly observed—require some way to discern close genetic relatives from more distant relatives and nonrelatives. It is for this reason we should expect to see mechanisms that carve the social world along lines of relatedness.

Following Marr's different level of analyses, and given that we've identified the goal of the system—kin detection—the next question is one of algorithmic structure. What systems are in the head that support this function? Such a system likely uses information (inputs) that were readily available in the environment of our hominid ancestors. Modern genetic analyses—paternity tests and the like—are so young that it doesn't even register on the evolutionary timescale. So any system designed to detect kin must therefore utilize the information that would have been available to it in the Pleistocene-like environment of our hunter-gatherer ancestors.

As suggested above, language couldn't be the primary mechanism because it blurs genetic boundaries. Another problem with language is that perceptions of kinship are perspective dependent. For instance, inclusive fitness theory posits that an individual should favor a full biological sister, who has a 0.5 chance of sharing a particular gene by virtue of sharing the same parents, over a maternal half-sister, who has only a 0.25 chance (the degree of relatedness, r, of 0.5 is twice as great as an r of 0.25). But the individual's mother sees the world differently, as she is related to both her children equally, $r = 0.5$. She will be motivated to have you "help your sister," without linguistically marking whether that sister is full or half, a factor that only affects *your* decisions, not hers. Given the perspective dependency of kinship, it is unlikely natural selection would have (or even could have) crafted systems to teach another person's relatedness to others, thus rendering language an imprecise mechanism for learning about kinship.

Last, there is good reason to suspect that alternative kin-detection mechanisms were in place long before language evolved. Indeed, many social species, including lions, voles, birds, bees, squirrels, elephants, wolves, and chimpanzees, treat close genetic relatives differently than more distantly related or unrelated individuals. Specifically, they tend to act more altruistically toward close genetic relatives and to avoid their close genetic relatives as sexual partners.[19] The existence of these behaviors implies that many species possess, somewhere in their psychology, systems for identifying relatives. But none of these species possess a verbal language, and so they cannot rely on it to learn or communicate "this is your sister, so be nice and don't have sex with her."

Instead, non-human animals use a variety of ecologically valid "kinship cues" to discern genetic relatives from nonrelatives.[20] For instance, some species use the cue of physical association to figure out who their relatives are. Many species of birds rely on this cue to detect offspring; only chicks that hatch in one's *own* nest are treated as offspring and are fed and protected. On average, this cue tends to do quite well, ensuring that males and females invest precious time and energy in their own genetic offspring. But the system can be fooled, a feature some parasitic birds such as the cuckoo evolved to take advantage of; cuckoos, for example, will lay their eggs in the nest of another species and let the parents raise their young.

Humans too use the kinship cue of association, but in our case, this cue helps to identify likely siblings, not offspring. Edward Westermarck, a Finnish social scientist, noted in the late 1890s that as a near rule children living in the same household tend to be genetic siblings. This led him to propose that *close childhood association* (childhood co-residence duration) serves as a primary cue to siblingship.[21] This makes good sense: over our species' evolutionary history, children receiving care from at least the same mother would have remained in close proximity, particularly throughout early childhood when demands on parental care were greatest.

But research has shown there is an even better cue to siblingship: seeing your mother pregnant and breastfeeding a newborn. So long as you've correctly identified which female is your own mother (likely determined by which female breastfed *you*), by tracking which child (of all the local children) she regularly nurses and cares for, you would be well on your way to accurately inferring relatedness.

The one hitch is that the cue of seeing one's mother caring for a newborn is only available to older siblings—children already present in the world and capable of observing this relationship. A younger sibling wasn't alive when their older siblings were born and nursed. Consequently, younger siblings must rely on an alternative cue to siblingship, one possibility being the childhood co-residence duration cue first proposed by Edward Westermarck.

On the table, then, is a prediction regarding the design of a sibling-detection system. To ascertain relatedness, the system is predicted to take as input two cues to kinship and use this information to compute an *internal estimate of genetic relatedness*. But given an input—a particular kinship cue—how does the system "know" how high to set the kinship estimate? It depends on the validity of the particular cue set in ancestral environments. Some cues act as a bolus, delivering highly valid and immediate information about the likelihood of relatedness. Birth is a good example of this, and is used by females to identify offspring; if the baby comes out of your body, it is yours (at least ancestrally this was always true). Likewise, seeing one's mom nursing an infant would also have served as a bolus, cueing younger siblingship, and should cause the genetic relatedness estimate to be set quite high. In contrast, other cues, such as co-residence duration, would have provided only incremental information regarding the likelihood of relatedness. Repeated observations of living with another (older) child who was receiving care from the same two parents should gradually ratchet up one's certainty of relatedness to that child. One instance of sharing a meal does not a sibling make, but repeated meals along with repeated co-sleeping and repeated care from the same parents would have increasingly cued greater and greater probabilities of relatedness.

Is there any evidence in favor of this model? Yes. Because estimates of relatedness should influence both cooperation and sexual attraction, it is possible to see how the presence of particular kinship cues affects behaviors and judgments in these domains. In a study of college undergraduates, evolutionary psychologists Debra Lieberman, Leda Cosmides, and John Tooby found that older siblings in a sibling pair reported elevated levels of altruism toward their younger sibling and, for younger opposite-sex siblings, very strong sexual aversions. Moreover, the level of altruism and sexual aversion reported was not affected by how long the subject had lived with their younger sibling. This suggests that when older siblings observe their younger siblings cared for by their own mom and dad as infants, this information acts as a bolus and produces an elevated estimate of relatedness, increasing the volume on the altruism and sexual avoidance knobs.

By contrast, for the younger siblings in a sib pair (and some older siblings who, for instance, had a different mother), the duration of childhood co-residence with an older sibling predicted the intensity of altruistic motivations and sexual avoidance, starting off low with shorter durations of co-residence, and gradually increasing year by year. It seems, then, that in the absence of information relating to early natal care such as breastfeeding, sibling detection relies on tracking how much parents invest in other children over the duration of childhood. In fact, data suggest that it takes approximately 13 to 14 years of co-residence duration to get to the same estimate of relatedness achieved when the cue of observing one's mom caring for an infant is present. Perhaps not coincidentally, this also happens to be approximately the age puberty begins. It appears as if evolution engineered a system whereby sexual aversion toward a younger sibling and that toward an older sibling are of approximately equal magnitudes upon reaching sexual maturity.

Kin detection is a prime example of instinct blindness. The mental systems that register "duration of co-residence" or "events of parental care directed toward another child" (e.g., feeding, soothing, and bathing) and then translate them into an internal probability of relatedness are hidden from us—part of the unconscious machinery that tends to work seamlessly. They simply produce a tacit sense that a particular male is a brother or a particular female is a sister—we just *know*. However, our conscious experience clouds our view of the complex underlying systems for figuring out relatedness and guiding motivations and behaviors in the cooperative and sexual domains. Instinct blindness renders invisible much of the information processing that generates, for instance, the sense that sex with a sibling is gross. We don't have access to how or why we learned to feel this way, and almost no one will make the connection that it is tied to seeing your mother care for them, or to how long you have lived together. Moreover, the mental barrier between the consciously produced feelings and underlying information-processing circuitry gives rise to the erroneous view that there must be a simple system that causes this feeling—for example, a general process of social learning that somehow enabled us to learn about relatedness and norms forbidding incest. But this intuition, much like Minsky's original conception of vision, is too simple and moreover cannot explain the absence of inbreeding in non-human species.

This isn't to say that social and cultural information are not important—they are. But they are important by virtue of mental systems that sift the social world for particular pieces of information that bear on the challenges our species faced in ancestral environments. That is, we don't take in *all* information and use it in *all* ways. This would be debilitating. Instead, cultural and social learning depend on the structure of the mind. The key is in discerning what kinds of social information each psychological adaptation takes as input, and how it might use that information. For kin detection, social arrangements are critical for learning about kinship. What happens when these systems are at sea in a novel environment? What happens, for instance, when genetically *unrelated* children are raised under the same roof? Given that kin-detection systems can only rely on cues that were *strongly indicative* of relatedness and not *actual* genetic relatedness, we should expect to see different patterns of cooperation and sexual avoidance. Do we?

The Kibbutz: A Natural Experiment on Kin Detection

The Kibbutz (Hebrew for communal settlement) was a social organization developed in Israel/Palestine in the early 1900s. The Kibbutz embodied the philosophy *from each according to ability, to each according to need* and was marked by joint ownership and the sharing of responsibilities such as food production, education, and, of particular relevance here, childrearing.[22]

On a Kibbutz, children born within a few months of one another were moved into a children's house, *bait yeladim*, where they lived and were cared for by a caretaker, a man or woman who was typically not the biological parent of any child in the house. Children slept, ate, and bathed in the children's home but were allowed to visit the home of their biological parents between 4 and 7 o'clock each evening. After 7, children—even infants—were returned to the children's home to be put to bed. This arrangement led to a group of genetically *unrelated* children being raised together in the same household.

Above we mentioned the hypothesis put forth by Edward Westermarck that close childhood association leads to sexual aversions later during adulthood. If this is true—that is, if childhood co-residence duration is one way the mind evolved to infer siblingship—then perhaps peers mistakenly categorize each other as siblings. Joseph Shepher and colleagues tested Westermarck's prediction by examining the marriage patterns of peers raised on the Kibbutz. Shepher found that *no* marriages occurred between peers who had lived together for at least four of the first six years of life. The lack of marriage between early childhood associates was interpreted as support for Westermarck's claim.[23]

But, as they say, marriage is one thing, sex quite another. A more direct test of whether the mind tracks childhood co-residence duration to infer genetic relatedness is to see if co-reared peers develop strong *sexual aversions* toward one another. After all, there are many reasons why peers might not marry—in Israel, upon turning 18, residents are required to complete mandatory military service, exposing them to a variety of potential mates outside the Kibbutz. But, independent of marriage or not, having categorized someone as a "sibling" should cause the reduction (or near-elimination) of motivations to pursue them as a sexual partner. And this is what we find. By and large, the longer two peers lived together in the same children's house, the greater the sexual aversion felt toward one another.[24] Converging lines of evidence that prolonged childhood association led to larger (nonconscious) estimates of relatedness come from the findings on cooperation: the longer two peers lived together throughout childhood, the more inclined they were to help one another in various situations as adults.

For peers on the Kibbutz, the mind appears to have miscategorized a nonrelative as a genetic relative by virtue of being exposed to the cues our species evolved to use to learn about relatedness. Because mental programs that assess relatedness serve as a front end to two different motivational systems, erroneously categorizing non-kin as kin led to the inhibition of sexual attraction and greater motivations prompting care.

The presence of the strong sexual aversion between co-reared peers and the lack of marriage between them cannot be explained by simple sociocultural learning mechanisms. This is because on the Kibbutz, families often *preferred* their children marry a peer. Because of the perspective dependency of kinship described above, from the parents' perspectives, they don't view a children's house as a "house of siblings"—they only see their own son or daughter. (After all, they didn't give birth to or sire all the children present in the house.) To parents, another child in the same children's house and by extension the child's family members are better known, perhaps making them more desirable as in-laws. But from the child's perspective, the children's house looks quite different. It is a house chock-full of individuals who feel like family and are therefore much less desirable as sexual and marriage partners.

In sum, the Kibbutz is an example of how novel cultural institutions can mislead kin-detection systems into categorizing genetically *unrelated* individuals as relatives. This example also helps to reveal the underlying workings of our psychology that guide relationships with family. Critically, genetic relatedness, while learned, is not blindly learned. It is learned by virtue of having mental systems organized to take as input particular shards of socially derived information that, in ancestral worlds, were relevant to inferring relatedness. Whether that information hits its target, as typically occurs when nuclear families remain under the same roof, or whether the information misleads, as occurred for the Kibbutz co-reared peers, depends on the structure of the social world. As we will see in later chapters, the structure of the social world can also lead to situations in which individuals fail to categorize an actual genetic relative as such, opening the door to *increased* sexual attraction. That is, the kin-detection system we have been discussing can help explain why incest sometimes occurs.

SUMMARY

Two persistent challenges face behavioral and social scientists investigating the form and function of the human mind/brain. First, explicit self-reports often do not reflect actual processes, and second, much of the internal processing of the mind is hidden from conscious view. Evolutionary biology and cognitive science offer potent solutions. Specifically, the conceptual tools of adaptive function and information-processing structure provide the means to reverse engineer the mind—they allow us to crack open the casing of our mysterious machine.[25] In this way, even our most sacred of shared intuitions, what we might consider the universals of human experience—the intense love of a parent for a child, the gnawing regret of a foregone relationship, our moral intuitions of right and wrong—can be elucidated as products of the evolutionary process, outputs of information-processing systems embedded in neural pathways whittled into the template of human cognition over evolutionary time. Kin detection is one example of how evolutionary psychology can generate hypotheses regarding the "design" of psychological systems. It also provides a nice illustration of how a uniform system can generate behavioral variation on the cultural scale by virtue of different social arrangements and informational inputs. Next, we'll take a closer look at how a specific subset of these processes—emotions—work, and then we'll delve into our particular emotion of interest: disgust.

The Emotions

To understand what emotions are, we need to start with where they live: the brain. Brains are for behaving. Generally speaking, no brain, no complex behavior. Consider the sea squirt, a tube-like marine animal. For the first portion of its life, the sea squirt is mobile and spends its time searching for a suitable habitat, in this case a rock, to which it will attach and remain fastened for the rest of its life. During this first stage of life, the sea squirt uses its brain to extract information from the environment to assess whether a particular location has favorable light conditions for the symbiotic oxygen-producing algae that attach to the sea squirt's body. If not, the sea squirt moves on and keeps looking. The assessment of local conditions and directed mobility requires the processing of information, hence the brain. But after the sea squirt attaches to its new home, it no longer needs to navigate the seas or make decisions about habitat suitability. In short, it no longer needs a brain. Consequently, during the adult life stage, instead of maintaining energetically expensive neural tissue, the sea squirt "eats" its brain.[1]

Humans are not sea squirts,[2] but the same point holds: brains are for behaving—interacting with environmentally derived information to navigate and interact with the world. But behavior—at least behavior that tends to lead to positive fitness outcomes—requires direction. Random movements tend not to aid an animal's survival. Put a different way, those of our ancestors who moved in survival-*enhancing* ways with respect to cliffs, predators, rivers, and mates tended to live to see another day or reproduce more often than individuals who moved randomly when, for instance, on the edge of a precipice.

In the simplest of cases, directionality can occur by moving along a chemical or electromagnetic gradient of some type. For instance, many single-celled organisms can detect local pH levels and move toward greater acidity or greater alkalinity. Gradient-directed cellular movements are ubiquitous in humans too: neural development and organization occurs because neurons travel along various concentration gradients to reach their destination.

At greater levels of organization—at the level of the individual, a multicellular mass—there are more complex systems that enable movement.[3] Such movements tend to be in the service of some goal—to flee a predator, to find food, to mount a mate, or, in the case of the sea squirt, to find a home. These behaviors don't arise from nothing and they are far from random and chaotic. Instead they are targeted, often with sniper-like precision.

Emotions are one type of program instantiated in neural tissue that helps direct behavior; they are one of nature's guidance systems. Imagine life without any emotion. No fear, anger, jealousy, disgust; no depression, shame, hunger, thirst; no gratitude, joy, lust, or love. What would you do all day? What would cause you to move? Need food? Well, unfortunately, you are not a sea squirt capable of dining on nutrients floating by your mouth, so your hope rests on a hamburger falling from the sky. Without hunger, an emotion causing movement to search the environment for matter to consume, you would waste away. Need to reproduce? Better hope a mate falls into your lap, and in exactly the right way. Without emotions to seek out mates bearing particular qualities (sexual attraction and lust), reproduction would be random, if it occurred at all. In short, emotions are programs that organize elements of psychology and physiology to react to situations that repeatedly occurred over our species' evolutionary history in a manner that led, on average, to fitness-enhancing outcomes.

The key point is that emotions are programs that initiate and regulate *action*. They are, ultimately and eventually, about movement. Indeed, the root of "emotive" is *movere*, the Latin verb "to move." Humans possess a number of emotion programs. In general, the emotion programs in a given species depend on the kinds of movements that tended to enhance survival and reproduction in that species' ancestral environment. This includes both human and non-human animals alike. Because emotions are programs that coordinate fitness-enhancing responses to situations that repeatedly occurred over many generations, it would be strange if they did not exist in other species, particularly in our primate ancestors and relatives.

To provide a conceptual framework for understanding our focal emotion, disgust, this chapter aims to define what an emotion is from an evolutionary perspective and to provide the tools for characterizing an emotion. We begin with a commonly held intuition about emotion, namely that "emotion" is distinct from "cognition." This dualist view also goes by "feeling versus thinking" or "passion versus reason." Coming to grips with the important and unimportant aspects of these dichotomies is critical, in part because they reflect our intuitions of how the mind works—intuitions that, as we've already seen, are subject to a debilitating instinct blindness.

MAKING THE NATURAL SEEM STRANGE

Intuition tells us there is something different about emotion—*feeling*—versus cognition—*thinking*. When you are angry, it *feels* different than when you are balancing your checkbook. When you are jealous that your partner is flirting with a stranger, it *feels* different than the mindset you adopt when playing chess. Emotions tend to have a characteristic feeling or quality—"qualia" in philosopher-speak. By contrast, "regular thinking," for instance, sorting laundry, doing math homework, or comparing nutrition labels, seems to lack any characteristic feeling, leading to the intuition that feeling and thinking are qualitatively different states.

These intuitions aren't *wrong*—the two categories do feel different to us. But while intuitional knowledge may be useful in our day-to-day lives, it can also lead to errors when it comes to scientific inquiry. Consider the lessons from physics. Newtonian mechanics held that, as intuition suggests, space and time are fixed dimensions, backdrops against which matter interacts. But Einstein, through his theories of relativity, revealed flaws in these assumptions and showed that the space–time relationship varies in systematic ways. Physicists also tell us that matter is made up of mostly empty space, but this completely defies our experience when we bump into walls rather than pass through them or when we attempt to overstuff a suitcase. To cap it all off, the theoretical framework of superstring theory posits the existence of ten different dimensions, yet our brain registers only four. Lessons from physics reinforce the idea that intuitions and experience with matter work for us—medium-sized animals with a particular evolutionary history—but might not reflect the "true" state of nature.[4]

Psychology has suffered a similar fate. Much as in physics, intuitions have led to (potentially) erroneous views. Take, for instance, the once-popular view of the human mind as a blank slate, a notion replaced over time with the view of the mind as a general-purpose computer. Both views entail computationally intractable problems, yet experientially they seem plausible.[5] Our intuitions regarding emotion have also misled investigations into how the mind works. Emotions tend to be billed as automatic, uncontrolled, and irrational processes, whereas cognition is lauded as voluntary, controlled, and rational. Naturally, there is both truth and misrepresentation with this characterization. The truth lies in the fact that feeling *is* different than not feeling. In other words, the subjective experience of emotions is different from our experience of deliberate calculation. But this consciously felt and intuitive difference fades away at the level of information processing, the true business of neurons.

Both "emotion" and "cognition" require circuitry—that is, some underlying program to carry out their function. Nothing highly organized and functional comes for free. Artificial intelligence engineers will sing the same song: robots adopt behaviors that were encoded into their circuitry, and even the flexible responses they exhibit occur by virtue of code enabling such flexibility. As programs, both emotion and cognition take inputs, perform operations on inputs, and generate outputs that, in turn, affect downstream systems.

With respect to emotion, much if not all input is decidedly "non-emotional." Color detection, movement analysis, reproductive value estimation, kin detection, expected welfare valuation, and categorization analysis are all stereotypically labeled by social and behavioral scientists as "cognitive" processes, but all are critical components of various emotions. Let's revisit fear. Part of the "fear program" includes visual and auditory systems that assess the presence of predators and an eye-gaze analysis system that determines whether the predator has seen you. If signal-detection analyses determine that there is likely a predator in your immediate environment and that it has indeed detected your presence, other systems are activated, such as those calculating escape (a highly coordinated response in its own right, requiring, among other things, physiological systems redirecting oxygen and fuel to muscles, and psychological systems governing spatial navigation). Where do the perceptual processing, decision-making circuitry, physiological regulation, and behavior modification shift from "cognition" to "emotion"? This is a difficult question to answer. But even if one did find the line of demarcation, it would just be an arbitrary way to label events. At the level of information processing, the distinction between cognition and emotion fades. Inputs associated with predators trigger a constellation of physiological, psychological, and behavioral components that coordinate an adaptive response: surviving an encounter with a predator. The sequence of information processing that achieves this goal is just that: a highly organized sequence of information processing, which was structured by the forces of natural selection. How we, as beneficiaries of these systems, choose to label them is one thing; what they *are* is another.

So what about the *feeling* of being scared? What is it and is it necessary for the adaptive response? There is much debate on these topics.[6] The physiological response associated with fear—the activation of the heart, musculature, and respiratory systems—might just happen to be associated with a particular feeling. Similarly, it could be that the stomach and esophageal activation associated with disgust just happen to be associated with a particular (nauseous) feeling. On this account, the particular quality of an emotion, its qualia, is a byproduct, just a feature that happens to go along with the functional response of the system. This is one plausible account—the sensation associated with an emotion might just be a property of our carbon-based physiology.

One could imagine programming a droid—R2D2 or C3PO—to avoid predators. It would likely possess many of the same information-processing procedures as the human mind (e.g., detection systems, decision-making algorithms, and learning mechanisms that store prior successes). By virtue of being composed of silicon chips and synthetic materials, the droid might not have a sense or "feeling" of activation. But it might. Does this make the response any different than the outputs of our predator-response system? Would the response to a predator be any less effective if the feelings were absent? This is hard to know.

Another possibility is that qualia, rather than being downstream consequences of system activation, represent the primary response and cause of activation. On this interpretation, you first feel the sense of fear, and then this prompts you to look around and determine its cause. The only problem with this account: What caused the sense of fear in the first place?[7] Feelings do occur—it just isn't clear that they are the primary movers.

The scientific focus on feelings has had another detrimental effect on the study of emotion. Many emotion researchers maintain that qualia are *defining features* of emotions. If a state does not have a characteristic feeling, it is not an emotion. Two additional "defining features" of an emotion are commonly thought to be the presence of a facial expression, and a short time course (clocked in minutes).[8] Running through the roster of states often discussed as universal emotions, we can see they all meet these three necessary and sufficient criteria: anger, disgust, fear, happiness, sadness, and surprise. They all have a typical feeling and a universally recognized facial expression, and they tend to occur over short durations. Check, check, check.

But what about jealousy? Gratitude? Depression? Shame? Illness? Hunger? Sexual arousal? These are typically not categorized as emotions. Instead, they are "drives" or prolonged "conditions," often termed *affective states* (oh, the curse of language). One reason for the different classification is that each violates one of the three canonical defining features, features that in our opinion were plucked from the (mine)field of intuition. Jealousy, gratitude, and sexual arousal might not have a stereotypical facial expression. Jealousy can last a long time, as could shame. These properties disqualify them from being labeled an emotion as conventionally understood. But they are nonetheless programs that, in response to an ancestrally recurring situation (e.g., jealousy: suspected mate infidelity; gratitude: jump-starting a cooperative relationship), cause a change in elements of the psychology and physiology in a manner that led to fitness-enhancing outcomes (e.g., prevention of cuckoldry and developing a friendship, respectively).

In our opinion, the focus on qualia and "feeling" has been a siren song in psychology, distracting researchers away from questions more susceptible to scientific analysis. With respect to facial expressions and time course, we suggest these are potential *properties* of emotions, not defining features. Starting from first principles grounded in evolutionary biology, we can generate predictions regarding *when* communication via facial expressions would have been adaptive and *how long* it would have taken our ancestors, on average, to deal with a particular recurring challenge.

EVOLUTIONARY LOGIC VERSUS CONSCIOUS MOTIVATIONS

Before we delve into an evolutionary analysis of emotions, there is a common misstep we'd like to address. The misstep: equating the explanation for *why* an emotion evolved (that is, the logic of how a particular sequence of behaviors affected survival or reproduction in ancestral environments), and the explanation of *how* the system operates in the human mind. Natural selection didn't code into our mental machinery the logic of why particular behaviors or states evolved. It just coded behavior that happened to have particular statistical effects over many generations. For instance, mothers love their children because of programs that evolved to direct intense care and attention to genetic descendants. But mothers need not know the logic by which such programs operate. Somewhere in these programs are lines of code assessing likelihood of relatedness and need state, but moms typically aren't consciously aware of this information when giving a child a piece of cheese. Moms just experience the motivational force of love. Similarly, siblings reared together typically never think about sex with each other and when they do, such thoughts tend to be met with disgust. But siblings need not know *why* such feelings arise—that is, they need not be aware of the evolutionary feedback process

that selected for psychological mechanisms generating inbreeding-avoidance behaviors. The same holds for other emotions including fear, jealousy, and anger. We
just feel and act. But we feel and act in the manner we do because these outputs
tended to have a positive effect on survival and reproduction in ancestral environments. Keeping these two explanations separate—the evolutionary logic for why
a program exists and the program itself—can be tricky, but it is important. As we
move forward into discussions of disgust, explanations of what disgust evolved
to do might at times seem foreign. This is because natural selection crafted procedures that cause us to think and behave in particular ways that led, on average,
to greater chances of survival, not procedures that allow us to understand the biochemical implications of, for instance, host–parasite interactions. Evolutionary
logic is different than psychological intuition.

AN EVOLUTIONARY APPROACH TO EMOTIONS

Our view of emotions is perhaps best described by way of analogy. Members of
a submarine crew cannot directly observe the outside world. To navigate, sub-
mariners must rely on a variety of guidance systems, like sonar. Imagine a hypothetical submarine with different sonar systems for detecting the presence of
different situations: one for detecting marine life, one for detecting land, and one
for detecting metal surfaces. These three sonars constantly sweep the environment, each with its own detection algorithm for knowing what counts as a fish,
what counts as land, and what counts as a likely military vessel. Blips will appear
on the sonar when detection circuitry (calibrated in just the right way) calculates
an above-average chance that something in its respective category is indeed "out
there." Response systems within the sub will differ depending on what is found.
Land will be avoided; fish will be ignored; enemy subs will be monitored and
possibly attacked. Furthermore, not all blips will affect the different crewmen on
board in the same way. The sonar operator, repairman, cook, chemist, hospital
corpsmen, engineering aide, gunner's mate, enginemen, missile tech, electrician's
mate, and logistics specialist will all take on specific duties given a specific situation: missile test, enemy engagement, radiation leak, speed test, or evacuation.

The highly orchestrated ballet that occurs on submarines in response to external situations (enemy attack, terrain navigation, resupply) and internal situations (water leak, foodborne illness, physical altercation) is an apt analogy for
emotions. From an evolutionary perspective, emotions are programs that monitor
internal and external environments for situations that, over human evolutionary
history, affected survival and reproduction and that activate a response that led,
on average, to fitness-enhancing outcomes in ancestral environments.[9] More specifically, emotions are organized, prepared responses to those situations that had,
on average, *a narrow range of solutions* that would have best promoted survival
and reproduction. For instance, when predators were present, programs that narrowed in on the particular behaviors associated with the best chance of survival
(run, hide, or freeze) would have done much better over evolutionary time than

programs that simulated outcomes associated with all possible behaviors (sleep, sing, strip, eat, sneeze, draw, dance, cook, walk, wink, run, laugh, cry, and cough) before selecting a winner.

Emotions orchestrate and prioritize. When two situations arise simultaneously—for instance, when one is hungry and one happens upon a predator—emotion programs prioritize responses in a manner that would have led to positive fitness outcomes. In the presence of both hunger and the threat of a predator, prioritizing escape over food acquisition would have, on average, led to better outcomes. Fear trumps hunger. Fear should also trump sexual arousal and jealousy, for the same reason. (Fear, however, seems not to trump nausea, as one of us white-knucklers recently discovered on a flight home.) In general, natural selection built rules or tinkered with weightings to prioritize which states get command over the body under particular circumstances. Sometimes these states are more or less compatible (boredom and hunger) and sometimes they are not (fleeing predators and seeking a mate).

If emotions are programs engineered by natural selection to navigate the opportunities and threats our ancestors repeatedly faced, then for each emotion we should be able to identify the situation to which it is yoked, and outline the kinds of information-processing systems required for the emotion to function adaptively. To relate this back to our discussion of Marr's levels of analysis (see Chapter 2), after we posit the survival challenge an emotion program helps overcome (satisficing a computational level of analysis), we should be able to provide an algorithmic level of analysis, which details how the emotion works in an individual's mind/brain. Here we roughly break down an algorithmic level of analysis of an emotion into three basic steps: situation detection, integration, and response.

Step 1: Detecting the Situation

Each emotion program is a response to a particular situation, or class of situations. Hunger is a program activated in response to perceived nutritional depletion; fear is a program activated in response to predators and other threats to physical safety; anger is a program activated in response to perceptions of exploitation or social undervaluation; male sexual jealousy is activated in response to perceptions of infidelity. But how do we know that a particular fitness-relevant situation is at hand? For instance, how does one know that a predator is about to attack? How does one know a mate is being unfaithful? We just "seem to know" when each is occurring, but as the lessons of instinct blindness have shown, we effortlessly just "know" by virtue of having dedicated systems for sussing each situation out. To put the matter a different way, how would you program a robot to "know" that a predator is looming or that its mate might have a secret lover? There would likely be specific lines of code directing the collection of particular types of information from the environment allowing the robot to learn when each situation was at hand.

The ability to detect situations depends on our ability to parse space–time into events and register the features that specifically cued the occurrence of a repeated event. No two events are identical, but many have properties in common. Seeing a large-fanged animal and hearing a roar were properties shared by states of the world in which predators were present. Moreover, fangs and roars reliably provided information about predator presence and not, for instance, mate infidelity, enemy ambush, genetic relatedness, or food palatability. By contrast, seeing one's mate in the arms of a rival reliably cued potential infidelity, not predator presence et alia. Indeed, a strange (and Monty Python-esque) inference upon seeing a predator would be to suspect one's mate was having an affair.

To the extent that particular cues reliably correlated with a specific recurring survival-jeopardizing or survival-enhancing situation, natural selection could have used these regularities to build programs to detect the situation and mount an adaptive response. By contrast, situations for which there were no reliable cues, or for which there was no reliable recurrence, preclude natural selection from engineering circuitry to specifically navigate that type of situation. Take climate change, for instance. Humans did not regularly experience the catastrophic consequences associated with intergenerational threats, such as climate change (or meteors posing extinction threats) over the course of their individual lifetimes, and thus there are likely no psychological adaptations that evolved to carry out the specific function of detecting climate change (or meteor impact) and motivating the adoption of protective and preventive measures. Of course, we *can* reason about these events, but reactions to many novel situations don't carry the same motivational force as reactions to, for instance, predators, disease, or mate infidelity.[10]

In sum, a first way to characterize an emotion is the ancestrally recurring situation to which it is adapted and the cues that indicate the presence of that situation. Box 3.1 presents a list of situations and cues. Try and match each with the relevant emotion.[11]

Step 2: Integration

Humans show great flexibility in behavior. This flexibility is afforded by the presence of yet additional circuitry that integrates information bearing on how, when, and to what extent an emotion response would have been adaptive in a given situation. Remember, no behavior comes for free. The question is, between situation detection and behavioral response, what additional factors would have had an effect on the survival value of a response? Given that a piece of food might show evidence of microorganisms (e.g., mold or rot), would it have been adaptive to avoid eating it under *all* situations? If the person next to you has a cold, would it have been adaptive to avoid that person regardless of who they were? Rather than being a purely reflexive response in which the presence of a situation leads invariably to the same behavior, emotions are in fact flexible devices (or at least more flexible than typically appreciated).

Box 3.1

PAIRS OF RECURRING SITUATIONS AND CUES INDICATING THEIR PRESENCE

Situation	Cues (ancestral)
1. Predator presence	fangs, fur, agency, snake-like, spider-like
2. Pathogen presence	filamentous appearance, dung, blood, body fluids, smell of volatile compounds, mushiness
3. Mate infidelity	prolonged absences, close physical association with rivals, poor relationship quality
4. Another person undervalues the self	person imposes a cost on self or avoids delivering benefit to self
5. Another person overvalues the self	person delivers benefit to self or avoids imposing cost on self
6. The self undervalues another person	inflicted cost on person, did not provide a benefit when could have
7. Nutritionally depleted	low blood sugar levels
8. Mating opportunity	presence of potential sexual partner
9. Investment in relatives	cues to kinship and need

Each emotion program, be it fear, lust, disgust, or sexual jealousy, integrates a range of information that would have helped generate an adaptive response. When in the presence of an attractive individual, the program of lust/sexual pursuit doesn't reflexively kick in. Rather, additional pieces of information are brought to bear on the problem of when to pursue a person as a sexual partner. Genetic relatedness is a critical piece of information; so too is their relationship status and thus cost of pursing the desired mate. Indeed, many factors are weighed to assess the costs and benefits of mate choice; sexual pursuit is not trivial. As we will discuss in the next section, the same is true for disgust. There are a variety of factors that disgust systems take as input to generate the flexible behaviors we observe with respect to food consumption, contact, and mate choice.

Learning, the guided extraction of information from the environment, is also a critical component of emotion programs. Some emotions require information from the surrounding *physical* environment (e.g., learning what counts as a predator); some require information from the surrounding *social* environment (e.g., learning the features of men and women in the local environment to calibrate mate-choice systems); and some require information from *internal* monitoring systems (e.g., blood glucose levels are monitored and, when low, trigger motivations to seek additional sources of food). In contrast to the common view that learning is a process that fills empty spaces in our blank-slate mind, it makes sense that only a mind rich in programs has the capacity to carry out the vast range of learning exhibited in humans. As the psychologist Martin Seligman has stated, humans and other animals come "prepared to learn" associations holding survival value.[12] These learning systems are thus components of the architecture of the mind, influencing how information is weighted and processed, and ultimately influencing the kinds of behaviors an emotion sets into action.

Step 3: Selecting a Plan of Action

After a situation has been detected and the relevant information integrated, the next step is a response. But what *is* the adaptive response when one has detected a predator or caught a mate in the sack with a rival? Theoretically, circuitry that detects a situation (a looming tiger or an unfaithful spouse) could be linked to any behavior (jumping, sleeping, crying, spinning, arousal, or vomiting). The situation–behavior pairings we observe in humans are those that led, on average, to an increased chance of survival and/or reproduction under ancestral conditions. Freezing, climbing, and running away are possible solutions to predator presence. Distancing oneself from the source of contamination and vomiting in the event a contaminated substance was consumed are adaptive responses to cues of pathogen presence. The presence of an attractive mate should trigger other situation-specific responses (note: vomiting, falling asleep, or running away would probably not have been among those selected).

In addition to overt behavior, emotions can exert control over many, if not all, of the different components of psychology and physiology. How each component of our psychology—for instance, memory, perception, learning, and reasoning— is activated or deactivated depends on the emotion and the situation at hand. For instance, when one is nauseated, memory systems recall the kinds of foods recently eaten, and reasoning systems infer that illness was caused by something one ate, not something one heard or something one wore. When one is angry, concepts like blame, harm, and punishment are activated in the service of changing the provoker's behavior in future interactions. And when one is afraid, memories of hiding places are primed and conceptual frameworks shift, turning pens from writing devices to possible weapons.

Emotions can also regulate perception. Fear, for instance, changes auditory and visual acuity. The common phenomenon of hearing noises in the house when home alone is due to a shift in perceptual sensitivities, not (necessarily) a change in the frequency of noises. Being alone, especially at night, was, under ancestral conditions, a strong cue of increased vulnerability to attack or ambush. Our fear system is designed to increase the sensitivity to perceptual systems that might detect such an attack in advance. Daytime or the presence of other people rendered ambush less likely. In the daytime, your house still makes all of the same sounds as it does at night; it's just that the reduced threat level downregulates perceptual sensitivities, making it less likely you will become aware of such noises.

With respect to physiology, emotions can exert control over a range of processes, including respiration, blood pressure, heart rate, immune function, water utilization, and glucose regulation. For instance, fear slows down digestion and halts sexual arousal, yet primes systems that release analgesics in the event of tissue damage (e.g., a snake bite). Which physiological systems each emotion entrains and whether particular systems get ramped up or turned down depend on the situation and the kind of response that would have improved the chances of survival and reproduction in ancestral environments.[13]

SUMMARY

Emotions are the musical chords of the mind, each with a particular tone and mood. They coordinate the activation of a particular constellation of psychological, physiological, and behavioral processes in response to ancestrally recurring situations. Although they are termed emotions, we can describe these functional responses in terms of their underlying information-processing procedures—that is, their inputs, algorithms that integrate information, and behavioral, physiological, and psychological outputs. In this respect, emotion *is* cognition.

As we move forward into the world of disgust, we will utilize the framework that we've spent these past two chapters outlining, asking questions such as: What is the function of disgust? What recurrent ancestral challenges was disgust naturally selected to help solve? How does it work—that is, what is the information-processing architecture that generates the subjective "feeling" we experience during disgust? Wading through the psychology of disgust is important. Before we can understand how disgust influences the law, we must first understand how disgust interacts with moral judgments. And before we can understand how disgust interacts with moral judgments, we must first understand what disgust was designed—via natural selection—to do in the first place.

In the next four chapters, we'll sketch a phylogeny of repugnance, showing how evolution engineered disgust to originally perform three functions, namely regulating decisions pertaining to consumption, physical contact, and sex. By sketching the information-processing systems that carry out each function, we will show how disgust can be activated in response to a heterogeneous mix of acts, both within and across cultures. Ultimately, understanding what causes disgust and how it operates provides the foundation for exploring the downstream relationships between disgust and morality, and disgust and the law.

PART II

Disgust

4
—

What to Eat?

The term disgust is intimately linked to food, coming from the Latin *dis* (negative or reversal) and *gustus* (taste). Not surprisingly, emotion researchers have long focused on the link between food and disgust. Darwin, in *The Expression of the Emotions in Man and Animals*, defined disgust as referring "to something revolting, primarily in relation to the sense of taste, as actually perceived or vividly imagined; and secondarily to anything which causes a similar feeling, through the sense of smell, touch, and even of eyesight."[1] Similarly, Andras Angyal, in another early consideration of disgust wrote, "the main threat against which disgust is directed, is the oral incorporation of certain substances," which he maintained include waste and body products of humans and other animals.[2] Paul Rozin, Jonathan Haidt, and Clark McCauley, current researchers in the field of disgust, built upon Darwin's and Angyal's conception and posit what they term *core disgust*, revulsion at the oral incorporation of contaminants.[3] Given the potential dangers associated with ingestion, it makes good sense why taste, the mouth, and oral incorporation have received such prominent attention.

The focus on consumption, however, raises an interesting question: What *is* food? Instinct blindness might render this question absurd. We naturally know what is and is not OK to eat—hamburgers, brownies, carrots, shrimp cocktail, apples = good; desk, carpet, bark, rocks, metal = bad. But by now, we hope it is evident that when such seemingly obvious conclusions occur, they occur by virtue of a sophisticated and complex underlying programming structure that makes them so.

Today, as in ancestral times, substances differ in their nutrient, and hence fitness, value. Had there been no variation in how consuming particular items affected our system and our ability to survive, then no food selection or discrimination mechanisms would be required; there would not even need to be a category "food"—anything would suffice. But in the environment in which we evolved, substances *did* vary according to their composition. And given that humans are omnivores consuming plants, animals, and, from time to time, fungi (e.g., mushrooms), it would have been adaptive to discern nutritional from harmful items within each Kingdom. Of course, humans don't just require food, we need water as well. Hunger and thirst, despite being labeled as "drives," are nonetheless information-processing programs that evolved to regulate decisions and behaviors in response to a recurring challenge of the ancestral environment: the need to obtain valuable nutrients. They are 'emotions' all the way. In this chapter, we provide a description of what our consumption system might look like and the role disgust plays in preventing the ingestion of many harmful substances.[4]

THE PHYSICS OF FOOD

Before we delve into human consumption psychology, it is perhaps worth ruminating over why we eat and drink. The answer is simple enough: we need energy. But more than this, consumption is a process that evolved because of its positive effects on maintaining, increasing, or restoring order. In the parlance of physics, eating helps fight entropy, the tendency of physical systems to move toward states of greater *dis*order. Energy obtained by foods is used to promote movement, respiration, repair, growth, and the maintenance of cellular structures and products. Thus, consuming substances containing high-energy bonds easily broken and translated into usable energy for these purposes would have conferred a fitness advantage. Because water is a critical ingredient of many biochemical reactions, an adequate supply of water, either obtained from food materials or straight from the source, would have likewise aided in the fight against entropy.

But indiscriminate ingestion would have been dangerous. Consuming matter that *increased* entropy would have carried severe negative outcomes for the organism in terms of survival, and hence reproduction. That is, not everything is "food." Our psychology of consumption, so viewed, is technically a selection system *seeking* order-promoting matter and *avoiding* entropy-promoting matter. The question is, what kinds of substances, if consumed, tend to cause an increase in entropy in our bodies?

In general, there are three different types of threat: biological, chemical, and mechanical. Every piece of food is a potential Trojan horse, harboring a destructive biological army, a brew of toxic plant chemicals, or an arsenal of thorns and barbs. Pathogens—bacteria, viruses, worms, and other microorganisms that rely on hosts to replicate and spread—actively disassemble our bodies for their own purposes. Over human history through today, the spread of influenza, smallpox, the black plague, cholera, malaria, and HIV reveals how lethal pathogens have been. Even chronic diseases, such as heart disease, diabetes, and various cancers, have been increasingly linked to infectious agents.[5] Whether fast or slow, pathogens have been a fierce biological threat, having evolved numerous strategies to dismantle their hosts in their own fight against entropy. Plant toxins likewise pose serious threats. Plants, in their defense against pathogens and predators alike, produce chemical weapons to prevent decimation. Toxins can be particularly pernicious as many interfere with critical physiological processes, including respiration and neural activity. Last, hot and sharp items such as barbs and thorns can cause cellular damage. Together, biological, chemical, and mechanical threats disrupt order and risk the ultimate entropic state of a living organism: death.

Humans and other organisms have evolved various protections against entropy-causing substances. In humans, mechanical and thermal threats are detected via the peripheral nervous system and cause one type of aversive response: pain. Our focus will be on biological and chemical threats—pathogens and plant toxins—as their detection is mediated via the central nervous system and is linked with our aversive response of interest: disgust.

Given the dangers of pathogens and plant toxins, how does one infer that a piece of food is "safe" to eat? Bacteria are hard to see with the naked eye. Likewise, plant toxins cannot necessarily be discerned via visual inspection. The best evolution could have done is to construct a "pathogen detection system" and a "toxin detection system" sensitive to properties that were reliably indicative of these harms *in ancestral environments*. Long ago, as today, our human ancestors could have relied on a variety of visual, olfactory, tactile, auditory, and taste cues to make inferences regarding the safety of consuming particular items.

CUES TO HIDDEN DANGER: DETECTING PATHOGENS

Compiling a list of the organic substances that disgust us is akin to sweeping the world with a high-powered magnifying glass, cataloging the various microscopic dangers that humans would do well to avoid. Because our eyes can't see at such fine levels of magnification, though, we are forced to rely on inferential cues. Visual and olfactory inspections provide first passes at foodborne pathogen risk assessment. Imagine yourself as a hunter-gatherer walking the savannah in search of food. You come across a dead gazelle. How do you know whether it is safe to eat? Of all the information you might collect (e.g., the pattern of spots on its fur; whether the fur is dark brown or light brown; the number of antlers present; whether its nose points north or its legs are crossed), only a very narrow range will provide information that bears upon infection risk. For instance, inferring the cause of death and time since death would have been informative. Animals that show no sign of predatory attack could have fallen ill or could have been struck with or ingested a fatal toxin. Visual cues about the animal's condition provide a means for inferring these possibilities. For instance, cues of perspiration (moist, matted fur) could reflect a fever; foam or drool could be indicative of viral contamination or toxin ingestion; and worms around the animal's orifices (at either end) suggest intestinal infestation. These cues can all be used to infer cause of death and the potential risks of consumption.

In addition to the likely cause of death, time matters. The longer the time since an animal's own immune system has stopped functioning, the longer the time resident pathogens have had free rein over host tissue and, thus, the greater the likely pathogen concentration. Luckily, nature provides humans with a few time stamps. One is the presence of fly larvae—better known as maggots. When flies find organic matter, they lay eggs out of which emerge, after a day or so, cute and cuddly maggots. The larval stage is the "eating stage" of flies and over approximately a four-day period, maggots feast on decaying matter, growing four times in size. After a two-week-long stage of metamorphosis, flies emerge, restarting the entire life cycle. Why do we find maggots so disgusting? The presence and size of maggots as well as their population density are one of nature's time stamps for how long an animal has been dead, cuing the safety (or lack thereof) of meat consumption.

Another time stamp is the olfactory bouquet of decomposition. Bacteria play a role in protein putrefaction by decomposing sulfur-containing amino acids. As they and other microorganisms feed on organic matter, they release noxious volatile compounds, many of which humans have evolved to detect: ammonia, hydrogen sulfide gas, and thiols (a particularly noxious class of compounds, used as an odorant for otherwise odorless natural gas). Only the smallest of concentrations are required to trip our nasal circuitry, a feature scientists often exploit when inducing disgust in the lab.[6] As with visual cues, natural selection linked many of these olfactory-detected chemical signatures with avoidance and aversiveness (as opposed to approach and appetitiveness) because they were associated with negative fitness outcomes when consumed.

There are a variety of other cues associated with contamination. Fungi such as molds can be visually detected via their filamentous hair-like structures ("hyphae") that spread over organic matter (you know, the green furry stuff in your fridge). Many kinds of worms are easy to see, particularly if they are on external surfaces. Internally embedded worms can likewise be detected, with the worst kind being those discovered half-gone after biting into fruit flesh. In plants, cell damage can lead to the breakdown of cell walls, making the plant more vulnerable to airborne spores and microbes. Bruised fruit with punctured skin can harbor foodborne pathogens such as fungi, molds, *Escherichia coli*, or salmonella. We can detect the extent to which a fruit has been damaged by assessing how mushy it feels. Recall the last time you shopped for peaches or apples and picked up a mushy one; chances are you quickly exchanged it for one that was more firm. Tactile-derived information regarding tension correlates with cell damage in plants, a state that, if present, would have coincided with an increased infection risk.

Moisture and sliminess function as additional cues to potential bacterial or fungal presence because microorganisms tend to flourish in wet conditions. More accurately, they tend to flourish in wet *and warm* conditions. There is good reason why we have well-funded fields of *tropical* medicine but not *tundral* (cold/wet) or *desert* (hot/dry) medicine. Empirically, in our own lab, research conducted by Robert Oum and Alison Aylward found that subjects rate mushy dough as more disgusting than solid rope, a difference that becomes more pronounced when the dough is wet.[7] Halloween games take advantage of the fact that humans use tactile properties relating to consistency and moisture to detect pathogens. Ask kids to put their hands into a bag to feel "eyeballs" (hard egg yolks covered in oil) or "worms" (spaghetti and sauce) and hit "record" on your camera—you will capture disgust at its best.

The use of tactile cues as a means for inferring safety is not limited to humans. Primatologist Cecile Sarabian and colleagues from the Primate Research Institute at Kyoto University conducted a study similar to the one conducted by Oum and

Aylward, but with chimps. Researchers placed banana slices on top of hidden pieces of dough or rope. Chimps were far less likely to eat the bananas when they were set atop the dough. More than this, their videos show that the chimps recoiled when their hand (unexpectedly) touched the dough in a manner virtually identical to what we observed in our own lab with humans.[8]

Although typically overlooked, auditory cues can also provide information regarding the safety of food consumption. If you've ever heard anyone retch, you've likely experienced the full effect of how audio cues can trigger disgust, nausea, and, if you're very unlucky, vomiting. The function of such a link is easy enough to see if you consider human ancestral environments where food sharing was common: if someone in your immediate environment has eaten something rotten and is now retching, chances are you, too, might have consumed something rotten. Researchers have recently explored the possibility that humans come prepared to associate particular sounds with pathogen presence. For instance, Disa Sauter, Paul Ekman, and colleagues studied whether auditory sounds linked to disgust are recognized across different cultures. Specifically, they compared the ability to identify disgust sounds in European native English speakers and the Himba, a northern Namibian pastoral society. In their study, subjects heard a short story (in their respective language) and then were asked to select which of two sounds matched the emotion depicted in the story. One of the stories was about a person who had eaten rotten food. After hearing the story, English-speaking subjects heard prerecorded vocalizations made by Himba speakers and Himba-speaking subjects heard prerecorded vocalizations made by English speakers. Far better than chance, all subjects selected the appropriate disgust sound, which in both languages ends up sounding something like "ech" or "blech."[9] Though this is only one study, these data point to the possibility that disgust has a universally recognized vocal signature in addition to a universally recognized facial expression.[10]

In the event that visual, olfactory, tactile, or auditory cues fail to reveal pathogen presence, there is one last sensory line of defense before ingestion: taste. Humans, like many species, evolved taste receptors to identify substances linked with positive as well as negative fitness outcomes. Carbohydrates (sugars), salts/minerals, and proteins were all substances that varied in their availability and contributed to our survival in ancestral environments. As a consequence, we evolved specialized behavioral systems to seek them out (e.g., cravings) and physiological systems to identify their presence (e.g., taste buds to identify sweet, salty, and savory).[11]

But we also possess taste receptors identifying substances that, if overconsumed or consumed at all, could be linked with deleterious outcomes. Sourness, for example, is the sense of taste that evolved to detect the presence of bacteria in potential foods. Microorganismic pathogens such as bacteria thrive in and on organic matter, particularly sources containing supplies of iron and lipids (e.g., animals). As bacteria invade, they produce, as part of their normal life cycle, many byproducts including ammonia and acids rich in hydrogen ions. Natural selection took advantage of bacterial production of acids and built taste receptors sensitive to hydrogen ions in species (like us) that consume substances potentially harboring bacteria. When these receptors get activated, they give rise to our experience of sourness. The twingy-tang on the tongue after sipping milk or tasting a yogurt sauce is our brain identifying a potential danger—microorganism presence. Sour taste receptors help detect bacteria populations in potential foods and activate our aversive response. But bacteria and other microorganisms represent only one class of danger.

CUES TO HIDDEN DANGER: DETECTING PLANT TOXINS

As stores of valuable energy-rich resources, plants, much like humans, need to protect themselves against invasion by pathogens and consumption by predators. Plants have engineered multiple solutions to these problems. One solution is the production of chemical compounds that interfere with the day-to-day cellular operations of would-be pathogens and predators. As an herbivore and plant "predator," humans thus faced the danger of ingesting these defensive toxic plant compounds.

How do we infer the presence of plant toxins? Visual cues will help identify a physical structure as a plant but do not necessarily provide information regarding its toxicity; a healthy-looking plant might still be quite lethal. The lack of apparent cues provides an important role for socially transmitted information regarding the consequences of consuming a particular plant. And for this reason, we should expect to see sensitivity to socially transmitted information regarding palatability. We will return to this point below but mention here that "poisonous" appears to be a privileged mental tag that, once learned via social transmission, is seldom tested.

In the absence of culturally transmitted knowledge or dead prey with plant parts hanging out of its mouth, or a royal taster, there is another way to carefully inspect the toxicity of plants: taste. Many plant toxins are alkaloids, compounds that adhere to particular proteins found on receptors in the mouth and that trigger the sense of bitterness. If ingested, many plant toxins can wreak havoc on the internal nervous systems of animals. You are probably familiar with many common plant alkaloids—they are chemicals that end in "-ine": morphine (poppy plant), cocaine (coca plant), nicotine (tobacco plant), caffeine (produced by about 60 plants), strychnine (strychnine tree), atropine (belladonna plant), and theobromine (cacao plant). If overconsumed or, in some cases if consumed at all, many plant toxins are poisonous and affect the central nervous system, the body's main command center, consisting of the brain and spinal cord. For instance, alkaloids can affect neuronal responses in the brain, leading to disorientation, hallucinations, misperceptions, or general confusion. They can also affect the nerves controlling respiration. This is one reason why it isn't a good idea to feed your dog chocolate—canines are over three times as sensitive as humans to the theobromine found in chocolate.

Beyond bitter-tasting alkaloids, plants evolved a variety of other toxins as measures of protection. For instance, species of onions and garlic use acids to protect themselves. Onions and garlic, when left alone, aren't a problem. Chances are you could hold an intact onion very close to your eye without shedding a tear. These plants get mean only when provoked—when they experience cellular damage (entropy) of the kind inflicted by teeth or a knife. Both onions and garlic produce the starting materials of sulfuric acid, safely tucked away in packets within the cell. When the cell is damaged, the starter materials combine. In onions, these sulfur compounds are small, enabling them to go airborne and, once combined with water (e.g., found on the wet surface of an animal's eyes or in the mouth), turn into caustic sulfuric acid. (So perhaps the old wives' tale about whistling while you cut onions isn't so farfetched.) By contrast, the sulfur-containing compounds in garlic are too large to go airborne and instead operate via contact, slowly burning the moist skin of would-be predators (or vampires).

Some toxins, however, are not detected via taste. When and if they make it inside, their trace quantities are dealt with differently. For instance, some plants produce glycosides (e.g., cyanogenic glycosides, which release cyanide). Should these and other compounds make it into the body, they are typically met with a destructive enzyme force in the digestive tract. Should enzymatic activity of the gut not suffice in denaturing the toxin, physiological adaptations of vomiting and diarrhea kick in, helping to rid the body of toxins. We should mention that some bacteria, for instance *Vibrio cholerae* and those associated with food poisoning (*Staphylococcus aureus*, *Bacillus cereus*, and strains of *E. coli*), possess their own toxins, termed enterotoxins, which aid in the bacteria's transportation from host to host. This represents a double whammy, activating the body's response to both bacterial *and* toxin presence.

The nasty effects of toxins on our system can explain some puzzling and bothersome novelties of modern environments. Take, for instance, motion sickness. Humans did not evolve alongside planes, trains, or automobiles. The phenomenon of motion sickness is an example of a modern environmental condition impacting a Stone Age mind. But what *is* motion sickness? We typically don't get sick while walking or running, so it couldn't just be about motion. To solve the riddle of motion sickness, consider how humans got around for most of our time on this planet: on foot. Our perceptual systems are calibrated to movements typical of our hominid ancestors. When we walk or run, the information detected by perceptual systems matches what the body is actually doing. That is, the internal sense of how our body is moving—our proprioception—matches the incoming perception (via vision, for instance) of how fast the external world is changing. Our nervous system expects muscular movements to coincide with perceptual changes and vice versa.

But toxins can interfere with neural communication and distort perception. So when a mismatch occurs between perceptual systems, for instance between the information coming from your eyes and your body's sense of motion, a good inductive bet—at least in ancestral times—was that you ingested a toxin. The solution? Vomit! In modern environments, the expression of a toxin defense system might vary between individuals—some people are just more sensitive to the information provided by their vestibular and perceptual systems, particularly in evolutionarily novel situations. For sensitive folks, culturally novel situations—riding in a car, on a roller coaster, or on a motion-simulated ride (e.g., Epcot's Mission to Mars and Universal Studio's Harry Potter and the Forbidden Journey)—can produce motion sickness and cause nausea and/or vomiting. Subtle mismatches between perceptions of movement through an environment without any muscular feedback of actual physical movement cues a state that would have been brought about ancestrally when one ingested a toxin.

The example of motion sickness, though a false alarm of sorts, reveals a system that evolved to respond to the ingestion of a toxin, particularly toxins that affect our central nervous system. But there is another class of plant toxins, one that takes advantage of our pain system and targets our *peripheral* nervous system— capsaicin, the chemical that makes hot chili peppers hot.[12]

Capsaicin works by binding to a special class of receptors in the mouth, nociceptors (also present on the skin), which transmit information to the brain regarding mechanical and thermal information.[13] When we consume enough capsaicin, this activates the cooling system, features of which include sweating and vascularization (reddening) of the skin. Capsaicin is an interesting plant toxin for a number of reasons. First, for most people, capsaicin causes pain/heat, not disgust. Second, many would argue that capsaicin, at least in small concentrations, is not *dis*tasteful but instead quite delightful. The fact that many humans learn to love the burn associated with hot peppers suggests they are not similar to other plant toxins.

Josh Tewksbury, a professor of biology at the University of Washington, has been investigating the evolutionary origin of capsaicin endemic to pepper plants of Bolivia and Peru. He and his colleagues have found that capsaicin safeguards the pepper plant against multiple threats. In South America, many pepper plants fall victim to insect predators. These insects use their proboscis to bore a hole into the plant's fruit (the pepper) to access valuable nutrients. The problem is that the holes leave the plant susceptible to fungal damage on its seeds. To protect their seeds from fungi, peppers produce and coat their seeds with capsaicin. Studies conducted by Tewksbury and colleagues have shown that fungal growth is indeed inhibited by capsaicin. Furthermore, they have found that chili plant populations that grow in wetter climates with more insects and more fungal infections contain greater concentrations of capsaicin than chili plants that grow in drier climates, with fewer insects and fungal infections.[14]

As a secondary benefit, capsaicins in the pepper fruit protect against attack from various rodents tempted to metabolize and digest the pepper fruit *and* seeds. These rodents—animals with teeth that crush—can feel the pain of the capsaicin. (At the very least, they contain similar receptors to us, so we can infer they feel something that registers as "painful" and deters them from dining on peppers.) By contrast, birds such as the thrasher that disperse pepper seeds (and do *not* crush them) do not possess receptors sensitive to capsaicin.

It is unclear whether capsaicin-producing plants were a recurrent feature of our evolutionary history. By virtue of the presence of heat and thermal receptors in the mouth we can detect the effects of capsaicin, because this chemical binds to (and won't let go of) receptors responsible for activating the pain/heat response.

(Indeed, capsaicin is now used in topical creams to help control pain, such as the arthritis pain reliever Capzasin; by overstimulating nerve endings, Capzasin prevents them from continually firing, eventually reducing the pain signals sent to the brain.) The fact that capsaicin doesn't trip the bitter system might mean that our body doesn't tag it as a toxin per se. Rather, it is a mimic. Instead of causing actual structural damage of the kind pain and heat nociceptors evolved to protect against, capsaicin is a chemical that happens to activate these systems, producing a sensation we have come to learn as relatively safe and now enjoy manipulating.

THE INFLUENCE OF PLANT TOXINS

Much like how pepper plants manufacture chemicals to protect against microorganisms, humans too have developed ways to utilize the anti-pathogenic effects of various plant compounds. Of course, in many cases, we don't realize that our consumption of plants has beneficial effects on our health and survival—just like we don't necessarily realize that our preference for symmetrical mates has beneficial effects on offspring survivability. Instead, evolution tinkered with preferences that tended to do well *in the long run*. Take, for an example, our preferences for, and consumption of, nicotine. Ed Hagen, an anthropologist at the University of Washington, Vancouver, has found that nicotine, the psychoactive component of tobacco, is linked with reduced worm load in the Aka, a group of Central African foragers that suffer from severe worm infestation. Hagen and research assistants collected saliva, which they assayed for a metabolite of nicotine, and stool samples, which allowed them to look for and quantify worm-egg concentrations. They found that the more nicotine in a person's saliva, the lower the worm concentration in his stool. Nicotine, an alkaloid, appears to be a natural plant compound humans conditionally use to treat worms.[15] The pharmaceutical industry has known about this link for some time; many modern drugs that serve to reduce worm load (anthelmintics) target the same receptors as nicotine. These drugs (and nicotine) cause paralysis in worms, leading to their expulsion from hosts.

Beyond tobacco, we use the firepower of many plants to help in the defense against pathogens. Specifically, cuisines around the globe appear to leverage the defense systems offered by plants to combat foodborne microorganisms that cause food spoilage. We are talking, of course, about seasonings and spices. Do spices—dried plants—actually have antimicrobial properties? The answer appears to be yes. We've already seen that capsaicin combats fungal growth on the seeds of pepper plants and that nicotine inhibits intestinal worm growth. Other spices/seasonings also have antimicrobial properties. Garlic, onion, and oregano inhibit the growth of every single bacterium they have been tested on (including various species of staphylococcus, pseudomonas, salmonella, and streptococcus). Thyme, cinnamon, tarragon, cumin, cloves, lemongrass, bay leaves, rosemary, and capsicums inhibit at least 75 percent of the bacteria they have been tested on.[16] Given this antimicrobial activity, Cornell University biologists Paul Sherman and Jennifer Billing investigated whether the use of spices in the cuisines of various cultures relates to the concentration of pathogens present in the environment. Their question: Why do some like it hot?

Sherman and Billing investigated the patterns of spice usage in the meat-based cuisines of 36 countries. They wanted to examine whether spice use was more common in environments in which pathogens flourish and in which foods, particularly meat, tend to spoil faster. They sifted through 4,500 meat-based recipes and recorded the type and amount of spices in each one. In addition, they gathered information regarding mean annual temperature for each region, a proxy for pathogen density (as mentioned earlier, pathogens tend to flourish in warmer climes, suggesting that the closer to the equator, the greater the risk of pathogen infection). As predicted, they found that the warmer the annual temperature of a given country, the greater the variety and quantity of spices used per recipe. So it ends up that there is an evolutionary logic for why some like it hot and spicy. Cultural cuisine—particularly the use of plant-borne compounds—is, in part, a manifestation of adaptations protecting against pathogens (and, incidentally, a reason why we often encounter Mexican, Asian, and South American cuisines, but rarely encounter Finnish, Icelandic, and Canadian cuisine).

To sum up, food has been a major focus of disgust researchers because the mouth is a main entry point for a variety of harmful substances. Pathogens, toxins, and mechanical/thermal irritants are three such harms. While mechanical/thermal threats trigger avoidance behaviors via pain generated by the peripheral nervous system, pathogens and (most) plant toxins activate avoidance via disgust, generated by the central nervous system. Though we've learned to harness the power of some plant compounds, we have done so sensitive to the quantities ingested.

As we discussed in the last chapter, an emotion can first be categorized according to the situation (challenge) it evolved to respond to and the cues indicating the presence of that situation. Here we have the situation—what to consume—and we have so far detailed the cues signaling the presence of our two threats of interest: pathogens and plant toxins. The next step is to consider the range of information that might bear on the adaptive response. Given the problem of what to consume, if, say, pathogens are detected, would the adaptive response have been to avoid consumption all of the time, no matter what? No. Context matters.

WHAT TO EAT? CONTEXTUAL FACTORS

Paul Rozin, one of the pioneers in the study of taste preferences and aversions, has discussed at length the factors that should influence decisions about what to eat.[17] Rozin points out that food availability, the local norms associated with consuming particular foods, nutritional state, and individual experience should all influence consumption decisions. Certainly the availability of foods in the local environment is critical in calibrating food-preference systems. Whether one tends to dine on gazelle, bear, python, octopus, or cow depends on where you live. Generally speaking, the variety of foods available in a particular ecology will generate patterns of within-group similarity and across-group differences—culture, if you will. But availability is a rather un-nuanced factor: either the food is there or it isn't. So here we will instead focus on more dynamic factors such as nutritional state, experience, and developmental stage to show how context can shape our preferences for what to eat.

Factor One: Nutritional State

When a person is hungry or dehydrated, mental systems regulating what counts as edible should shift to include a wider range of substances that would help address the current depleted state. Coming home late at night hungry, we tend to be open to eating things we wouldn't otherwise consider (perhaps even the green furry pizza in the fridge). Ancestrally, prolonged states of hunger or dehydration would have been a matter of life or death. It is perhaps better to risk disease— from which one had a chance of recovering—than risk starving to death. (Note, though, that this would not be the calculus for lethal plant toxins, which would have been bad to eat regardless of nutritional state. That is, no matter how hungry you were, eating jequirity seeds, belladonna, nightshade, desert-rose, hemlock, or foxglove—all plants known to be highly poisonous—would have been a bad idea.)

Evidence that our pathogen-avoidance psychology relaxes under stress comes from studies on the effects of dehydration and food deprivation. In a study conducted in Bern, Switzerland, researchers examined men who underwent 18 hours of water deprivation. When thirsty, men rated the odor of fermented fish as far less disgusting than when they were hydrated. In addition, their reduction in disgust was associated with reduced neural activity in brain regions known to govern the disgust response.[18] The moderation or suppression of disgust under nutritional stress appears to be an adaptive response. When the body is in dire need of water, it should cause the person to be less picky—more accepting—of potential substances that could address this need. In a similar vein, a separate group of researchers found that after being deprived of food for 15 hours, subjects smiled more when viewing palatable foods and showed reduced disgust expressions toward moldy corn.[19]

Our food psychology thus displays an *adaptive flexibility*, restricting or broadening the value assigned to substances in the environment, depending on condition. The consumption system, rather than being a reflexive response that invariably yokes pathogen detection to all-out avoidance, integrates via internal processing circuitry information that had survival consequences in ancestral environments. One such input would have been hydration and nutrient status.[20] Another input is experience.

Factor Two: Prior Experience

Disgust is a flexible adaption, but not infinitely so. Built into the disgust adaptation are prior expectations of how the world works. This brings us to experience, a second factor that should influence decisions about what to eat. There is strong evidence that humans and likely many other species evolved to learn about the things that tend to make us sick. Specifically, the mind appears to make connections between illness felt currently and foods consumed earlier. In a classic study, John Garcia and Robert Koelling[21] showed evidence for this specialized taste-aversion learning. In their study, they gave saccharine-flavored water to rats and paired their drinking with a bright light and a clicking noise. Half of the rats were then exposed to an electric shock; the other half to x-ray radiation. The point was to induce either pain or nausea, respectively. So as a rat, you were having a good day drinking sweet water in a disco-like environment with some light and noise, and then you were either shocked or made to feel very sick. This was part one of the experiment (Fig. 4.1).

In part two of the experiment, Garcia and Koelling wanted to see what the rats had learned. They offered half the shocked and half the x-rayed rats the saccharine-flavored water without the bright light or clicking noise; they offered the other half of each group unflavored water with the light and noise. The question: In the mind of the rat, can pain and nausea be equally associated with a sight/sound as with a taste? More generally, can the mind learn the association between *any* two stimuli equally well?

The answer: no. Rats that were shocked had no problem drinking the saccharine-flavored water when there was *no light or clicking noise*. But they avoided drinking completely when water—*unflavored* water—was presented after the light and clicking noise. These rats came to associate the pain of being shocked with the physical stimuli of light and noise—not the taste of sweetness. On the other hand, rats that were doused with radiation and made to feel nauseated had no problem drinking *unflavored* water paired with the light and clicking. However, they avoided the saccharine-flavored water, even when there was no light or sound. It appears that these rats came to associate nausea with a particular taste—not with light or noise. The rat mind, it seems, comes prepared to make certain assumptions about the world: things you eat make you sick.

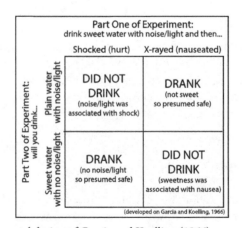

Figure 4.1. Experimental design of Garcia and Koelling (1966).

Humans, too, carry assumptions about the kinds of things that tend to make us sick (and, by extension, the things that cause pain). If you've ever suffered food poisoning, you have likely experienced food-primed learning. While hunched over the toilet thinking about what caused your illness, here are things that typically aren't under consideration: What did I wear today? Is the garage door open? Where should I go on vacation? Did I pay the electric bill? Instead, one tends to (non-randomly) wonder: What the heck did I *eat*?

Learning mechanisms relating to detecting pathogens and toxins are structured to infer that "if I am sick, then it is something I ate." This process of learning has come to be known as the *sauce béarnaise effect*, coined by psychologist Martin Seligman.[22] As Seligman recounts, "Sauce béarnaise, an egg thickened tarragon-flavored sauce, used to be one of my favorite foods in the world. One evening, in 1966, I had sauce béarnaise on filet mignon. About six hours later I began to throw up and spent the next several hours retching. After that, sauce béarnaise tasted foul to me."

Toxin- or pathogen-induced emesis activates learning systems to store specific information regarding what was consumed, not about the weather or one's social status. The take-home message is that the minds of humans and other animals make causal bets. In the natural environment, when one got sick, it was because of what one ate, not what one heard, saw, or felt. Natural selection took advantage of this regularity to shape the learning systems that guide consumption.

Factor Three: Developmental Stage

Across the lifespan, pathogens and toxins alike can have different effects on the body. The threats of foodborne pathogens and toxins begin well before birth. Early on during development, toxins can have particularly nasty effects. One reason why is because organs develop during the first trimester of pregnancy, and it is during this time that the developing fetus is most prone to harm from toxins. Toxins ingested by mom enter the fetus via the placenta and can cause genetic mutations and interfere with DNA replication and cell division. Evolutionary biologist Margie Profet has argued that the food aversions, nausea, and vomiting that peak during the first stages of pregnancy evolved to protect the growing fetus from harmful toxins. As Profet mentions, "Red cabbage, Brussels sprouts, cabbage, all these contain L-isothiocyanate, which can break chromosomes."[23] Evidence that supports the idea that pregnancy sickness serves as fetal protection comes from the devastating effects of drugs such as thalidomide, which decreased nausea and vomiting during pregnancy but contributed to birth defects such as limb deformation. By eliminating the unpleasant experiences of nausea and vomiting, medicine was removing an evolved layer of protection against the consumption of plant toxins and pathogens, substances that interfere with fetal development.

As another line of defense, food preferences, specifically for meat, appear to change during the early stages of pregnancy. Compared to later stages, during the first trimester, the immune system of the mother is suppressed, a function thought to protect newly inhabiting "non-self" paternally derived fetal tissue from attack by the mom's immune system. Suppressing the immune system leaves the body a bit more vulnerable to infection. To offset this vulnerability, according to evolutionary anthropologist Dan Fessler, women avoid consuming items associated with an increased infection risk during the first trimester. In particular, Fessler suggests that women avoid eating meat to reduce the possibility of ingesting harmful microorganisms. To test this idea, Fessler and colleagues administered a web-based survey to approximately 500 women. They found that women in the first trimester reported greater disgust sensitivity toward food than women in later stages of pregnancy. This pattern held even after controlling for the amount of nausea experienced.[24] So women appear to "beef up" their defense against pathogens during pregnancy by adjusting the sensitivity of physiological reactions such as nausea and vomiting and by adjusting psychological food preferences such as those for meat.

After birth, the focus shifts from maternal food consumption to infant food consumption. Anthropologist Elizabeth Cashdan has studied food learning and food aversions in children and has found that between the ages roughly of six months and three years, children are prone to put just about anything in their mouths. In terms of diet, they show much greater breadth. Paul Rozin and colleagues have also found that young children will put all sorts of items—disgusting items such as hair, dangerous items such as soap, and inappropriate items such as paper and leaves—in their mouth.[25] But this tends to end around age three, when the range of items that children consume shrinks considerably. Not surprisingly, the frequency of poisonings tracks the range of consumed foods, with far more poisonings occurring in children under age three. What could account for this blip in preferences for *greater* food breadth (and greater poisonings) during the first few years of life? It would seem this pattern strikes a blow at the notion that psychological machinery evolved to protect humans against pathogens and toxins.

But don't throw the baby out with the bath water just yet. Consider the social ecology of our human ancestors. For much of human evolution, and as is still the case in modern foraging societies and among other primate species, females more or less *continuously carried* their young during infancy. In addition, our foremothers breastfed children up until approximately age three, at which time they were weaned off breast milk and slowly introduced to the local cuisine. This means that for much of human evolution, for very young children from birth up to around age three, there was only one food source: mom. The preference to orient the suckling response toward a dark skin spot would have been well on its way to solving the problem of food acquisition for quite a long time. In fact, the piece of coding "put anything and everything available into your mouth as much as possible" would have been fitness-*promoting* in ancestral environments, leading young infants who were carried around to feed more or less continuously. No other food preferences would really be required. No food aversions would be required either. Evolution took care of this by tinkering with *mom's* food psychology. If a child was carried around continuously and had around-the-clock access to a food source with few exceptions, why would natural selection spend precious energy on brain processes assessing the suitability of various food sources? Children can free-ride off the systems already present in mom to ensure the safety of breast milk.

Another interesting feature of infant consumption psychology is that there would have been less of a need for a feedback system that decreased consumption over time. That is, there might not have been a need for a system that indicates "I'm full, stop eating" in newborn minds. While hunger might initiate an infant's feeding, mom ends it. The reason why moms "take control" of how much their infants feed is because, from the mom's point of view, it is quite costly to provide an endless supply of nutrients to a growing child. Female psychology is organized to make trade-offs, specifically trade-offs between the amount of time and energy spent nurturing the current child versus the next. And how do moms slyly (and of course nonconsciously) control access to the flow of resources? Moms lace breast milk with benzodiazepine-like compounds.[26] It's hard to nurse if you're asleep! Ever seen the "angelic" face of a baby napping after being breastfed?

In modern environments, the absence of adaptations terminating infant feeding becomes evident. Formula-fed babies do not experience the same soporific interventions that breastfed babies do, sometimes resulting in a messy cycle of binge and purge. Likewise, in modern environments, infants are not continuously carried around, and they frequently encounter evolutionarily novel plastic toys and other objects on the ground. Today, the lack of an adaptation preventing ingestion becomes a bit more obvious. This perhaps is one of the reasons why, as Cashdan reports, children under the age of three are more prone to poisoning and choking; adaptations guiding food preferences and food aversions have yet to kick in, putting young children at risk in modern environments. Indeed, evidence from Cashdan's studies as well as those on food neophobia and pickiness suggest that human developmental systems are organized to expect the introduction of (non-breast-derived) foods starting around age three.[27]

But even as children are beginning to pick up their local cuisine, there are foods that continue to remain dangerous to a growing brain. To kids, whose brains and entire bodies are still in the process of self-organizing, toxins are extremely dangerous, and this changes their perception. Kids being pushed around in a grocery cart through the produce section of the local food market see a landscape of enemies lying in wait. For instance, plants from the genus *Brassica*, which includes broccoli, turnips, cauliflower, Brussels sprouts, and cabbage, contain a derivative of cyanide called thiocyanate, a chemical that prevents the absorption of iodine by the thyroid, causing the stressed gland to enlarge and ultimately leading to the condition of goiter. The genus *Allium* gives us onions, garlic, and chives, which contain sulfoxides, chemicals associated with the production of sulfuric acid as mentioned earlier, and apoptosis, programmed cell death.

Adults can stomach (liver?) these compounds in limited amounts because of the enzymes that accumulate over time. But in children, small doses of toxins can have large physiological effects, leading to an increased sensitivity and a tenacious resistance to plated vegetables. Evidence of toxin aversion in young children is also apparent when you consider the things you rarely hear young kids request. Despite being bombarded with demands such as "Give me candy!" and "I want ice cream," parents never hear a six-year-old say "Can I bum a smoke, mom?" or "Will you make me an espresso?" Yes, of course, there are norms against children going outside for a smoke and taking coffee breaks, but our point is that kids *aren't even asking* to do these rule-breaking behaviors. This is strange, given that kids push the envelope in almost every other domain, sometimes on an hourly basis. It seems that children's food preferences steer them toward carbohydrates, salts, and lipids but away from pathogens and plant toxins (e.g., alkaloids such as nicotine and caffeine).

But children do learn to eat their vegetables and many go on to enjoy escargot, carpaccio, sushi, olives, red onions, and even Brussels sprouts. The peak stages of food neophobia, which occur between two and six years of age, relax and enable the expansion of diet even in the pickiest of eaters. Patricia Pliner, a social psychologist at the University of Toronto, has been one of the main researchers of food prefer-ences and food-learning systems. She and colleagues have investigated the manner in which children learn about food suitability. Interestingly, they report that in chil-dren seven to nine years old, exposure to novel foods *decreases* further willingness to try subsequent novel foods.[28] One explanation for this pattern is that children are learning what works and what doesn't. Children, acting in a scientific manner, at-tempt to run controlled experiments: taste this new food, wait, and make sure you don't get sick over the next day or so before trying anything else novel. This way, if illness ensues, a good inductive bet can be made regarding the likely source of illness. Introducing multiple novel foods at once, much akin to introducing multiple con-founding variables in an experiment, can interfere with inferred causality. Our food-learning system is impressively sophisticated—all by design.

ENGINEERING: EXPECTED VALUE OF CONSUMPTION

If you were tasked with writing a software program that enabled a robot to seek out or avoid food based on particular qualities and circumstances, what would it look like? What kinds of information would you program it to incorporate? How would you weight those different inputs?

Natural selection tinkered with our neural circuitry to guide consumption be-havior by first enabling the detection of fitness-promoting substances (sugar, salts, proteins) as well as the detection of fitness-jeopardizing substances (pathogens and, typically, toxins). Then it linked detection with behaviors motivating con-sumption versus avoidance, while at the same time regulating the strength of the response according to context. Figure 4.2 is a rough sketch of the types of psycho-logical computations at work in calculating a specific variable—the *expected value of consumption*—that serves as a fulcrum for the disgust system in decisions on what to consume. (Later, in Chapter 8, we'll show how this variable is seized by moral systems that generate intuitions as to what counts as acceptable and unac-ceptable behavior.)

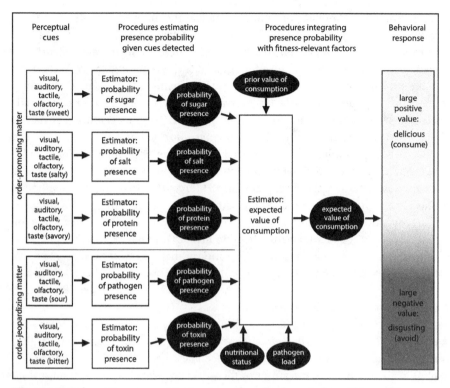

Figure 4.2. Information processing structure of our food psychology. This model is a theoretical diagram of how our food psychology might be organized. Detection systems monitor the environment for substances that possess cues associated with the presence of order-promoting matter (substances we detect as sweet, salty, and savory) and order-jeopardizing matter (substances we detect as bitter and sour). For each, there are dedicated procedures that estimate the probability that a particular substance is "out there" given the cues detected. This generates internal estimates of the probabilities of sugar, salt, amino acid, pathogen, and toxin presence, here identified as black ovals, which are taken as input by a compiler that outputs a critical regulatory variable associated with disgust, *expected value of consumption*. One's nutritional status and health status (pathogen load) modulate consumption. Likewise, memory helps to store prior values of consumption as experienced firsthand or learned via social transmission. Developmental changes in food preferences might occur via the changing of weightings (here represented as arrows) of how probabilities of toxin (pathogen, etc.) presence influence the expected value of consumption, which, when low, gives rise to our sense of disgust.

Working from left to right in the model in Figure 4.2, cues to the presence of order-promoting matter versus order-jeopardizing matter are perceived by our senses. Because different sets of cues would have corresponded with the presence of sugars, salts, amino acids (proteins), pathogens (e.g., bacteria), and toxins, there are likely *different detection systems* that feed into a dedicated compiler that estimates the probability that a particular substance is present.

Each of these compilers, or estimators, solves the following problem: *given the pattern of firings from cells linked to visual, olfactory, tactile, auditory, and taste receptors, what is the probability of actual pathogen [toxin, sugar, salt, protein] presence?* For instance, given I taste a hint of acid (e.g., something tastes "off"), what is the probability that bacteria are present? Remember, this calculation is done almost wholly subconsciously; only certain steps in the process ever consciously register. Uncertainty in any domain, but particularly with regard to substances that might be harmful, motivates additional information-collection behaviors. When we suspect milk, meat, or derived products to have "gone bad," we can investigate via tentative sipping or nibbling. We sniff, re-sniff, visually inspect with greater care, and perhaps nibble again. Don't forget the tried-and-true method of outsourcing the problem of detecting pathogens by handing the item to someone else (you trust) and asking, "Does this taste funny to you?" Attention focused on perceptual and social information helps to firm up internal estimates of pathogen or toxin presence. An interesting observation is that we rarely need to outsource the job of determining if something tastes yummy; one rarely hears, "Will you taste this to see if it is sweet?" Corroboration appears to be a process engaged by systems assessing possible threats, not treats.

All of the compiled estimates—the *probability of pathogen presence, toxin presence, as well as sugar, salt, and protein presence*—are values that have been tweaked and re-tweaked by natural selection via feedback occurring over many generations as to how particular features of the world correlated with the results of ingestion. That is, the risks (or benefits) of ingesting a particular substance bearing particular qualities were "learned" across generations and codified in our neural programming. Our circuitry is thus set with default weightings that link specific cues to pathogen and toxin presence. Of course, the possibility that harm probabilities come "preloaded" on our neural operating system says nothing about how easy or difficult it might be to alter these weightings. Knowledge regarding alterability can be obtained only by investigation. Likely, our system is designed to take social information as input so as to help inform the individual of what counts as harmful versus harmless in the current environment. Thus, a set programming structure with a few open parameters to be set by incoming information (that is calibrated via "learning") is to be expected in our food psychology.[29]

As we discussed earlier, it might not have been adaptive to mount an all-out avoidance response in all cases once a particular threat was detected. Context matters. In order to calibrate a response that most effectively weights the potential advantage and disadvantages of consumption, the system should take as input not just the probability of harm presence, but also nutritional status, hydration status, prior experience, developmental stage, and other variables bearing on the potential value of consuming a particular item. The system then integrates these relevant inputs and calculates a key variable, the *expected value of consumption* for a given item.

There is a large range over which the expected value of consumption acts. It can range from extremely high and positive ("I'm starving! I'll eat my shoe if I have to!") to extremely low and negative ("That *hárkal* [rotten shark] is going to make me vomit"). When positive (e.g., there are no cues to pathogen or toxin presence, but instead cues to the presence of sugars, fats, and amino acids, and nutritional status indicates low levels of vital nutrients), the expected value of consumption motivates ingestion (and perhaps the sensation of yumminess). When negative (e.g., cues to pathogens are present—sour taste buds have fired—and one is not in a depleted nutritional state), the expected value of consumption motivates avoidance and maps onto an aversive response, *disgust*. Disgust is caused by—and in a sense *is*—a low expected value of consumption. That is, computation-wise, a low expected value of consumption gives rise to the feelings—the qualia—we call disgust.[30]

CONTEXTUAL FACTORS AND ADAPTIVE FLEXIBILITY

The model in Figure 4.2 reveals how contextual factors influence disgust at the level of information-processing structure and enable flexibility. For instance, consumption behaviors and perceptions of what seems yummy or not can change by increasing or decreasing any of the inputs to the *expected value of consumption*. Take nutritional status. When one is hungry and in a depleted state—that is, when the nutritional status estimate is low—this *increases* the expected value of consumption, and promotes eating. Of course, with each bite, there are diminishing returns for the next bite because systems assessing nutrient status dynamically change. This is why the first bite of the first slice of pizza tends to be valued much more than the last bite of the fourth piece. If you have ever gorged on food to the point of discomfort, or ever witnessed someone do the same, you've been privy to statements such as, "If I have another bite, I'll barf" or "I'm grossed out by how full I am right now." It might not be with the same intensity inspired by maggots (and for good reason), but disgust it is. A lowered expected value of consumption *changes* perceptions, rendering previously appetitive substances as substances no longer viewed as currently desirable. (But note, because nothing negative was experienced, for instance, no illness ensued, these foods remain on the menu of desirables in the future when hungry.)

Importantly, when hungry, the value of consumption is not raised for all substances with equal force. For instance, no level of hunger should motivate the consumption of bitter-tasting poisons. Likely there are priorities assigned to which nutrients are valued most given one's current physiological state. One could even imagine an impressively designed consumption system that was sensitive to particular amino acids, lipids, carbohydrates, or even pathogen-fighting, plant-borne chemicals (we will discuss this later) and upregulate a specific "hunger for" what was needed. Thus, our model, while it illustrates that nutritional status is integrated with incoming information regarding sugar, salt, protein, pathogen, and toxin presence, it is not fully fleshed out in that it doesn't provide enough detail for *how* this incoming information modulates preferences and risk tolerance. The weights of the arrows in the system (and how they change) are as of yet unknown and a matter for further investigation.

Another source of flexibility relates to experience and social learning. For plant toxins, learning which plants are and are not safe to consume (or touch) would have been a critical feature of childhood development. Indeed, the more ancestrally hazardous the item, the more likely one-trial (or even no-trial) learning procedures handle the assignment of probable harm. Though we have listed only perceptual cues, linguistically transferred information about these perceptual cues is an important input to systems estimating and storing the probability of harm (e.g., "Don't eat the plant that has red spots on its leaves").

Another variable that enables "learning" is the *prior value of consumption*. After consuming each meal, information is stored regarding the effects of what was consumed. When nothing happens—well, that is, when nothing bad happens— the body ratchets up the *prior value of consumption*. This occurs without any conscious awareness. All that registers is "That tasted good; I'd have that again." When one gets sick, the body lowers the estimated *prior value of consumption*, causing the foods just consumed to be tagged with *lower* expected values of consumption and typically preventing them from being considered in the future. This helps explain the mechanism behind the *sauce béarnaise effect* discussed above as well as food pickiness.

Our food psychology system also shows an impressive flexibility to meet the changing costs of consumption throughout development. Natural selection could have engineered our consumption psychology such that during infancy the *expected value of consumption* of everything is set to high, because rationing decisions were, ancestrally, left to mom. Around the time that young children start to roam freely and are introduced to the local cuisine, the *expected value of consumption* should dial back and reflect the fitness costs versus benefits of consuming particular items. Given that toxins are particularly pernicious during early development, the input coming from receptors attached to bitter taste buds should be weighted very heavily when calculating the expected value of consumption. Only when children develop a healthy population of enzymes ready to denature plant toxins should bitter aversions begin to ease (i.e., a given probability of toxin presence might no longer have *as* strong an effect on the computed estimated value of consumption). Likewise, in the adult female mind, weightings assigned to particular perceptual properties (bitterness and sourness) might be more pronounced during pregnancy, functioning to reduce consumption of foods dangerous to a growing fetus.

Our main point here is that over the course of development, there are likely triggers that change the weighting of each input to the *expected value of consumption*, leading to behaviors that would have been adaptive in ancestral environments. This is one way in which flexibility can be programmed—enabled—into the system.

Last, current health status or pathogen load likely modulates the *expected value of consumption*. When one is ill, fighting an infection, it wouldn't have been a good idea to further burden the system with the ingestion of additional pathogens (e.g., worms or bacteria). Tastes change when we are sick, and this is all regulated via the system we model. Bacterial infection, for instance, should reduce consumption of red meat, which contains iron, a component critical for bacterial replication. By tinkering with the "taste for" certain compounds when ill, natural selection could increase the efficiency of clearing an infection. So, for instance, to reduce the possible complications of ingesting additional meat-borne pathogens, natural selection could have caused our preferences specifically for umami to decrease when ill.

But not all taste preferences decrease during illness. One kind of taste that appears to be enhanced is the taste for particular bitter-tasting plants.[31] This might seem strange—wouldn't it seem silly to overburden our physiology with plant toxins while trying to combat microorganisms? Not if plant toxins offered a way to combat microorganismic growth. As our discussion on spices and nicotine revealed, many plants contain substances that curtail the growth of mold, bacteria, and worms. The benefits of consuming plants, particularly when ill, could have outweighed the costs of toxin denaturation. Evidence that primates consume plant matter when ill suggests this might be so.[32] The mechanism enabling this behavior could be as simple as upregulating the desire for bitterness and accessing stored information regarding the types of plants one has observed others consuming (and, of course, not dying from).[33]

CONCLUSIONS: WHAT TO EAT?

Darwin's quote at the beginning of this chapter indicates that taste is the primary cause of disgust, but that this feeling can also be triggered by other senses. Here we explained why this is. Our consumption psychology depends on the generation of an internal variable, *the expected value of consumption*, which is formed based on inputs regarding cues indicative of nutrient status and threat potential as well as a host of contextual factors that would have affected survival in ancestral environments. When the brain computes a low *expected value of consumption*, an aversive response occurs, one we call disgust. The magnitude of the expected value of consumption modulates the intensity of disgust and, at the other end of the spectrum, appetitiveness. Just because an all-out disgust response is not felt, for example, when one is full or thinking about eating rocks, does not mean that expected values of consumption are not at work. They are. The computed value might be low, but not low enough to cause the same physical feeling we feel when seeing maggots crawl out of our meat and onto our plate (and for good reason). Substances vary in their fitness value and only those seriously jeopardizing fitness in the moment will trigger extreme disgust avoidance responses.

Disgust, often poetically referred to as a type of *behavioral immune system*,[34] motivates avoidance and serves in part to protect us from ingesting substances, particularly pathogenic microorganisms and plant toxins that often would have had negative consequences on survival and reproduction in ancestral environments. As part of the behavioral immune system, disgust oversees another important function regarding protection, and one we turn to now: the avoidance of contact with surfaces and other individuals who display cues to disease and infection.

What to Touch?

Pathogens and infectious agents aren't transmitted solely through eating or drinking, and they aren't just transmitted via plants and non-human animals, either. Touching pathogen-rich surfaces—whether it's the feces of a caribou or the infected flesh of your coworker—poses a risk of disease transmission. There are a variety of fungal, viral, and bacterial diseases that spread from host to host via physical contact. The transmission of infectious agents via contact posed the same type of recurrent ancestral threat—pathogen colonization—that transmission via ingestion posed. And so, in addition to a consumption psychology that estimates the value of eating particular substances, we should expect to find evidence of a *contact psychology* that estimates the value of touching them. This chapter is about just that. Of course, the systems for detecting and avoiding harmful substances from contact will undoubtedly share many of the same attributes with the systems that avoid consuming them, and so we won't belabor their similarities. Instead, we'll take a few pages to emphasize the novel aspects of disgust when it comes to deciding: what to touch?

CONTACT

From a pathogen's point of view, transmission requires some form of physical contact. For this reason we should expect to see strategies that evolved in hosts to mitigate the costs of infection that can occur via (a) contact with substances harboring pathogens (e.g., feces and rotting carcasses), (b) contact with animal vectors that transmit disease (flies and mosquitoes), and (c) contact with conspecifics showing signs of infection. We briefly discuss each in turn.[1]

First, humans and many non-human species alike avoid not just consuming but having any contact at all with substances bearing cues of parasite presence and the presence of disease-causing agents. As we discussed in the last chapter, humans and chimps, for instance, show increased sensitivities to tactile properties of pathogens, recoiling when their hands touch slimy surfaces. Many animals engage in behaviors to reduce the presence of contaminated substances in their immediate environment. Sheep avoid grazing on feces-contaminated grass; rainbow trout swim away from parasitic worms that cause blindness; and even the worm *Caenorhabditis elegans* will avoid the bacterium *Bacillus thuringiensis* when placed in its petri dish.[2] Nest- and hive-cleansing behaviors likewise serve to clear the environment of disease-causing agents. Wood ants bring into their nest pieces of resin from coniferous trees, which inhibit the growth of both bacteria and fungi; wood rats collect bay leaves, which act like DEET and kill off flea larvae in the nest; many species of birds use plant materials to fumigate their nests; and canines will eat feces produced in the den to keep the den clear of parasites and safe for developing offspring.[3] (So there is a reason why your [artificially selected] dog eats poo—dogs inherited adaptations that were naturally selected in wolves to prevent contamination!) Indeed, across the animal kingdom, researchers have identified a variety of behaviors linked with avoiding contact with substances harboring disease-causing agents.

Some pathogen-avoidance behaviors, however, target the vectors of disease transmission. Flies, ticks, and mosquitoes can inject viruses and bacteria into each host they visit. In response, grooming behaviors are one type of adaptation that evolved to reduce parasite load. For instance, elephants will obtain branches with leaves or fronds and use them to swat flies; cattle will swish their tails; vampire bats will scratch; impala will tongue-comb; and rats will lick—all for the purpose of reducing parasites that exploit contact with the epidermis of their hosts and the transmission of disease-causing agents.[4]

Many animal species also avoid contact with other animals showing signs of infection. Ants will remove dead colony members from their nest; the spiny lobster, despite being a highly social creature, will refuse to share dens with lobsters showing signs of disease; killifish will avoid other killifish with markings indicative of disease; mandrills will avoid grooming group members infected with parasites; and bees will clear out the cells of infected kin.[5] In general, a remarkable array of behaviors have evolved to mitigate the costs associated with contacting contaminated surfaces and individuals.

Not surprisingly, humans too show a heightened sensitivity toward contact with potentially contaminated surfaces and individuals. We avoid contact with substances bearing the hallmarks of pathogen presence (feces, vomit, spit, blood, guts, and gore); we attempt, when possible, to avoid assault by flies, mosquitoes, and other vectors of disease; and we steer clear of touching other people who show signs of infection. Even if not infected, for instance with cold sores or skin rashes, we still tend to avoid physical contact with strangers, at least initially.

Importantly, not all locations on the body are equally likely to house pathogens. Hotbeds of pathogen presence include the mouth, anus (and products), genitals (and fluids), and (broken) skin. The mouth serves as an entry point for many pathogens (including molds, fungi, *E. coli*, and salmonella), but it is also a pathogen's way out. This renders other people's mouths as potential sources of contamination. Consider the various exit strategies the mouth offers. The bacterium causing tuberculosis sails from host to host on saliva droplets expelled when an infected host speaks, coughs, or sneezes. The common cold and the flu likewise hitch rides on airborne water droplets. The bacteria causing cholera ride the vomit train, contaminating water sources and other surfaces. The anus and genitals are also major sources of contamination. Diarrhea is a bowel rinse and can occur either because the body is attempting to rid itself of infection, as appears to be the case for shigella infections, or because the pathogen is trying to spread, as occurs in cholera and Ebola virus. Regardless, feces of any kind are potentially dangerous sources of contaminants. Similarly, the fluids and cells transmitted during sex are handy transports exploited by a variety of disease-causing organisms, such as those that cause chlamydia and gonorrhea, rendering our genitals potential hotspots as well.

As an outer covering, the skin is a common battleground of infectious attacks. One line of defense against invading pathogens is the rapid replication of skin cells. Skin cells are constantly turning over, replacing older exposed skin with newer cells (which is one reason why tans never last). Another line of defense is the relative dryness of the skin. As mentioned earlier, bacteria tend to flourish in warm, wet environments, so the dryness of our skin is one way to prevent bacterial colonization. Concentrations of bacteria vary throughout the body, pooling in areas with greater moisture and heat content.

Several scientists have recently been investigating the various cues humans use to assess "touchability." Among them is Val Curtis (whom we mentioned in Chapter 1), a scientist at the London School of Disease and Tropical Medicine. Curtis and colleagues found that images depicting disease risks such as biological fluids (e.g., blood and pus) and open, wet skin lesions elicited far more disgust than non-biological fluids such as blue goo and lesions that had scabbed over. They also found that an image of man with damp hair and reddish skin blotches was rated as more disgusting than a man depicted with dry hair and no skin blotches. Although it is tough to say whether subjects were responding to the wet versus dry hair and/or the presence of a skin infection, results are consistent with the notion that humans are sensitive to cues indicative of a body fighting an infection (e.g., fever and inflammation).

Of course, not *all* people are equally disgusting—perspective and context matter. Just as our food system weighs information regarding pathogen presence against other factors such as toxin, sugar, salt, and amino acid presence and nutritional state in decisions regarding what to consume, our contact-evaluation system also considers factors beyond cues to pathogen presence to regulate touch. We don't avoid contact with everybody all of the time. In fact, there are good reasons to expect trade-offs in decisions about whom to touch and when.

WHAT TO TOUCH? CONTEXTUAL FACTORS

There are at least three important contexts in which we might expect to see decisions to trade off the risks of contamination and infection in favor of physical contact. The first is genetic relatedness. In a study by Trevor Case and colleagues entitled "My baby doesn't smell as bad as yours," the researchers asked moms to smell the soiled diapers of their own baby and another woman's baby. They found that in a blind sniff test, moms rated their own baby's feces as far less disgusting.[6] One would expect this same pattern to hold for the scrapes, boogers, vomit, and so forth of one's offspring, and the adaptive explanation is clear: systems that relaxed the pathogen-avoidance response in the presence of offspring enabled caregiving behaviors.

In a similar vein, researchers Richard Stevenson and Betty Rapacholi investigated how disgust differs when pathogen cues emanate from different groups of people.[7] They found that bad odors from kin elicited far less disgust than the same odors from strangers. Despite the very same physical properties, our brain appears to use information regarding relatedness to regulate our perceptions of the costs versus benefits of contact. This cost/benefit analysis manifests as different levels of disgust.

Another context in which physical contact is favored occurs when in the presence of "close associates." Beyond family members, humans and many other species also engage in regular contact with other, unrelated individuals: friends. In non-human primates, friends groom one another, a behavior that evolved to rid individuals of external parasites. In humans, friendships are marked by physical and emotional "closeness" and the sharing of food, hairbrushes, and, under the direst of circumstances, even underwear. An interesting possibility is that motivations to form social bonds and initial physical contact share similar features with our food psychology. Perhaps we engage in "social sampling" much like we sample an unknown food source. That is, upon meeting, humans often do not immediately bear-hug and rub bodies together (at least not without the help of alcohol). Instead, there is a gradual familiarization with a stranger, a behavior that perhaps, on a nonconscious level, serves as a way to sample their pathogens.[8] On the flip side of the coin, when we dislike someone, we increase physical distance and we avoid contact. Motivations to increase or close the distance are thus cues to social "closeness" (an apt descriptor).

The third and final context we'll discuss that should influence preferences regarding touch is sexual arousal. Reproduction is the name of the evolutionary game. Those features of individuals that tended to increase the rate and success of reproduction tended to increase in frequency down the generations. But if other people represent planets of pathogens just waiting to leap from host to host, how in the world does sex occur? In other words, if we have a pathogen-detection psychology that identifies other people's bodily fluids as potentially infectious and that motivates avoidance, how can two people overcome this intense disgust to do the things people tend to do in the process of sex?

Not surprisingly, natural selection engineered a solution to this problem. As we'll discuss in more detail in the next chapter, we possess systems that evaluate others according to their suitability as a sexual partner. That is, individuals assign other people a "sexual value," which generates the obvious and immediate sense of another's *sexual* attractiveness for oneself. There are many factors involved in computing sexual value, and we'll save the bulk of this discussion for the next chapter. For now, it suffices to note that when someone has a high sexual value— when they are perceived to be a very attractive potential sexual partner—this tends to decrease the perceived costs associated with contact. Reduced disgust toward another person's pathogen portals—their skin, mouth, and particularly their genitals—facilitates sexual reproduction.

A handful of studies reveal that pathogen disgust is indeed downregulated during sexual arousal. In one of them, Charmaine Borg and Peter de Jong asked women to view either sexually explicit or neutral videos in the lab. After the video, women were asked to engage in various disgust-eliciting behaviors, for instance touching an apparently used condom. Women who watched the sexual video reported far less disgust toward engaging in these acts. A similar pattern has also been found in men.[9] The extent to which disgust can be turned down during sexual arousal is also colorfully evidenced by the panoply of human sexual fetishes. When in a heightened state of sexual arousal, humans have been known to play with many body products (e.g., feces and urine) to the utter disgust of those *not* in such heightened states.

In sum, the pathogen-avoidance response in terms of whom to touch and when is a flexible response that takes into account those dimensions that would have influenced survival and reproduction in ancestral environments. Three such dimensions are genetic relatedness, social closeness, and mating. As we'll discuss next, the pathogen disgust software program takes these factors into consideration when regulating decisions about contact. As with consumption, there is a critical variable that regulates the level of disgust produced in response to contacting different surfaces and individuals, a second variable that is subject to use by our moral psychology.

ENGINEERING: EXPECTED VALUE OF CONTACT

The model in Figure 5.1—a counterpart to the food-centric model shown in the last chapter—represents the information-processing structure of a system designed to make decisions regarding whom and, more broadly, what to touch. The first thing you will notice is that the left-hand portion of the model is similar to the pathogen-detection system involved in regulating decisions regarding what to eat. Likely, the very same system that sifts the world for cues to pathogen presence for the purpose of guiding consumption behaviors uses those cues to guide contact behaviors. This is why in the model there is an arrow leading from the black oval representing the probability of pathogen presence to two different estimators: one that estimates the expected value of consumption discussed in the last chapter, and one that estimates the *expected value of contact*.

For decisions regarding what to touch, the probability of pathogen presence is integrated with factors bearing on the question of contact suitability. This requires a different compiler, one that estimates an *expected value of contact* based on the unique set of information pertaining to contact. One reason for positing a new compiler is because the factors that modulate contact are different than those that modulate consumption. An individual's relatedness, social closeness, and sexual value are factors that should influence the expected value of contact, not consumption.[10]

Much like the expected value of consumption, the expected value of contact ranges from very low—causing disgust—to very high—causing a longing to be

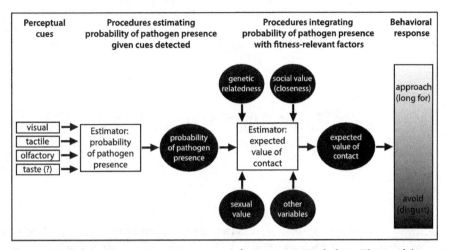

Figure 5.1. Information-processing structure of our contact psychology. This model is a theoretical diagram of how our contact psychology might be organized. Decisions about what and whom to touch share the same pathogen-detection system as used by our food psychology. That is, once the internal variable probability of pathogen presence has been computed, it is taken as input by systems that compute *expected values of consumption* (see Fig. 4.2) and *expected values of contact*, the second critical internal regulatory variable associated with disgust. Contact decisions depend on factors such as relatedness, social value, and sexual value. Low expected values of contact motivate avoidance and give rise to our sense of disgust.

near. When, for instance, there are elevated cues to pathogen presence, the expected value of contact is decreased, increasing the disgust response and motivations to avoid. Sexual value is one factor that should modulate avoidance: when aroused, contact becomes more likely. Genetic relatedness is another factor that should modulate the avoidance response. Given a high degree of relatedness, for instance one's child, cues to pathogen presence such as a runny nose, diarrhea, and vomit do not decrease the expected value of contact. That is, kinship suspends or at least dampens *contact* (and only contact) disgust.

The fact that kinship has a very different effect in the sexual domain, where it actually *intensifies* disgust, suggests there is a separate system governing *sexual* contact. That is, disgust, as a response designed to guard against the communication of pathogens via contact, does not automatically buy you sexual avoidance, even though disgust is a common reaction to certain sexual situations. Cold sores all over a person's mouth would probably render that person unsuitable to touch and less desirable as a sexual partner. If we take away those cold sores, is that person now a suitable sexual partner? What if that person is your sister or brother? The reason you don't French kiss someone with herpes is much different than the reason you don't kiss your sister, even though the response ("eww, gross!") may feel the same. In the next chapter, we'll explain why this is, and how, even in the absence of cues to infection, disgust still works to guide contact-related behavior, specifically sexual avoidance.

With Whom to Have Sex?

In the last two chapters we addressed two ancestral problems disgust evolved to solve: what to eat and what to touch. The avoidance of pathogenic microorganisms plays a prominent role in each domain. But as we left off in the last chapter, pathogen avoidance can only go so far in explaining the intuitive repulsion that humans often feel at the thought of certain sexual activities. It could, for example, help account for disgust at the thought of sex with someone who has open wounds, infections, bad hygiene, or other potential indicators of pathogens. But a mechanism geared to mobilize disgust in response to cues of pathogen presence cannot account for the oft-reported disgust felt at the thought of sexual encounters that do not involve any additional pathogen hazards above and beyond those encountered during sex between an adult man and an adult woman. To wit, people often report feeling disgust at the thought of sex with family members, young children, the elderly, individuals of the same sex, or non-human animals, none of which, as a general matter, necessarily present a heightened pathogen threat.

As a result, a complete explanation of disgust must include an account of how this emotion is involved in sexual behaviors not related to the *proximate* avoidance of pathogens. Moreover, for this explanation to pass the sniff test, it must also be able to account for why these various sexual acts sometimes do happen. As we'll see in later chapters, laws against homosexuality, incest, sex with children, sodomy, bestiality, and the like have persisted across cultures since the advent of codified law, and persist in many (or most) places today. If people weren't doing these things, there would be no reason to proscribe them. Consequently, any model of sexual disgust must both (a) explain why certain sexual behaviors trigger a similar response to that triggered by systems regulating consumption and contact avoidance and (b) explain why, if humans are engineered to avoid those behaviors, they still occur in non-trivial frequencies. In this chapter, we'll do just that by showing how disgust was naturally selected to solve a third problem: avoiding sexual partners that potentially jeopardized the production of healthy, viable offspring.

WHY SEX?

To see how disgust influences our selection of sexual partners, let's start with why we have sex to reproduce. It ends up that pathogens play a key role in this story, too. As we touched on in the "What to Eat" chapter, pathogens have been quite deadly. And one of the reasons pathogens are so deadly is that there is a vast difference between the rates of replication of pathogens as compared to their hosts. Whereas it takes approximately 20 years for humans to reproduce, bacteria, for instance, reproduce every 30 minutes. This amounts to approximately 350,000 generations for every one of ours. To put it another way, in one human lifetime, bacteria in the gut will undergo as many generations as have occurred since the chimp–human split approximately 6 million years ago.[1] The result is a pathogen–host dynamic with asymmetrical rates of evolution. During one host generation, infectious pathogens cycle through numerous iterations of selection and reproduction, learning how to evade components of internal defense systems and how to capture host resources in their own struggle to survive and replicate.[2] This relative time lag in host reproduction presents pathogens with a more or less stable environment to which they can adapt, ultimately increasing their ability to exploit their hosts. Not surprisingly, hosts, in return, have evolved a set of defenses to stem the tide of invasive microorganisms.

One major line of defense for hosts is the immune system, a kind of special ops force that specifically seeks out and targets pathogenic microorganisms that have breached our borders. Another defense is gene variability. Within a species' genome, there are often many different versions, or *alleles*, of a gene. Indeed, for genes involved in the ability to recognize foreign cells entering the body, there can be as many as 50 to 100 different alleles. In addition to gene variability *between* individuals, there are differences in gene expression *within* the individual over the lifetime. A common feature of long-lived multicellular creatures is that different genes "turn on" at different developmental time periods and in different locations throughout the body. Both the variability observed in the time course of gene expression within a cell, and the exact type of genes expressed across individuals (groups of cells), help to vary the array of expressed genes and gene products, the chemical targets of microorganisms.[3]

Perhaps the most important long-term defense against pathogens, however, and one for which we can all be grateful, is sex. Sex evolved to thwart the disorganizing (entropic) effects of pathogens.[4] To understand the benefits of sex, consider "asex." Asexual reproduction (cloning) maintains a more or less constant genetic environment down the generations; that is, offspring resemble parents in almost every respect. Imagine a set of cells from your finger (or rib if you like) separates from your body and begins to sprout a new person: a clone of you. Under these conditions, bacteria, viruses, and other microorganisms on the original "you" would have an advantage when colonizing and adapting to the "new you." In general, all of the generations pathogens spent adapting to the specific characteristics of an asexually reproducing host would still be useful when the pathogens got transferred to new, identical offspring. The pathogen thus stays ahead in the pathogen–host arms race, increasing the risk of pathogen exploitation. This is one reason why many cloned animals suffer such high rates of mortality—biochemical uniformity favors pathogen evolution.

Some species do reproduce asexually, either all of the time or facultatively, and this delicate state of affairs is maintained because for them, pathogens pose less of a survival threat: either pathogens are not a stable feature of their environment (e.g., these species inhabit regions of high altitude or low temperatures), punctuated events of sexual reproduction are enough to prevent exploitation, they have evolved alternative mechanisms to vary gene expression (as appears to be the case for the polyploid root-knot nematode), or asexual organisms have generational times that more closely match those of their resident pathogens. With lockstep reproduction, hosts can evolve countermeasures against pathogen offensive strategies much more rapidly, slowing pathogens' rates of adaptation.

But for long-lived, multicellular beasts like us, sex provides genetic mixing and impedes pathogen evolution. Sexual reproduction, as compared to the clonal process of asexual reproduction, generates *new* combinations of genes. With sex, pathogens that might have been well adapted to a particular DNA sequence or its protein product are no longer as well adapted after genomes recombine and produce novel—yet still functional—sequences. Sexual reproduction changes the internal biochemistry of hosts and pushes pathogens back to square one in their progress toward host domination. Importantly, the advantages of sex are obtained only if individuals recombine genomes with others who *do not share the same genes*. Sex with a clone, though perhaps a distinctive experience, is no different than asexual reproduction in that it maintains a similar environment to which pathogens can learn to adapt and exploit. We'll return to this point when we discuss the biological costs of inbreeding.

FINDING A MATE: REPRODUCTIVE TASTE BUDS

The fact that we reproduce sexually means that we need to find a mate, have sex, and rear young. If everyone in the social environment represented an equally good sexual partner, we'd all be in good shape: select the first person you bump into and begin procreating. But not all individuals in the social environment represent—from a biological point of view—suitable mate choices. Humans, far from mating at random, show (sometimes extremely strong) preferences when it comes to selecting a mate. We are not alone in this respect: many of the selective forces that shaped our mating preferences also shaped the mating preferences of non-human animals.

What are these forces, and what is the nature of the software that underpins decisions for choosing a sexual partner? Again, answering these questions requires an investigation into the dynamics of the ancestral milieu. The mate preferences we hold today are very much a reflection of the kinds of traits that led, on average, to the production of a larger number of healthier offspring over evolutionary time. Our modern preferences were forged in Stone Age times and, in many respects, serve as a time machine, revealing the conditions of our species' past. In this way, sexual preferences are like the taste buds we discussed in the previous chapter. Taste buds evolved to detect and prefer compounds that contributed to survival in ancestral environments (sugar [sweet], salt [salty], and protein [umami]) and reject compounds that jeopardized survival (bacteria [sour] and toxins [bitter]).

In much the same way, we have preferences to pursue sexual partners with qualities that were, on average, linked with greater reproductive success and to avoid partners with qualities that were not.

Importantly, our reproductive taste buds today are a reflection not only of the kinds of traits that affected reproduction and childrearing, but of traits that *varied* in ancestral conditions. Put differently, without variation there would be little need for preferences directing choice. This applies to all preference systems, including those for food—we evolved appetites for fitness-enhancing substances that varied in the local environment. We like sugar and fats and are motivated to go get them precisely because they were rare and valuable in ancestral environments. Fruits and wild game needed to be sought and collected or hunted—hence the powerful motivational systems to get us moving. In stark contrast, fiber was plentiful and less variable. As a hunter-gatherer, you couldn't escape fiber. The regularity of fiber in the hominid diet reduced the selection pressures to fashion neural circuitry motivating its consumption. By and large, if you were a hunter-gatherer and you were eating, you were getting fiber. This explains, today, our dietary apathy toward fiber and the lack of fast-food restaurants peddling fiber.

The same logic holds for mate preferences. For dimensions that did not vary across individuals or did not affect reproduction, there would have been no need for dedicated systems directing preferences along that dimension. As a silly example, take, for instance, the fine hairs that grow, for some, on the fingers close to the knuckle. Within reason, this attribute did not affect survival and reproduction, nor did it influence "mate-ability." The lack of influence of this trait on reproductive success is why the content of our mate-choice system does not include explicit preferences for or against these hair follicles and why you rarely, if ever, hear two men who are discussing the attractiveness of a woman say, "Did you see the hairs on her fingers? They were so cute!"

So, then, the question becomes: For our foremothers and forefathers, what dimensions would have affected reproduction *and* varied when it came to selecting a sexual partner?

SEXUAL VALUE COMPONENT ONE: MATE VALUE

Mate value is a general term for physical attractiveness, the intuitive sense that someone is a "7" or a "10." We all have a pretty good sense of where we belong on that scale, owing to both mirrors and the feedback we get from others. We also register the mate value of each person—male *and* female—we encounter. But when we assess a man's mate value (his attractiveness), exactly which features are we taking stock of? And are these the same features we use to assess a woman's mate value (her attractiveness)? The short answer is "no," and there are sound biological reasons why.

The features that go into computing mate value are, in large part, a reflection of the attributes that promoted reproductive success in ancestral environments. What promoted the reproductive success of men was not always what promoted the reproductive success of women. Thus, in addition to some commonality, there are important differences, and these differences stem from a fact of the biological world: men and women experience different limitations in their ability to produce and rear young. To see what this means, consider the maximum number of children each sex can produce.

According to the *Guinness Book of World Records*, the most children born to one woman is 69.[5] The record-holder—a Russian woman in the 1800s—reportedly gave birth to 16 pairs of twins, 7 triplets, and 4 quadruplets! 27 birthing episodes in all. As impressive as this number is (and it *is* impressive), the maximum number of children sired by a man is an order of magnitude larger. Limiting ourselves to old-school, biblical insemination techniques (we're excluding Bertold Wiesner, a physiologist who sired about 600 children by contributing his own sperm for artificial insemination for couples looking for high-IQ sperm donors), the winner is either Genghis Khan, for whom no number has been calculated but presumed to be in the thousands, or Moulay Ismail Ibn Sharif (1672–1727), a former sultan of Morocco, who, with 4 wives and over 500 concubines, reportedly sired an estimated 1,042 children (raised from the prior estimate of 888). These numbers sound impossible, but anthropologists from the University of Vienna, who created various models to explore the veracity of this claim, contend that, at least in theory, it can be done. To produce this number of children in approximately 30 years of power, they claim the sultan would have had to have sex with at least three different (fertile) women every two days.[6]

But even if these numbers aren't precisely accurate, the point stands that the ceiling on reproduction is quite different for men and women. The primary reason for this is because males and females incur different *minimum* levels of time and energy required to produce a child. Whereas women are on the hook for 9 to 10 months of pregnancy followed by 2 to 3 years of breastfeeding, men can clock their minimum investment on an egg timer. The difference in obligatory commitment to get a child up and running (literally) is what creates the differences in reproductive capacity described above. As the anthropologist Laura Betzig remarks, "In the time taken for a woman to complete the menstrual cycle that releases one ovum, a man could ejaculate 10 to 100 times."[7]

Not surprisingly, differences in minimum levels of parental investment have shaped male and female physiology and psychology. The evolutionary biologist Robert Trivers explains that the extent of the differences in parental investment for the sexes in a given species determines the intensity of *intra*sexual competition (the extent to which males, who are typically the less-investing sex, fight for access to females, who are typically the more-investing sex) and also the intensity of *inter*sexual competition (the extent to which females express greater levels of choosiness in sexual partners as compared to males). To wit, in "come-and-go" species where males invest relatively little in offspring, there are reproductive advantages to inseminating as many fertile females as possible. To this end, males in these species evolved various strategies to compete with other males to control access to available mates. Sexually dimorphic features such as horns, antlers, and large body size are features that evolved because of the differences in parental investment between the sexes; they aid males in their competition with each other over access to higher-investing females. In humans, males invest quite a bit in offspring yet still exhibit physiological features (e.g., greater musculature in the upper body; larger body size) indicative of a species in which men continue to compete for access to fertile females.

As for the second component, choosiness, the more equal the sexes in their levels of parental investment, the more similar the sexes will be when it comes to selectiveness. But where the sexes differ in parental investment—typically, creating a situation in which females invest much more—females will be the choosier sex. Greater investment translates into programs that evaluate mates more carefully for the features indicative of producing and raising healthy young. Consider the dung beetle. Female dung beetles evaluate males based on their ability to provide a very large meal made of dung. Male dung beetles thus expertly collect and roll perfectly spherical balls of dung with one goal in mind: sex. Humans, of course, are different: men don't roll balls of poo to entice potential mates. But at least in Western societies, women have been known to evaluate males on their ability to produce other spherical gifts.

In terms of psychology, differences in *minimum* parental investment shape many preferences. Take, for instance, preferences for partner variety. Whereas men can increase the number of offspring sired by mating with successive (fertile) women, the same is not true for women. Once an egg is fertilized, that's it for approximately four more years (the timeframe for gestation plus lactation): one and done. The ability for a male to increase the number of copies of his genes by mating with many different females has led to a common pattern: men (and males of many other species) tend to get re-aroused at the sight of novel females. This pattern is called the *Coolidge effect*, named after President and Mrs. Coolidge. As the psychologist Gordon Bermant tells it,[8] the story goes that President and Mrs. Coolidge once visited a government farm. Soon after their arrival they were taken off on separate tours. When Mrs. Coolidge passed the chicken pens she paused to ask the man in charge if the rooster copulates more than once each day. "Dozens of times" was the reply. "Please tell that to the president," Mrs. Coolidge requested. When the president passed the pens and was told about the rooster, he asked, "Same hen every time?" "Oh no, Mr. President, a different one each time." The president nodded slowly, then said, "Tell that to Mrs. Coolidge."

There have been a number of empirical studies that lend support to the Coolidge effect in humans. For instance, evolutionary psychologists David Buss and David Schmitt explored the sex differences in the desire for short-term versus long-term sexual partners. Whereas men and women reported an equal desire to seek a long-term relationship, males expressed stronger desires than women to seek short-term relationships. When they asked men and women to indicate how many sexual partners they'd generally like to have over various durations of time ranging from one month to one's entire lifetime, men reported far more partners than did women.

Additional evidence of sex differences in mating preferences comes from studies examining receptivity to sexual offers. If men in general prefer a greater

variety of sexual partners than do women, one might also expect men to more en-
thusiastically take advantage of new mating opportunities. Not surprisingly, they
do. In a now-famous study, the psychologists Russell Clark and Elaine Hatfield
conducted two field experiments on the campus of Florida State University. Male
and female research assistants approached members of the opposite sex and first
said, "I have been noticing you around campus. I find you to be very attractive."
Then the researcher asked one of three questions: "Would you go out with me
tonight?" "Would you come over to my apartment tonight?" or "Would you go
to bed with me tonight?" Researchers simply recorded whether the target said
"yes" or "no." For men approached by a female researcher, the more sexual the
offer, the more researchers heard "yes": 50 percent of men said "yes" to the date,
69 percent said "yes" to coming over to the apartment, and 75 percent said "yes"
to sex. For women approached by a male researcher, about the same percentage
said "yes" to a date: 56 percent. But this is where the similarity ends: only 6 percent of women said "yes" to coming to the apartment and 0 percent said "yes" to
sex. For women, the more sexual the offer, the *less* enthusiastic their response. In
fact, in their second study, every single woman said "no" to both the apartment
and to having sex—in contrast to the 69 percent of males who said "yes" to both.
The researchers also reported that men were at ease with the researchers' requests
and often apologized when they said no, saying they were in a relationship or had
other plans. Women, however, were extremely *uneasy* about the requests and were
reported saying, "You've got to be kidding" or "What is wrong with you? Leave
me alone."[9]

The Clark and Hatfield studies have been replicated many times.[10] By and large,
they provide robust evidence that males, much more than females, are willing
to take risks when it comes to sexual engagements. Buss and Schmitt found a
similar pattern as well: they found that men were far more likely than women to
consent to sex after knowing someone for only an hour (the shortest duration of
time examined). Women's willingness to consent to sex was lower than men's *for
all durations of time examined*—that is, until five years. After this time (and only
after this time), males and females were equal in their willingness to consent to
sex. Even if these data are inflated, which they might be due to the nature of self-
report, the general pattern holds: men are more eager and more willing to engage
in sex, at least with partners known for less than five years. This calculus stems
from psychologies sensitive to the opportunity costs associated with mating. Due
to their much larger minimum investments, female psychology is more sensitive
to the costs of making poor reproductive decisions. That is, the opportunity costs
associated with each sexual encounter are potentially high, and so, all else being
equal, women tend to exhibit extreme reticence to engage in (sober) sex without
having properly vetted a particular male. For men, by contrast, the opportunity
costs for reproducing are lower, and so male minds have been fashioned to take
relative advantage of additional mating opportunities. These preferences lead to
general patterns of behavior that differ between men and women.

By and large, the different obligatory levels of parental investment were powerful selection pressures that shaped mental systems assessing the suitability of

potential mates. And because different sets of information bore on the question of "mate-ability" for a given male or female, different systems likely evolved to compute a man's versus a woman's mate value.

Female Mate Value: Fertility, Fidelity, and Health

As we mentioned, the main dimension limiting (or facilitating, if you like) the reproductive success of a female is her fertility. Over evolutionary time, men who preferred women who were closer to peak fertility as sexual partners tended to produce, on average, more offspring than men who selected a mate at random. The variation in a female's ability to conceive over the lifetime would have selected for programs to assess a female's reproductive potential and, in the male brain, target sexual motivations accordingly. In humans and many non-humans species alike, then, a main component of female mate value—a female's attractiveness—is her fertility status.

How can you tell which women are fertile and which ones are not? Although menstruation and ovulation begin around age 12 to 14, less than 10 percent of the menstrual cycles during this time include actual ovulation. It is not until ages 21 to 25 that the percentage of fertile menstrual cycles increases to 50 percent.[11] Indeed, data from various sources, including psychological studies and online dating sites, are in accord that men of most—if not all—ages show the greatest preference, on average, for women who are in their early 20s.[12] In a landmark study investigating the mate preferences of men and women from 37 different cultures around the globe, David Buss found that the average age men prefer in a marriage partner is 24, an age very close to a female's peak fertility. Other researchers have found a similar pattern. For instance, Doug Kenrick, Abraham Buunk, and colleagues have shown that as men age, they tend to prefer women who are progressively younger than them, again because they are preferring women who are in their early 20s.[13] Similarly, data examining the age of the wife and husband in first versus later marriages show that regardless of whether it is a man's first or second marriage, the older he is, the larger the age gap with his bride.[14]

But, in the environment of our ancestors, how would one have known the age of a particular female? The ovaries don't generate a red neon sign reading "fertile"— at least not in humans. Instead, there are a number of traits that would have cued fertility (read: not too young but not too old): hair color that isn't gray; smooth skin; the presence of secondary sexual characteristics including breasts, hair patches, and the deposition of fats in the thighs and buttocks; agility; and particular vocal qualities. Men who possessed mental circuitry that caused a preference for these traits would have left, on average, more offspring than men with mental circuitry that caused a preference, for example, for gray hair, reduced agility, and wrinkled skin. Moreover, sons would have inherited these preferences, increasing their frequency in subsequent generations.

In addition to fertility, sexual fidelity is a critical dimension of a female's mate value. For a given male, a highly fertile female might be desirable, but for those seeking a long-term partner, confidence that a female was a sexually faithful partner was important. For reasons we'll discuss shortly, men, relative to women, tend to particularly prize sexual fidelity as a trait in long-term mates (though they are also willing to trade off that fidelity for ease of access—in other words, when the woman required little or no courting).

The last main component of female mate value worth noting is health. In an age where there were no hospitals, minute clinics, or antibiotics, our ancestors would have been at the mercy of their own immune system (and knowledge of medicinal herbs). Cues to reduced health—lethargy, paleness, skin blotchiness and bumpiness, coughing, sneezing, and vomiting—not only indicate potential pathogen presence but signal a reduced ability to bring a child to term and to nurture the child throughout infancy.

In sum, then, the main components of female mate value are fertility, sexual fidelity, and health. And men?

Male Mate Value: Status, Resources, Intelligence, and Kindness

Many of the dimensions along which we assess the mate value of males differ from those used to assess the mate value of females. For men, the factor that limited their ability to produce young wasn't their own fertility. Males, once sexually mature, maintain a more or less consistent ability to fertilize an egg. The lack of variation in sperm production and ability to donate DNA means that females had little issue discerning the fertility of men. Instead, the factor that limited a male's reproductive success was access to and the ability to attract fertile females. And so what are women attracted to?

From a female's perspective, a main issue when selecting a mate was choosing a male who was both capable and willing to provide resources she could use in the production and rearing of her children. Together, the capability and willingness to provide are main components of *male* mate value. How might natural selection have engineered the software to perform this function? That is, what are the clues that enable a woman to infer "that man over there will be able to provide for me and my offspring?"

One cue indicating the ability to obtain resources was the amount of resources the male currently has—current success is as good a bet as any for future success. Likewise, social connectedness indicates the number of other people who value the male and might be willing to provide him with resources. That is, one can observe the number of kin present and the frequency of cooperative versus antagonistic interactions a male has with others to gauge his "social status" and, hence, access to resources. General intelligence, too, would have enabled one to assess a male's ability to solve problems relevant to resource acquisition. Last, motivations to go and find resources would have been indicative of a man's ability to obtain resources. Most women tend to find men who are lazy and "underemployed" not so attractive, all else being equal. Instead, attributes such as industriousness, creativity, and curiosity are predictors of a man who might seek resources of value. David Buss, in his 37-culture study, found that females rate good financial prospects, and ambition and industriousness as highly desirable in a mate. All around the world, females prize resources.

To the list, we can also add strength and kindness, and especially a combination of the two. In ancestral conditions, a male's physical size would have correlated with his ability to obtain and control access to resources. In addition, greater formidability provides a female and her offspring protection against agonists. In the mating realm, then, from a female's perspective, a physically dominant male is desirable to the extent he poses no physical threat to her or her offspring. But if a male—capable and physically dominant though he may be—is not willing to share the resources he has acquired with *you*, what's the point? One way to evaluate a man's propensity to share is to see how cooperative he is with others. We have an intuitive sense of how "nice" people are, and this no doubt comes from the nonconscious assessment of how willing the person is to share versus compete with others. Perhaps most striking, David Buss has found that being honest, affectionate, kind, and understanding are traits rated highest in terms of desirability. It's not just about the gold.

Last, as with female mate value, an important component of male mate value is health. Because females incur much larger opportunity costs associated with producing an offspring than do men, females are a bit more sensitive to mate quality. Put differently, females are after males with "good genes" for their children. Each genetic blueprint guides the developmental programs that build and calibrate our physiological and psychological features. As we discussed in one of the examples of instinct blindness in Chapter 2, the ability of underlying developmental processes to build successful design features is evidenced by symmetry, a state easily disrupted by genetic mutations, disease-causing organisms, and other environmental perturbations. Likewise, because testosterone suppresses the immune system, males showing enhanced secondary sexual characteristics (squarer jaw, larger musculature, deeper voices), which are caused by testosterone and its derivatives, provide evidence of good health and "good genes."

The desire for "good genes" is evident in many other species. For instance, a peahen studying a peacock is evaluating the male on the symmetry of his design, how bright his colors are, and his train rattling.[15] These features allow the peahen to infer how healthy the peacock is—symmetry, iridescent coloration, and large tails are easily disrupted by disease, genetic mutations, and developmental systems not as robust against environmental insults. In humans, male musculature, masculine facial features, and vocal tone are secondary sexual characteristics dependent on testosterone and good indications of health and the robustness of a man's developmental blueprints.

In sum, a man's health and ability to acquire, defend, and share resources are dimensions that would have been relevant to a woman's ability to produce and care for young. As a result, these have been naturally selected as primary (not sole) factors in the assessment of a man's mate value. In ancestral times, as today, men varied along each of these dimensions. Not all men exhibit the same motivation or prowess in securing valuable resources (e.g., calories), the same ability to defend oneself and one's mate against rivals, or the same willingness to direct resources toward a particular female (as opposed to multiple or other females). Females— both human and non-human—appear to be sensitive to these dimensions when evaluating potential mates.[16]

The Architecture of Mate Value

The adaptive challenges males and females faced when selecting a mate suggest that somewhere in our psychological architecture are programs that use mate value to evaluate potential partners. What might such a system look like? A representative schematic is pictured in Figure 6.1. Starting on the left is a column that lists the various selection pressures that affected reproductive success for males and females in ancestral environments. Linked to each selection pressure are the systems that detect and assess the various dimensions we might use to identify fitness-promoting mates. So, for instance, male mate value derives from the ability to obtain, defend, and share resources. Cues signaling the presence of these abilities in addition to health are taken as input and combined by an estimator to generate an estimate of *male mate value*. Very young males, because they tend to lack resources, the social networking required to obtain them, and the upper body strength to protect them (in addition to their inability to reproduce if they are prepubescent), tend to register as having lower mate value than older males with such capability.

For women, the game is a bit different. The key selection pressures influencing a female's reproductive potential are her health and fertility. Thus, cues signaling these dimensions are taken as input by a separate estimator to create an estimate of *female mate value*. All else being equal, women at the far ends of the spectrum—the very young and the very old—have less reproductive potential, and thus hold lower mate value, than do women of fertile ages. Not coincidently, neither of these demographics exhibit many of the cues to fertility. The young do not yet possess secondary sexual characteristics, and as women age after their reproductive window has closed, skin begins to wrinkle and sag, hair begins to gray, and muscle tone begins to decrease.

Practically speaking, then, our ability to assign mate value to others depends first on the ability to categorize a person as male or female, and second on the application of gender-specific mate value criteria. When evaluating a male, programs particularly assess resource-acquisition dimensions; when evaluating a female, programs particularly assess fertility. (We'll visit the subject of sexual orientation later and show how crisscrossing inputs can generate some of the variation we observe in sexuality and sexual preferences.)

But mate value can't be the only factor guiding *sexual* attraction. Men, for instance, are able to assess the mate value of other men, yet this does not mean that

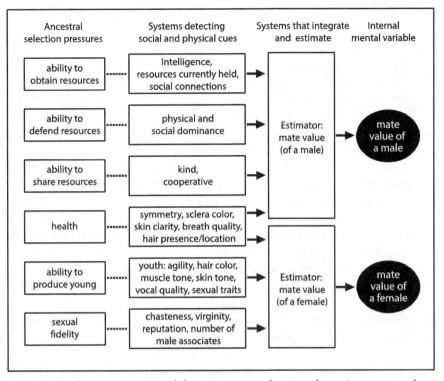

Figure 6.1. Selection pressures and the proximate mechanisms that estimate mate value for males and females. This model is a theoretical diagram of how mate value is computed in humans. The abilities of a male to obtain, defend, and share resources were critical factors that contributed to a female's reproductive success in ancestral environments and therefore made up a male's mate value. By contrast, female fertility was a critical factor that contributed to a male's reproductive success, and thus made up female mate value. One source of variation in sexual preferences, as discussed below, could stem from how mate values are assigned; traits used to assess female mate value could be applied to males and traits used to assess male mate value could be applied to females.

when they see a man of high mate value they find him sexually attractive. The same is true of women. Women are devilishly keen about how they and other women stack up according to attractiveness, and such scrutiny can occur without sexual arousal. So mate-value assessment cannot be the only internal variable that regulates *sexual* attractiveness (as opposed to just *physical* attractiveness). There has to be a system that takes into account the value a member of each sex holds as a *sexual partner for oneself*. After all, we can determine how attractive our family members are—both same-sex and opposite-sex relatives—without being sexually attracted to them ourselves. Indeed, this is one way fathers in some cultures determine bride price—the closer to optimal fertility age the daughter is, the greater the bridewealth she commands.[17] In addition to mate value, then, genetic relatedness is an important factor weighting the sexual desirability of another person.

SEXUAL VALUE COMPONENT 2: GENETIC RELATEDNESS

Oddly, when it comes to sexual attraction, many social scientists have overlooked the effects of relatedness. It's not that they are pro-incest, but rather they have been struck by a severe case of instinct blindness. So good are the systems that prevent kin from entering the mind as possible sexual partners that they are typically excluded from the discussion without notice. Entire chapters in psychology textbooks on sexual attraction discuss the ins and outs of sexual attraction without mentioning family, genetic relatedness, or kinship.

As evidence, social psychologists have identified three general factors that regulate who we find attractive as a sexual partner: familiarity, similarity, and proximity. Intuitively, these make good sense, until you consider the demographic that best meets these criteria: family! They're familiar—you've known them your entire life. They're similar—chances are you share the same religion and culture and even have a strong physical resemblance. Last, they are close by and easily accessible—perhaps even under the same roof and down the hall. Yet family members are, typically, the last group of individuals considered as potential mates for oneself. So despite a potentially high mate value (e.g., one's sister can be very *physically* attractive), genetic relatedness turns an otherwise perfect mate into one we typically avoid like the plague.

Why Not Sex with Relatives?

Why is it that humans and many non-human species avoid mating with close genetic relatives? There are at least two good biological reasons. The first has to do with the reasons why sexual reproduction evolved in the first place. The evolutionary benefits of sex come by virtue of swapping genes with another individual likely to possess *different* alleles. Genetic relatives, by virtue of sharing a common ancestor, have a greater chance of sharing the same genes and, by extension, a similar internal biochemistry. Mating with a genetic relative runs the risk of generating offspring who are more "clone-like" and who will suffer from an increased risk of pathogen infection. The closer the relative, the greater the overlap in shared genes and the greater the risk of producing a child vulnerable to disease. The pathogen-induced decrease in the reproductive success of individuals who happen to select more genetically similar mates is one of the main reasons why evolution favored (in humans and in many other species) neural software that causes inbreeding avoidance—the avoidance of close genetic relatives as sexual partners.

Another reason why inbreeding-avoidance systems evolved is because of the existence of harmful genetic mutations. Humans are a diploid species. We inherit one copy of genes from our mother and one copy from our father. This inheritance system has built-in redundancy: when the gene inherited from one parent is damaged, the gene inherited from the other parent can typically fulfill the required function. We all have damaged genes, which can range in their effects from deadly to slight. Geneticists have estimated that each human has roughly a dozen or so mutations peppered throughout the genome that, if present in a double dose (because mom and dad both donated the same broken gene), would be fatal. We are not dead 10 times over because when we inherit one of these mutations, its effects are masked by the functioning allele inherited from the other parent. Redundancy works. But this redundancy is severely compromised when parents are closely related.

Take a full biological brother and sister, and, to pick a gene at random, let's take a gene involved in DNA replication. Say both brother and sister inherited from dad a working copy of this gene, but they each inherited a damaged copy of this gene from mom. However, the brother and sister are healthy and show no abnormalities because the working copy of the gene (from dad) masks the harmful effects of the damaged gene (from mom). If the brother and sister now mate, they run the risk of passing two copies of the damaged gene to their child. It isn't guaranteed to happen—they could both pass on their father's working gene, or only one of them might pass along the damaged gene. But there is a one in four chance that the inbred child will end up with a double dose of this particular damaged gene. And this is just for one gene. Summing the probabilities of inheriting a double damaged dose *across the entire genome* means that the risks of producing a child with harmful genetic mutations increase quickly when parents are closely related.

There is a large body of evidence showing that inbred children experience a wide range of physical disabilities and cognitive deficits.[18] In one study conducted on Czech women, children sired by the mother's father or brother were six times more likely to suffer severe birth defects or early mortality than children born of the same women sired by an unrelated man. "Kissing cousins" are relatively less affected but certainly not exempt from these risks: the rate of infant and early childhood mortality for children of first cousins is over 4 percent greater than that for children of unrelated parents.[19] The same trend holds for non-human species too. By and large, where it's been studied, be it in plants or animals, inbreeding reduces the health and survivability of offspring.

Mating with close genetic relatives, then, increases the risks of transmitting harmful genetic mutations to offspring and creates in offspring internal biochemical environments more hospitable to invading microorganisms. Given these strong selection pressures, one should expect to see systems for identifying close genetic relatives. Indeed, evolutionary biologists have uncovered various mechanisms by which individuals of different species detect their kin. In humans, these mechanisms have been a topic of recent investigation.

Cues to Kinship

If genetic relatedness is an important factor governing the choice of sexual partners, then a complete understanding of mate choice includes a description of how we come to know that a particular individual is a genetic relative. This is important for at least two reasons. First, we can learn which cues to kinship lead to the development of strong sexual aversions. And second, we can identify those situations in which kinship cues are absent, leading to greater risks of both consensual and nonconsensual sex between genetic relatives. That is, we can better understand why incest sometimes occurs.

In Chapter 2 we discussed the logic of sibling detection. Two cues—co-residence duration and observations of maternal–neonate investment—are taken as input by systems that infer the genetic relatedness of another child. When present, these cues predict sexual and altruistic motivations, two separate systems that both rely on information regarding genetic relatedness. By and large, cues to relatedness decrease sexual desire and increase motivations to help and care. However, co-residence duration and seeing one's own mother caring for a newborn are good cues for detecting *siblings*; to the extent that different cues identified different family members in the environment of our hunter-gatherer ancestors, different kin-detection systems should exist. The negative consequences of inbreeding and the genetic benefits of altruism are most pronounced for nuclear family members and quickly drop off as you move further out on the family tree. It is likely that we possess systems to infer the relatedness of uncles, aunts, nieces, nephews, cousins, and grandparents. However, these relationships are most likely based on the inferences drawn regarding who counts as a mother, father, offspring, and sibling. Consequently, we'll focus our discussion here on the most robust kin-detection mechanisms: those that evolved to detect *nuclear* family.

MOTHERS AND OFFSPRING

Of all the bonds in nature, none is more certain than the relatedness of mother and offspring. In humans, because fertilization occurs internally, women have an unmistakable cue for identifying their young: birth. Long before the advent of modern medicine, a woman could always be 100 percent certain that the baby coming out of her body was indeed her own. Prolonged care (including breastfeeding) would have allowed mothers to imprint on features of the baby, enabling continued recognition. For the baby in question, a good bet for identifying "mom" or "primary attachment figure" would have been to simply determine who fed you. Ancestrally, babies nursed for two to four years, and the primary person doing the breastfeeding was mom. Circuitry in the baby's head that caused him or her to remember the olfactory, visual, or aural features associated with the feeding machine would have helped to detect which woman, of the group of surrounding women, was most likely mom and thus willing to extend care. Much of the literature in developmental psychology talks about attachment. Kin-detection systems that sift for cues used to infer relatedness are likely a good part of this larger attachment process.

FATHERS AND OFFSPRING

In stark contrast to women, men cannot be 100 percent certain who their child is (hence the expression "mommy's baby, daddy's maybe"). The question each man has to answer is: What is the probability that the child coming out of a particular woman is mine? The field is cut substantially by first determining which women the man has had sex with: no sex, no baby. After narrowing the field down to women with whom a man has lain, the questions get more specific: *When* did I have sex with her—many years ago or a few months ago? A pregnant woman with whom a man slept once five years ago could not be carrying his child today, but a woman with whom he slept five months ago could be. Somewhere in the male mind is a timer that indicates the probability of paternity.

While not directly applicable, studies of male langurs provide evidence for how such a mechanism might manifest. In langurs, there is one alpha male that controls access to a group of females. When a reigning alpha male is replaced by a new male, the new alpha typically begins to kill all of the nursing young and newborns. This causes the females to begin ovulating again (ovulation is inhibited by the hormones that ramp up milk production). The new alpha will continue to try to kill newborns up until the time that he could have sired the child.[20] Somehow langur males "know" the timing of their species' reproductive cycle. It is thus not farfetched to believe that in humans, men do too.

In addition to having a tacit understanding of timing, men also need to assess whether the woman in question has had sex with other men and whether this has occurred in the relevant time period. Sexual fidelity is critical to men's ability to infer their relatedness to offspring, and not surprisingly, men around the world tend to hold this trait dear. But sexual fidelity is only half the story. Even if a man believed his mate to be 100 percent sexually faithful, would this mean that *any* child she held or fed was his? No. Under ancestral conditions women frequently collaborated in childcare, often passing infants around for extended periods of being held by other women.[21] Thus, basing paternity on which baby one's mate held, independent of other information, would have led to many false positives.

Instead, what is needed beyond assessments of fidelity is the repeated and extended observation of one's mate caring for—breastfeeding—the infant, a "fidelity-feeding" combination of paternity cues.[22] This would allow the man to know that *this particular child* is mine (not the one she carried around for just an hour yesterday). So the logic for paternity assessment might go something like this: "(1) I had sex with a woman in roughly the right time window, (2) she is pregnant, and (3) to my knowledge and according to the local gossip mill she did not sleep with anyone else, so (4) the particular child I see her birthing, feeding, and caring for I can be relatively certain is mine."

What about the other direction—offspring detection of fathers? Notably, very little research has attempted to pinpoint how children identify their father. But while it's an open question, we can make some educated guesses based on the information available when these systems were formed. For example, humans often had reliable cues to motherness, which included breastfeeding and intensive care. Since males—both human and other mammalian species—do not breastfeed, much of infant caregiving fell on the shoulders of females. What are the cues that would have enabled a child to infer which man, out of the community of men, was likely "dad"? One possibility is that children merely rely on the paternity assessment of men. To the extent that a man is certain that a child is his own, he will likely be motivated to help care for the child. All the child would have to do, then, is to register which man provided the largest investment (in other words, who's doting on me the most? Who's bringing me meat home from the hunt?). Another possibility is that children rely on mom to figure out "fatherness." The man in a relationship with mom starting from when the child was born has a better chance of being dad than a stranger encountered from the next village when the child is 10. Identifying the man in close physical association with mom, sleeping in the same bed as mom, arguing with mom, and caring for mom has a better-than-zero shot at being dad (that is, most of the time).

The Architecture of Kin Detection

What might a system for kin detection look like? One possibility is shown in Figure 6.2.[23] The left-hand column lists the various ancestral pressures that would have selected for a system that computes an estimate of genetic relatedness. The next column lists cues that could have correlated with genetic relatedness in ancestral environments. These cues are taken as input by an intermediate system that computes, *for each individual* in the social environment, an estimate of relatedness. The absence of any kinship cues for a given individual leads to a low, baseline estimate of relatedness. The presence of kinship cues ratchets this estimate upward. The effect that each cue has on the magnitude of the computed relatedness

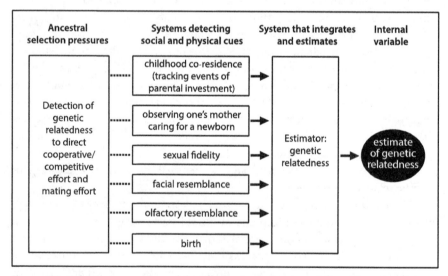

Figure 6.2. Selection pressures and the proximate mechanisms that estimate genetic relatedness. This model is a theoretical diagram of how genetic relatedness might be computed in humans. Given the evolutionary benefits of helping kin and avoiding kin as sexual partners, there are likely programs that evolved for assessing the probability a given individual is a genetic relative. Such a system is purported to take as input cues associated with relatedness to generate a single *estimate of genetic relatedness* that modulates decisions regarding both cooperation and, of relevance here, sexual attraction.

estimate has been set by selection based on the manner in which each cue statistically predicted genetic relatedness over many thousands of generations. (This is just like the effect each cue to pathogen presence has on estimates of harm of consumption and contact.) That is, the links between kinship cues and the probability of relatedness were "learned" across generations and codified in our neural programming. Once formed, the *estimate of genetic relatedness* is an internal psychological variable that can be taken as input by systems guiding altruism and, as we shall see in the next section, sexual preferences. By and large, greater estimates of genetic relatedness translate into greater sexual avoidance and disgust.

Wait, Whatever Happened to Freud! Don't People Harbor Sexual Desires for Their Family?

The short answer to the above question is a simple "no," but there are, as always, exceptions. Situations vary, and kin-detection systems sometimes don't correctly identify all genetic relatives as such. Every now and then a story shows up in the media of two siblings, a father and daughter, or even a mother and son, who meet and fall in love. If we have systems that evolved to prevent inbreeding, how does this happen?

There are three possible answers to this question. First, in cases where two individuals are *not* exposed to the cues the mind uses to infer relatedness, then the individuals are tagged with estimates of relatedness that are low—just like most strangers. For instance, siblings raised apart because they were adopted or because they share the same sperm donor didn't live together throughout childhood and were thus not exposed to the cues the mind privileges when categorizing another person as a genetic sibling. The same holds for men who meet a daughter for the first time during adulthood. These men did not observe their mate caring for their daughter as an infant and throughout childhood, and also perhaps carry doubts about their mate's fidelity, regardless of what a DNA paternity test reveals. Finally, women who give a child up for adoption at birth prevent the requisite imprinting of "mother" and "son." During adulthood, should son and mother meet, to the extent the younger male finds the older female attractive, there is no natural kinship aversion standing in the way of a sexual relationship. Freud, for example, is rumored to have been wet-nursed, which perhaps interfered with the proper categorization of his mother as "mom" and contributed to his sexual attraction toward her.[24]

A second reason why kin might engage in sexual behaviors is due to context. When sexual choices are constrained, as they can be due to geographical limitations or cultural institutions that require particular pairings (e.g., cases of Egyptian royalty), individuals might treat their family members as sexual partners. Of course, contextual reasons encompass both consensual and nonconsensual sexual interactions. Drugs and alcohol can impair kin-detection mechanisms and mute disgust reactions. Likewise, one member of a dyad might have inferred a high degree of relatedness whereas the other might not have, as can happen in cases where stepparents enter families with young children. Fathers have low estimates of relatedness, but children, by virtue of the cues of investment, might have higher estimates.

Finally, there is always the possibility that the machinery guiding kin detection is just broken. That is, there may be deficits present in particular brain regions that trigger sexual aversions based on the detection of kin. There is evidence, for instance, that particular regions of the brain govern the emotion of disgust—the insula, caudate, and anterior cingulate cortex (a region involved in error detection)—and that these regions are associated with various conditions linked to deficits in disgust, such as Huntington's disease and obsessive-compulsive disorder.[25]

In sum, there are principled reasons why people typically do not have sex with close family members and likewise principled reasons why they sometimes do.

WITH WHOM TO HAVE SEX? CONTEXTUAL FACTORS

In addition to another individual's mate value and genetic relatedness, context matters when it comes to making decisions about the suitability of a particular individual as a sexual partner for oneself. Two factors we'll consider here are one's *own* mate value and the perceived availability of mates.

Contextual Factor One: One's Own Mate Value

In the absence of mirrors, our ancestors would have had to form an idea of how they rated in terms of their attractiveness, particularly their facial attractiveness, by the feedback they received from others in the environment. The frequency with which others made eye contact versus looked away, smiled versus frowned, approached versus avoided, or delivered benefits (such as gifts) versus imposed costs (such as physical harm) would have enabled both men and women to make inferences regarding their own mate value.

Once a person has an idea of where they stand relative to others in the social environment, they can more efficiently target their mating effort. A female at the top of the mate-value scale has the leverage to obtain a male with correspondingly high mate value. All other things being equal, a female at the lower end of the mate-value scale does not. Put more colloquially, 10s tend to mate with 10s, 9s with 9s, 8s with 8s, and so forth.[26] That is, at least with respect to long-term mating relationships; for short-term mating opportunities, the rules can change, especially if there is alcohol involved. A female 7 may be able to secure a male 10 for a one-night stand, but keeping him around is a different story.

Mental systems that calibrated the perceived attractiveness of others according to one's own assessed mate value would have prevented the loss of valuable time and energy. Most women agree upon who counts as attractive at the top of the male mate-value scale. As you work your way down this scale, however, women diverge in their assessment, with more attractive females having more stringent criteria for what counts as an attractive partner than less attractive females. This same pattern holds for men. At the top end of the scale, although most men would have no problem with having sex with a supermodel, not all men have the mate value (status and good looks) to get in the door. As one slides down the scale of female attractiveness, men will differ in their judgments according to their sense of their *own* attractiveness.

In sum, one's own mate value should moderate the sexual value placed on potential mates. When one believes oneself to be of high mate value, this increases the minimum acceptability threshold, restricting sexual motivations to only partners of very high mate value and causing avoidance (or the investment of very little effort) of all who fall in the lower range. And, conversely, when one believes oneself to be of low mate value, this should lower the threshold of acceptability, increasing the range of suitable partners, and decreasing the probability that one will reject or avoid other willing partners.

Recent studies on mate preferences lend support to the idea that one's own mate value factors into perceptions of attractiveness.[27] In one such study, Laura Morgan and Michael Kinsley manipulated males' sense of their own attractiveness via feedback and then presented them with attractive and unattractive faces. All males attended to attractive faces, regardless of whether they were given feedback that they were of high or low market value. The difference came for attention spent looking at the unattractive faces: males told they were of high market value spent significantly *less* time attending to unattractive faces as compared to males told they were of low market value. It seems that we modulate our goals based on our perceived condition.

Another study, conducted by psychologists Leonard Lee, George Loewenstein, Dan Ariely, and colleagues from HOTorNOT.com, examined over 2 million requests made by approximately 16,000 individuals to meet people encountered on the website HOTorNOT.com. The researchers also had in hand the attractiveness of each individual a member wished or did not wish to meet as well as the attractiveness of the member himself or herself (taken from the ratings of other members). They found that

> less attractive members were more likely to accept less attractive people as dates, and, conversely, more attractive members were more likely to accept more attractive people. These results suggest that less attractive members not only were less selective overall, but also tended to be less selective in the rated (consensus) attractiveness of potential dates.[28]

Similar effects have been found in the lab. Psychologists Jose Yong and Norm Li had both men and women hold a small sum (~$84) or large sum (~$2,100) of money. They found that the men—but not the women—who held the large sum of money *increased* their minimum requirements in the attractiveness of a potential date. A windfall of cash caused men to aim higher in the mate market. But women are not immune—they too show sex-specific effects of self-assessed mate value. Psychologists David Buss and Todd Shackelford found that more physically attractive women held higher standards for an acceptable mate in terms of his masculinity, income, desire for a home and children, and devotion as a partner.[29] Both sexes, it seems, leverage their assets to obtain a mate that, at least ancestrally, improved the chances of reproduction and offspring survivability.

The notion that one's own mate value influences decisions in the mating arena might explain, in part, the individual variation in preferences we observe. For instance, men of low mate value who have by and large "struck out" with reproductive-age (read: higher mate value) women may perceive their mating pools to have narrowed, causing them to extend their range of what is considered attractive to include pre- or post-reproductive females. While most men—even those who do become attracted to pre- and post-reproductive females—will avoid kin, the hundreds of biological incest cases reported each year (which probably constitutes a vast underreporting) show that even the kinship wall may be breached under certain circumstances. Thus, contributing to the collection of sexual preferences observed in humans are systems that evolved to guide mating decisions based on an individual's own mate value—actual or merely perceived.

Contextual Factor Two: Mate Availability

What if the pool of potential mates were small? How might this affect sexual attraction? If you were on a desert island with just your sister or brother, how long would you forgo sex? Forever? Likely men and women evolved to view such a predicament in different ways. Recall that the costs of reproduction are lower for men. So, in general, men should be less resistant to and more willing to engage in "risky" sex, especially in circumstances in which the mating pool is severely limited. One category of "risky" sex, by which we mean sex carrying potential biological costs (not sex involving trapezes), is incest. On the other hand, women, given their larger investments in reproduction, are likely to remain resistant to engaging in sexual behaviors potentially jeopardizing the health and viability of offspring far longer than men. Nevertheless, a general prediction is that the more restricted the perceived mating pool, the more relaxed one's preferences. And, depending on how limited one might be, one might even begin to find kin, same-sex friends, or other animals as potential sexual outlets. To our evolved mind, some sex might be perceived as better than no sex.

Perhaps the best evidence regarding the effect of restricted mating pools comes from data on Taiwanese minor marriages, a form of marriage common in the 16th century in which a young infant girl was adopted into her future husband's family and reared alongside him throughout childhood. Similar to the Israeli Kibbutzim example we discussed in Chapter 2, Taiwanese minor marriages presented a natural experiment in which genetically *unrelated* children were reared together in sibling-like environments. In stark contrast to the Kibbutz, however, these Taiwanese children, after being raised together throughout childhood, were forced to marry in adulthood.

Like the co-reared peers of the Kibbutz, co-reared minor marriage partners probably developed strong sexual aversions toward one another. Recall from Chapter 2 that childhood co-residence is a cue to siblingship and leads to the development of sexual aversions in adulthood. Indeed, anthropologist Arthur Wolf found that couples married in the minor fashion were more likely to get divorced, have extramarital affairs, and produce fewer children than other couples who were not raised together throughout childhood.[30] Although the case of the Taiwanese minor marriage is held up as support for the Westermarck effect, namely that childhood association leads to strong sexual aversions in adulthood, there is another lesson that applies to our discussion of mate availability: children raised as siblings *will* have sex and *will* produce children under circumstances in which cultural norms severely restrict the pool of potential mates. Indeed, many co-reared couples remained married throughout their lives. The case of Taiwanese minor marriages is certainly extreme, but it illustrates how restricting the mating pool can offset perceived genetic relatedness in evaluations of sexual attraction. For members of both sexes, a limited pool of available mates will influence the sexual attractiveness of those present. In other words, we're sensitive to what's available.

And never more so than when one is incarcerated. For incarcerated men, the unavailability of females as sexual partners changes behavior, leading some men to engage in sexual behavior with other men. The fact that bestiality cases arise with some regularity also suggests that members of other species aren't off the table, either. Of course, there are a myriad of factors that might lead to these different cases, and it's difficult to disentangle them (as we mentioned above, for instance, sex with kin may often result from the absence of cues that the brain normally uses to identify family members). But the lack of ideal prospects (from a biological point of view) should be kept on the list of usual suspects in attempting to predict and explain this behavior.

ENGINEERING: EXPECTED SEXUAL VALUE

Given the factors that influence mate choice, what is the design of the information-processing systems that govern motivations to pursue or avoid another person as a sexual partner? We illustrate one possibility in Figure 6.3: estimates of mate value and genetic relatedness combine, weighted by various contextual factors, to generate the last of three critical internal regulatory variables associated with disgust, *expected sexual value*. The *expected sexual value* of another individual registers the reproductive gains (or losses) associated with selecting him or her as a sexual partner *for oneself*. When positive and elevated, expected sexual value triggers sexual pursuit (read: lust); when negative and low, it triggers sexual avoidance (read: disgust).

Let's walk through this model to illustrate how our sexual motivations and preferences might operate. First, notice that both female mate value and male mate value are inputs to the expected sexual-value estimator. Once an individual

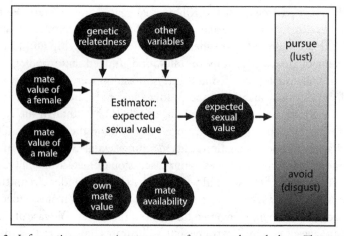

Figure 6.3. Information-processing structure of our sexual psychology. This model is a theoretical diagram of how sexual value is computed in humans. Mate values of both males and females are taken as input by a system that computes the third internal regulatory variable associated with disgust, *expected sexual value*. The effects of mate value on sexual value are modulated by a variety of factors including genetic relatedness, one's own mate value, and the perceived availability of mates in the social environment. These factors lead to the production of a dynamic representation of *expected sexual value*, which when low motivates avoidance in sexual contexts and gives rise to our sense of disgust.

has been categorized as male or female—a process that itself requires additional circuitry—then the category-appropriate mate-value criteria are applied, generating either a value for female mate value or male mate value. So for a heterosexual man evaluating an individual categorized as female, *expected sexual value* is a function of *female mate value*. When her mate value is high (e.g., cues to fertility and of good health are present), this leads to an elevated expected sexual value, activating lust and motivating sexual pursuit. When her mate value is low (e.g., she lacks cues to fertility or shows signs of severe illness), this leads to a lower expected sexual value (though perhaps still not zero due to the low opportunity costs associated with mating for males) and will motivate sexual avoidance.

Genetic relatedness, however, moderates the importance of mate value. When an internal estimate of genetic relatedness is high (because cues to kinship were detected), attractiveness tends not to matter. Due to the severe negative consequences of inbreeding, high certainties of relatedness under most circumstances lead to very *low* estimates of expected sexual value, regardless of how attractive a man's sister, mother, or daughter might be. At lower certainties of relatedness, however, the mate value of a particular female begins to carry more weight. For instance, during adulthood, when a man meets a woman he has never before met (that is, cues to kinship are virtually absent), decisions about how sexually attractive she is are based on the attributes that determine female mate value. The tendency for mate value to vary with a woman's age (and her cues to reproductive potential) means that males will tend to hold, all other things being equal, lower expected sexual values for very young and very old females, that is females not exhibiting secondary sexual characteristics and those exhibiting cues to post-reproductive age. For most men under most circumstances, thoughts of sex with a young child and octogenarians generate low expected sexual values, leading to intense sexual disgust when such acts are considered.

As mentioned earlier, context matters. One's own mate value and the available pool of mates are two parameters that should shift perceptions and motivations. One way this information could be integrated is by dynamically tinkering with the weights of various inputs. For instance, when one is of low mate value (you perceive you are not the target of anyone's affections; members of the desired sex avoid talking to you), estimates of the perceived mate value of other people (of the desired sex) might be modified upward, causing the broadening of the range of acceptable mates. Conversely, when one is of high mate value (you are frequently the target of attention by sexually desirable others), estimates of the mate value of others (of the desired sex) might shift down. Likewise, when few mates are available, the mate value assigned to all others of the desired sex could be increased, whereas when mates abound, the mate value assigned to any one particular individual might be lower.

A feature of the sexual value system we posit here is that it takes as input the mate value of *both* men and women. The system in heterosexual men that generates sexual attraction toward women is also responsible for producing sexual disgust toward other men. This is because, in the heterosexual male mind, the system for assessing sexual value is configured to weight the mate value of other males very low (negative) in calculations of expected sexual value. By contrast, the mate value of females is prioritized and given a much higher weighting when computing sexual value and hence sexual attractiveness.

Much like when a man encounters a female, when a man encounters another male, there is an automatic assessment of the male's mate value (which could range from very low to very high). All to say, men size each other up. Upon detecting a man of very high mate value, heterosexual men typically do not get sexually aroused. This is because for heterosexual men under most circumstances, assessments of male mate values are linked with *negative* expected sexual values. With a low expected sexual value, males don't experience the motivational push to pursue other men as sexual partners. But this doesn't mean that disgust is automatically deployed—to wit, when most men meet, they don't exchange disgust expressions. Sexual disgust is activated *only in sexual contexts*. Low sexual-value estimates mean that a man will not possess motivations himself to sexually pursue another man. That is, the thought never enters the conscious mind. Sexual avoidance will be triggered only when there is a reason to do so—for instance, when another man makes a sexual advance, or when a man is asked to imagine engaging in sexual acts with another man.

We've just focused on heterosexual men. How does this model apply to heterosexual women? Women too evaluate the mate value of both men and women, but for women, the system assessing sexual value weights the mate value of other women very low (negative), leading to a low sexual value. The sexual value of men depends in large part on their assessed mate value. Very young males do not possess the cues to resource acquisition and defense, leading to low sexual values and intense disgust when such acts are thought of—nor are they reproductively viable before puberty. Relatively much older males might likewise be viewed as less sexually desirable, perhaps because of the reduced time the male will be around to invest in a woman and her children.

(As an aside, it's important to make clear that we're not talking about anyone's willingness to enter into a relationship or a marriage—a decision that might be influenced by a massive range of factors that both include and extend well beyond those integrated into mate and sexual value. People enter into relationships and marriages all the time without a strong sense of sexual attraction [and vice versa—some people have sex without desiring a relationship]. Anna Nicole Smith may indeed have been more attracted to 89-year-old oil tycoon J. Howard Marshall because of his vast fortune. But she could also have very well entered into that relationship without the least bit of attraction whatsoever, for more pragmatic reasons.)

But as with male mating psychology, genetic relatedness trumps mate value in female minds too. In fact, because females expend greater minimum levels of parental investment and have more at risk for each sexual encounter than do males, estimates of genetic relatedness likely carry *greater* weight in calculations of sexual value in the female mind than in the male mind. That is, in humans and many other species, an event of inbreeding is far more costly for a given female than a given male. In studies examining the level of disgust associated with various acts, women find incest-related acts to be far more disgusting than do males. Further, men tend to vary in their disgust toward incest, with some objecting as much as most women and others objecting only slightly. Women, on the other hand, tend to respond at ceiling—the highest value possible on the scale, leaving little variation in responses.[31] The differences in intensity of disgust and patterns of variation support the theoretical claim that natural selection tinkered with female psychology in a manner consistent with the greater biological costs associated with events of inbreeding.

In terms of *how* the different costs associated with inbreeding are realized in the systems computing sexual value, here is one possibility: a given estimate of relatedness could translate into a *lower* sexual value in the mind of a female as compared to the mind of a male. We are not saying that the way men and women compute the probability of relatedness differs—exposure to the same kinship cues should lead to the *same* estimates of relatedness in the minds of males and females. What differs is how these estimates are weighted when computing sexual value. By weighting the genetic-relatedness estimate more in female circuitry, thereby causing an even lower—more negative—sexual value, natural selection engineered stronger, more intense inbreeding aversions in women.

With respect to contextual factors, similar to heterosexual men, in the mind of heterosexual women, one's own mate value and the availability of mates should influence the sexual value assigned to others. For instance, the higher a female's mate value, the greater the minimum threshold of what counts as sexually attractive.

That is, fewer males will be perceived as having a high *expected sexual value*. By contrast, a female of lower mate value might assign a greater range of males as having a higher sexual value. However, given the costs associated with reproduction for females, one prediction is that the sexual value system isn't as labile as it is in men. It should take very dire circumstances to render a brother or an unrelated individual of very low mate value a suitable sexual partner. Yes, very dire indeed.

In the Mating Domain, a Low Sexual Value Translates into Disgust

There is much evidence that individuals with low estimated sexual values evoke strong disgust when the topic of sex is on the table. To many, thoughts of incest evoke disgust. Given elevated estimates of kinship, the mind turns otherwise attractive individuals into bottom-of-the-barrel mates. Empirical evidence corroborates this commonly held attitude. For instance, in our own lab, subjects rate having sex with and tongue-kissing an opposite-sex sibling quite disgusting. As we have already discussed, there is a rhyme and reason to the variation in disgust reactions to incest: females tend to react with greater horror toward events of incest because they possess mental circuitry tuned to reflect the higher costs of investing in a potentially unhealthy offspring.

Beyond incest, homosexuality is another category of behaviors often topping the disgust charts (that is, for heterosexuals). To illustrate, here is an anonymous post from a presumably heterosexual man on his attitude toward gay men from a forum on Ethics, Morality, and Justice:[32]

> I don't have a problem with women giving me the eye. What I mean by "the eye" is the look a person gives you when it's clear that they're interested in you, and they find you sexually appealing. When a person gives you the eye, a lot [is] communicated. When a woman gives a man the look, it means he can have sex with her if he puts in a little effort. It is unmistakable when it happens to you. Personally, I find it flattering, no matter who gives me the eye. Even if it's an ugly chick, my ego gets a boost. If it's a hot chick, it gets an even greater boost.
>
> Usually men don't give women the eye, because it's presupposed that the man will have sex with the girl. A man giving a woman amorous eyes would be redundant. Thus, it is questionable when a man does it.
>
> However, when I get the eye from homosexuals, I am put off. I don't know why this would ever need to be explained to homosexuals, but here it is: Don't ever assume a random person is gay. Don't put the moves on another person, unless you're sure he/she is also a homosexual. Heterosexual males don't appreciate it when homosexual males hit on them. It is disgusting, because men know men. We know [that] they want to violate our corn holes and we are disgusted by it. It doesn't just apply to being hit on. It also applies to compliments. If a homosexual man compliments me on my looks, I don't take it the

same way I would from a woman, or even a fat, ugly woman. I take it that he wants to violate my corn hole.

There are two features of this post to notice. First, from a male heterosexual's point of view, male homosexuality can cause disgust because of the way in which male mate value is negatively weighted (typically) in assessments of sexual value. But disgust is amplified to the extent men focus on contact with another man's anus, a source of pathogenic microorganisms. That is, to men, other males trigger thoughts not just of low sexual value, but low contact value. It is a disgust double whammy. It doesn't necessarily have to be about pathogens, though: men might take issue with another man using his "corn hole" for pleasure.

In our own lab, we have collected data on the level of disgust heterosexual men report in response to gay men (and lesbians) as well as the concepts that contribute to their sense that homosexuality is disgusting. We find that for heterosexual men, two ideas that most inform opinions about gay men are the idea of touching a man's genitals and the idea of anal intercourse. Least important were the ideas that male homosexuality involves choosing an inappropriate sexual partner and that male homosexuality potentially involves two individuals of similar dominance.

Returning to the level of disgust expressed by heterosexual men in response to gay men, when we examine the literature, few studies actually ask about disgust. Instead, many examine the negative attitudes or stereotypes people hold regarding gay men, what happens to moral opinions regarding homosexuality when you prime disgust via smells or images, or how sensitivity to disgust elicitors relates to attitudes toward gay men. Few come straight out and ask "how disgusting do you find homosexuality?" One exception was a national study of 1,459 males between the ages of 15 and 19. Researchers found that close to 96 percent of the young men surveyed agreed with the statement "The thought of men having sex with each other is disgusting."[33] In our lab, we recently asked undergraduate students to report on their level of different types of disgust toward gay men and lesbians. We found that heterosexual men reported the highest levels of pathogen (contact)-related disgust and sexual disgust toward gay men. In Figure 6.4, we chart the contact-related and sexual disgust levels heterosexual men and women report toward gay men and lesbians. As you can see, limiting the discussion to heterosexual men's attitudes toward gay men leaves out a large portion of the story.

When it comes to lesbians, heterosexual men hold very different attitudes. In fact, the lowest levels of disgust were reported by heterosexual men in response to lesbians. We can make some educated guesses as to why, when you ask heterosexual men to think about two naked women having sex, they report low(er) levels of disgust. Likely, and as you might have guessed, disgust toward lesbians depends on the attractiveness of the women imagined. The more attractive the women (and the more women who are attractive) depicted engaging in sexual activities, the more desirable and the less sexually disgusting. Women, regardless of their own sexual preferences, are evaluated by heterosexual men in terms of their mate value, which boils down to cues of health and fertility. Furthermore, because in the heterosexual male mind female mate value is weighted more positively (on

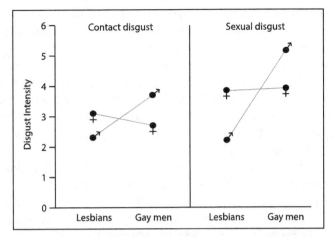

Figure 6.4. Heterosexuals' attitudes towards lesbians and gay men. Unpublished data on male and female heterosexual subjects' (N = 88) responses to two questions regarding lesbians and gay men: (1) How physically disgusting (i.e., how icky or gross) do you think male (female) homosexuality is? (2) How sexually disgusting do you think male (female) homosexuality is? Responses were recorded on a 7-point scale ranging from 0 (not disgusting at all) to 6 (very disgusting). In both the physical (contact) and sexual domains, heterosexual men report the greatest levels of disgust toward gay men and the lowest levels of disgust toward lesbians. Heterosexual women show intermediate yet more or less equal levels of contact and sexual disgust toward lesbians and gay men.

average) than male mate value, one would expect greater disgust reactions toward gay men than toward lesbians. This is what we find as depicted in Figure 6.4 and is what others report as well.[34] By and large, heterosexual men tend to rate gay men far more negatively than they do lesbians.

What about heterosexual women? Do they find homosexuality disgusting, and are there any differences between their attitudes toward gay men versus lesbians? A general pattern in the literature is that heterosexual women show equally low rates of bias and hold equally low negative attitudes toward gay men and lesbians. One exception appears to be attitudes regarding contact: heterosexual women rate contact with lesbians as worse than contact with gay men.[35]

This finding accords with our model: women don't experience the same lowering of disgust (heightening of arousal) in response to other women. To the extent that heterosexual women picture contact with a lesbian to mean genital contact, this likely heightens disgust reactions. (Note that one would expect the opposite reaction from homosexual women.)

In sum, our main point is that disgust is the output of mental systems that evaluate *sexual value*. Specifically, disgust is produced when the mind computes a very low sexual value. What counts as low sexual value will differ among males and females, heterosexual and homosexual.

A facet of our model that might have occurred to you is that if sexual value is a mental variable that produces both lust (when sexual value is estimated to be quite high) and disgust (when low), then we should find that feelings of sexual arousal and sexual disgust are zero–sum—the more of one, the less of the other. In the last chapter, we mentioned how heightened sexual arousal makes subjects more willing to come into contact with objects associated with pathogens (e.g., a used condom), a result of a lowered sense of disgust. It is also the case that heightened sexual arousal decreases the disgust associated with various sexual acts. One particular study nicely illustrates this pattern. psychologists Dan Ariely and George Loewenstein assigned men to a neutral condition or a condition in which they were asked to masturbate (with the help of erotic videos). While in a heightened state of arousal but before orgasm, the researchers asked questions regarding the attractiveness of various individuals and activities. Compared to men in the neutral (and presumably unaroused) condition, men in the sexually aroused condition found it easier to imagine being attracted to a 12-year-old girl, having sex with a 60-year-old woman, having sex with a man, having anal sex, and getting sexually excited by contact with an animal.[36]

A heightened state of arousal brought on by videos depicting women of high sexual value had the effect of muting disgust toward almost all other sexual activities. An interesting question is whether the same effect would hold in women. Our prediction would be that female inclinations are very target-specific. So while a heterosexual woman might be sexually aroused by a particular male, swap that male for an animal, a young boy, or another woman, and likely the mood does not transfer in the same way it does in the mind of a male. Male mating psychology, by virtue of the reduced costs of reproduction, is just more labile than female mating psychology.

Why Disgust?

Empirical evidence suggests that disgust is the primary emotion governing sexual avoidance—that is, low or negative expected sexual values are linked to feelings of disgust. But from a theoretical perspective, this leaves something wanting. Why wouldn't the *absence* of sexual attraction suffice? Why recruit disgust to avoid certain sexual behaviors?

If there were no system of sexual avoidance and the only system in place guiding mate choice was a sexual-attraction system, decisions would range from extreme sexual attraction causing pursuit, to the absence of sexual attraction, which simply kept an individual in neutral, no particular preference. (Keep in mind that the absence of sexual attraction does not automatically buy motivated avoidance—nothing organized and targeted comes for free.) But while a simple sexual-attraction system would work well for an individual behaving on his or her *own* preferences, the world is full of other people, who have their own designs. Although you might have a list of individuals you sexually prefer, you might be the target of pursuit by another to whom you are *not* attracted. One possible explanation for the need of sexual avoidance is that, in the absence of a program motivating the active avoidance of an undesirable other, infrequent sexual encounters might still occur. Indifference isn't strong enough to counteract unwanted sexual acts initiated by others. You might be indifferent toward having sex with a cat or cow, but the cat or cow isn't going to chase you down the hall—at least not for the purpose of having sex. Indifference might be strong enough for you to personally avoid others as mates, but indifference won't combat another person's desire. A stronger emotion is required to motivate avoidance.

As it happens, disgust was a felicitous system to co-opt for sexual avoidance because it was already linked to sex. Initiation of sexual contact requires the suspension of systems that motivate the avoidance of pathogens (in other words, the suspension of disgust). If instead of being lowered, disgust was raised in response to particular cues (e.g., genetic relatedness and low mate value), natural selection would well be in its way to engineering a sexual-avoidance system.

In sum, our mind computes the sexual value of other individuals and regulates motivations to pursue or avoid them accordingly. In addition to mate value and genetic relatedness, the mind weighs the availability of mates and one's own mate value in the assessment of how sexually attractive another person is for oneself. Whereas high magnitudes of expected sexual value activate lust, low computed magnitudes of expected sexual value activate disgust, particularly in sexual contexts. We have focused mainly on sexual value because our interest is in explaining sexual attraction. If you have sensed we are leaving out a large part of the discussion when it comes to finding a sexual partner, particularly a long-term partner, you are indeed correct. There are certainly other aspects of individuals that factor into partner choice, including those factors that generate a sense of closeness between two people (which might have little to do with fertility assessments or wealth). Our focus is on sexual disgust and the factors that influence sexual behaviors, not necessarily cooperative behaviors. We direct you to the work of other authors for a more in-depth view on the multitude of factors involved in partner choice and relationship satisfaction.[37]

VARIATIONS IN SEXUAL PREFERENCES

So far we have discussed how a mate-choice system can produce variation in sexual preferences. And we have mainly focused on heterosexual mate preferences. This begs the question of what, *from an information-processing perspective*, is going on with respect to homosexuality and other manifestations of human sexuality. In this section, we address how a system engineered to generate sexual preferences in heterosexuals is also responsible for producing much of the variety of sexual preferences we observe. We focus our discussion on homosexuality and frame our discussion with four questions:

1. What is homosexuality?
2. Is homosexuality a learned behavior or is it innate?
3. How does the mind generate homosexual preferences?
4. Is homosexuality a psychological adaptation that evolved because it provided an advantage in the struggle for survival and reproduction in

ancestral environments, is it a byproduct of an adaptation, or is it natural system variation?

What Is Homosexuality? Is It Learned or Innate?

Homosexuality is generally defined as the sexual preference for individuals of the same sex. (Now, of course, it matters how you define sex: genes? gonads? gametes? brain organization? We'll operate under the assumption people use the term *homosexuality* to refer to sexual behavior between two people who share the same external body parts.) Second, homosexuality is no more learned and no less genetic than is heterosexuality. Homosexuality, like heterosexuality, is a set of preferences formed via the development of many genetically based programs that rely on environmental information for organization and calibration.

There are many potential causes of the variation we observe in sexual orientations and preferences. For instance, variation could be caused by the effects genetic mutations or environmental perturbations have on the developing fetus. The potential causes of sexual variation get even more complicated when you introduce intragenomic conflict.[38,39]

But sexual variation, and in particular variations in sexual behavior, need not be explained by genetic mutations or genomic conflict. "Heterosexual blueprints" can result in homosexuality due to changes in sexual developmental and differentiation resulting from non-genetic factors. And then, of course, there is circumstance and culture. Recall that incarcerated heterosexual men can be "gay for the stay," engaging in sexual behaviors with other men when their sexual options are restricted to only men. Sexual variation can result from changes in those contextual factors that the system is designed to take as input (e.g., mate variability). Likewise, cultural pressures can change behavior. Recall the Taiwanese couples married in the minor fashion. Despite developing a sexual aversion toward one another, these individuals married and often produced children. Social costs of disobeying a norm and social benefits of conforming can cause behaviors that sometimes depart from strict preferences. But generally speaking it would be a mistake to attribute homosexuality and other forms of sexual variation to "learning" or "choice." If you are heterosexual, did you learn to be so? If so, who taught you? Perhaps the media, culture, family, and friends all discussed heterosexual behavior while you were growing up and this is why you are heterosexual. But remember, homosexuals too were exposed to this information, yet they hold different preferences (and often do so despite social and cultural pressures). Certainly there are many reasons why an individual might engage in homosexual behaviors (cultural norms, limited mate choice), but the expression of unfettered preferences in homosexuals is likely caused by the same complex system responsible for unfettered preferences in heterosexuals.

In sum, there are many factors that contribute to the architecture of our body, brain, and sexual preferences. Notably, there is variation in *every single system* that makes up our species. And so it would be strange if we didn't see variation in every component of the mate-choice system. While some variation might be genetically based, some might not. Nevertheless, we should expect to see variation crop up every generation anew. Sexual reproduction generates variations in designs, and it is precisely because variation crops up anew each generation that we need to understand how the mind generates sexual attraction and sexual disgust.

How Does the Mind Generate Homosexual Preferences?

If we start with basic engineering principles, namely the notions that patterned behavior must have a cause and that complex behaviors such as mate choice require sophisticated underlying procedures, then we are back at the design of mate-choice systems to explain homosexual preferences. Recall our discussion of how expected sexual value is computed. For heterosexual men, the mate value of other men is usually weighted low—let's say it is negative for ease of discussion—and the mate value of women is weighted high, positive. If instead, in the mind of a male, the program for computing sexual value was organized to weight the mate value of a *male* positively and that of a *female* negatively, we would see a different set of preferences: men would then assign higher sexual values to men than to women. A change in how the mate value of each sex is weighted when computing the value another holds as a sexual partner can begin to explain the difference between heterosexual and homosexual preferences.

In addition to how mate value is weighted as an input in the computation of an expected sexual value, there can also be variation in how mate value is computed in the first place. As we discussed above, there were specific selection pressures leading to psychological systems enabling females to assess males along dimensions associated with resource acquisition, defense, and sharing, and systems enabling males to assess females along dimensions associated with youth, fertility, and health. Another source of variation in our mating psychology comes from how these indices of mate value are computed for a given individual. In heterosexual men, upon detecting a female, cues, especially those associated with fertility and health, are applied to generate an index of mate value. But what if instead of applying these dimensions to females, they were applied to males? That is, one source of variation in our mating psychology comes from the application of standard female mate-value criteria to males and, conversely, the application of standard male mate-value criteria to females.

Evidence in favor of this explanation comes from the anxiety some heterosexual women and some gay men seem to share regarding the aging process. As the novelist John Rechy phrased it: "Age is the monster figure of the gay world."[40] And, so far as we can tell given the multi-billion-dollar cosmetics industry, age is also the monster figure of the heterosexual female world. One explanation for why this might be so is if the traits some gay men prefer—and traits some men choose to emphasize in themselves—are those indicating fertility and health. The psychologist Doug Kenrick at Arizona State University investigated the age preferences of heterosexual and homosexual men by comparing singles ads and found that men, regardless of orientation, preferred younger-looking sexual partners.[41] It seems that the same criteria are being applied to generate perceptions of attractiveness in at least some homosexual and some heterosexual men.

Likewise, for some lesbians, the mate value of women is driven less by cues to fertility and youth and more so by cues to resource acquisition (e.g., physical dominance). For other lesbians, the mate value of women is assigned in the same way heterosexual men assign it: according to youth and fertility. Common, if not outdated, terms for lesbians expressing different kinds of preferences include "butch" lesbians and "lipstick" or "femme" lesbians, which could be thought of as reflecting the different attributes women wish to express to emphasize their mate value to other women, and, by inference, the preferences women hold for who counts as an attractive mate. In general, the different application of particular criteria in forming an estimate of another person's mate value and whether this mate value is weighted negatively or positively when assessing that person's value as a sexual partner explains some of the variations in sexual preferences observed in homosexuality.

But how do these crisscrossed weightings happen in the first place? In other words, *why* would some males apply standard female mate-value criteria to other males, and vice versa? At least some of this variation can be explained if we take into account how (at least) five different sources of variation can combine to pattern mating psychology.

GENETIC SEX

The first is *genetic sex*. As with many other sexual species, the chromosomal structure of female genetic sex is XX, whereas male genetic sex is XY. The Y chromosome contains the "testes-determining factor," which leads to the production of testes and resulting androgens such as testosterone.

GONADAL SEX

This brings us to *gonadal sex*, which can differ from genetic sex. During sexual development and differentiation, we all start off with proto-gonads that could either develop into sperm-producing testes or egg-producing ovaries. We also all start off with *both* male and female tubing. That is, we have tubing that could become the vas deferens *as well as* the tubing that could become the fallopian tubes. Which set we keep depends on the organizational effects of testosterone and its derivatives. In XY individuals, expression of the testes-determining factor on the Y chromosome causes the proto-gonads to turn into testes. The testes, once formed, then start producing testosterone and other hormones. The result is that the male tubing is kept and the female tubing degenerates. Without the Y chromosome, the proto-gonads turn into ovaries (because there is no testes-determining factor) and the male gonadal system degenerates, leaving the (default) female tubing to develop.

But mutations can occur, and they can cause all sorts of variation. For instance, in a condition termed androgen insensitivity syndrome (AIS), an XY individual might develop testes (because the testes-determining factor is expressed on the

Y chromosome and causes the gonads to develop into testes), but might be *insensitive* to the testosterone and other androgens the testes produce. This means that the male tubing (vas deferens and epididymis), which requires the detection of testosterone to persist and develop, will degenerate! Testes also produce what is known as Müllerian-inhibiting substance (MIS), the hormone that causes the degeneration of the female tubing (the fallopian tubes). To the extent MIS and the receptors that detect their presence are intact, the female gonadal structures will also degenerate. This means that a person with AIS might not possess any internal reproductive tubing.

Externally, an androgen-insensitive XY individual can appear female or male. They will appear female if there is complete androgen insensitivity. This is because their cells, in addition to being unresponsive to testosterone (so no male tubing), are also unresponsive to a derivative of testosterone, dihydroxytestosterone (DHT), which is responsible for the masculinization of the genitals (no penis). If they are *only* insensitive to testosterone, however, then there will be no internal male tubing, but the external genitalia will develop in typical male fashion because their cells still respond to DHT. So the extent of masculinization/feminization will depend on the type of mutations present.

As another example of how genetic sex can differ from gonadal sex, consider the condition of congenital adrenal hyperplasia (CAH). CAH is caused by a mutation in the adrenal gland and leads to the production of a hormone that mimics testosterone. Depending on when this occurs and the extent of the mutation, genetically XX individuals could retain male internal tubing (maintained by the presence of testosterone) alongside the female tubing (because with no testes no MIS was produced, so female tubing did not degenerate). Externally, CAH individuals vary depending on the extent of exposure to androgens in utero; some have male genitalia (because DHT, derived from adrenally produced testosterone, led to masculinization of the genitals) or they can have ambiguous genitalia (ranging from a large clitoris to very small penis—it's all the same tissue developmentally).

To sum up, the development of internal tubing and external genitalia is anything but simple. Mutations can cause a variety of conditions, and this begins to explain some of the variation we observe in the bundle of adaptations that enable sexual reproduction, including our mating psychology.

PSYCHOLOGICAL SEX
Our discussion so far has pertained to internal and external sex organs, but hormones play key roles organizing neural as well as gonadal tissue in the developing fetus. In a "healthy" XY male, testosterone (and derivatives) produced by the testes will travel to the developing neural circuitry and lead to the development of mental operations that evolved to promote survival and reproduction in males. During puberty, testosterone activates male-specific adaptations leading to many of the male-typical behaviors we observe across cultures. However, in XY males with AIS, the brain might not undergo these changes. It will depend in large part on the status of the testosterone and testosterone-receptor system. Developmental insensitivities to androgens potentially change the way the gonads and brain

circuits develop and deploy. Similarly, an XX individual with CAH might have experienced during fetal development a masculinization of the brain. Depending on the extent to which the adrenal gland continues to produce testosterone, "pubertal" changes could entail activation of these male brain adaptations or could entail no such activity. An important lesson from fetal development is that the observable gender of the gonads (or internal tubing) does not always match the gender of the brain. That is, hormones have organizational and activational effects not just on "visible" gonads but "hidden" psychology, and various mutations can decouple the sex-typical manner in which these systems develop.[42]

Our model of sexual value provides some clues for the kinds of psychological variation we can expect to see. For instance, the mechanism that produces a sense of one's own mate value is a source of variation. Let's call this *internal gender identification*—that is, what gender one "feels," and consequently the traits one is motivated to emphasize in the display of one's own mate value. Masculinized brains (independent of genetic or gonadal sex) will likely "feel" male and promote the expression of mate-value qualities stereotypically desired by females (i.e., social status, dominance, resource acquisition). Feminized brains (again, independent of genetic or gonadal sex) will likely "feel" female and promote the expression of mate-value qualities stereotypically desired by males (e.g., cues to youth and fertility). And, of course, there is a long spectrum in between these two generalizations.

Another source of variation is in the set of *mate-value criteria* one uses to assess the mate value of a person identified as male or female. As mentioned above, the applied criteria can get crisscrossed, leading to female-typical mate-value criteria (fertility and health) being applied to males and male-typical criteria (resource acquisition) being applied to females.

A last source of variation we mention here is *how mate value affects sexual value*. Given that you have computed mate value for a given individual (regardless of the criteria you used), how does this value affect sexual attraction? A masculinized brain (in an XY or XX individual who has either male or female genitalia) could lead to male mate value being weighted *negatively* when computing the value of that individual as a sexual partner for oneself. Or, it could be weighted positively. Changing something as simple as a weighting in computed expected sexual value can have large behavioral effects.

Our point is that *each* adaptation that contributes to "psychological sex"—what gender one feels, the mate value criteria applied to a given person, and how that mate value affects the computed sexual value—can vary, leading to a veritable smorgasbord of preferences and orientations. Mix and match each psychological system with a type of genetic sex and a type of gonadal sex and you can see how you get the wide range of variation we observe in human sexuality. Identifying the components of each evolved system provides a better understanding of variation within the sexual-preference and mate-choice systems. It allows us to see why some people find certain acts arousing and certain acts disgusting. In each person's mind there is a sexual value computed for each person encountered, a value that systematically varies according to one's own conditions. Sexual disgust, while a universal feature of human psychology, is not universally directed toward the same acts for all individuals. Universal blue prints can generate vast variation.[43]

Is Homosexuality an Adaptation?

Some evolutionary theorists claim that homosexuality is an adaptation, a feature of our species that evolved because it conferred a reproductive advantage. The theoretical rationale is that although individuals preferring as sexual partners those of the same gender are less likely to reproduce themselves, they would be able to provide help to those family members that do. This has been called the "helper at the nest" hypothesis.[44] For a female tasked with rearing several young, might there have been an advantage to having a child who won't reproduce himself or herself so that he or she can help raise the young? From the mom's point of view, yes. But for the genes in the child, perhaps not. The reproductive success of a gene is best optimized, all things equal, by causing the individual it is in to reproduce.

The parent–offspring conflict inherent in devoting oneself to one's mother and her children is a problem for the helper at the nest hypothesis. And other questions remain, too: If homosexuality is an adaptation, why isn't it present in every family? Is it context-sensitive—and if so, to what contexts? Family size? The sex ratio of children? Is there even evidence that homosexual children help out more than heterosexual children? The answer to this appears to be "no."[45] And, last, is homosexuality the best way to engineer childcare? Wouldn't finding another mate or cultivating friendships have been a more efficient and fitness-promoting solution? Without answers to these and other questions, scientists are currently (or at least should be, given the dearth of evidence) hard pressed to categorize homosexuality as a biological adaptation. But, as we will argue in greater detail later, whether or not a feature is classified as an adaptation is of no normative consequence. Homosexuality, intersex, transgender, and other forms of variations in our sexual reproductive adaptations are forms of natural variation that result from the development and calibration of a complex system tasked with building itself from a single cell into a multi-trillion-celled animal. There is no a priori reason why the distinction between adaptation and byproduct should come to bear on larger societal issues involving equality, morality, or legality.

CONCLUSION

In this chapter we showed how disgust functions in the mating realm. As an emotion involved in the prevention of consumption of harmful substances and the prevention of contact with surfaces displaying cues of pathogen presence (and sensitive to sexual arousal), disgust was a fortuitous emotion to preside over a third evolutionary challenge: avoiding sexual behaviors with individuals jeopardizing the production and rearing of offspring. Estimates of another person's mate value and degree of genetic relatedness are two main factors that contribute to estimates of the expected value another person holds as a sexual partner. But context matters, too: one's own gender, one's own mate value, and the perceived availability of sexual partners interact to guide decisions regarding mate suitability. Sexual motivations, with respect to both pursuit and avoidance, are governed by the computation of an *expected sexual value*, an internal regulatory variable that can range from extremely high to extremely low. When the expected sexual value is high, motivations for pursuit can be context-sensitively deployed; when low, disgust works to motivate sexual avoidance.

Variations in the manner in which the sexual attraction system develops and calibrates can lead to a range of preferences. Indeed, homosexual, transgender, and intersex preferences can be understood using the same information-processing model that explains heterosexual preferences. The presence of a system that computes expected sexual value for oneself is capable of simulating the acceptability and suitability of any individual (or non-human animal or pie) as a sexual partner. This simulation can produce reactions that range from intense arousal to the deepest of disgusts.

A New Model

In the last three chapters, we have described three different adaptive challenges our ancestors repeatedly faced: what to eat, what to touch, and who to . . . with whom to have sex. Over our species' evolutionary history, mental programs evolved to address each challenge. Specifically, we have programs that motivate the avoidance of ingesting harmful substances, contacting surfaces and individuals showing signs of infection, and engaging in sex with partners jeopardizing the probability of producing and nurturing healthy offspring. We have provided a sketch for how these programs operate and how they generate flexible behavior. Specifically, we have identified three central regulatory variables—expected value of consumption, expected value of contact, and expected sexual value, which govern decision-making and behavior in the domains of consumption, contact, and sex, respectively. Disgust, a term applied to the feeling that arises when a low expected value of consumption, contact, or sex is generated, motivates context-specific avoidance.

If you have read anything about disgust in the last 20 years, chances are you have run across a very different model of disgust proposed by Paul Rozin, Jonathan Haidt, and their colleagues (for ease of discussion we refer to this as the Rozin–Haidt [R-H] model, though Rozin and Haidt had numerous co-authors on supporting research). Although there is some overlap between their model and ours, there are also key conceptual differences that have important downstream consequences when disgust becomes enmeshed in moral judgments and legal affairs. We'll discuss those conceptual differences here, though if you find this a bit too academic, you can skip to the next chapter without missing a beat. This chapter is really meant for those familiar with recent treatments of disgust, morality, and law that have relied heavily on the R-H model.[1]

According to the R-H model, there are three domains of disgust, which fractionate into eight categories of elicitors. The first domain, *core disgust*, is conceptualized as the original function of disgust and involves the rejection of offensive food substances, as well as certain animals and their body products. A second general domain of disgust is *animal-reminder disgust*, which "reflects the human concern to be distinguished from other animals or to not be considered as an animal at all."[2] Accordingly, death, body envelope violations (e.g., guts and gore), "inappropriate" sexual behavior (e.g., incest, homosexuality, and bestiality), and bad hygiene are all thought to be states or behaviors that remind us of our animal nature and mortality and, as a result, are actively avoided. A last domain (or expansion) of disgust, *sociomoral disgust*, pertains to social interactions: interpersonal contamination and moral offenses.[3] So, boiled down, the R-H model of disgust suggests eight different types of disgust elicitors: (1) offensive food substances, (2) certain animals, (3) body products, (4) death, (5) body envelope violations, (6) bad hygiene, (7) inappropriate sexual behavior, and (8) moral offenses.

Seven of the eight categories fit very nicely into the evolutionary information-processing model advanced in the last three chapters. Certain foods elicit disgust because they possess cues to pathogen or toxin presence and generate low expected values of consumption. Likewise, certain animals, like maggots and other insects that feast on decaying matter, cue the presence of foods that could cause harm, thus lowering the expected value of the foods they are near. Animals, for instance cockroaches and rats, are also vectors of disease (because of what they dine on) and are perceived as disgusting due to risks of infection. Thus, offensive food substances and certain animals elicit disgust because they relate to the problem of what to eat. The next four categories—body products, death, body envelope violations, and bad hygiene—relate to interpersonal contact and the problem of what to touch. Observing cues to pathogen presence in another person's body lowers the expected value of contact (of course, context-sensitively) and generates avoidance and disgust. Inappropriate sex (depending on your definition of inappropriate) relates to the third function of disgust discussed in the last chapter: avoiding sexual partners that would jeopardize the health and viability of resulting offspring. But despite seven of these eight elicitors fitting nicely into our model, there are serious disagreements as to *why* many of them elicit disgust.

ANIMAL-REMINDER DISGUST?

Rozin and colleagues maintain that the reason why we find things like various sexual acts and death disgusting is because they remind us that we are animals. As they've written, "anything that reminds us that we are animals elicits disgust."[4] Why? Because, according to the R-H model, thinking about our animal nature elicits an existential concern over our mortality. Thus, animal-reminder disgust is said to protect both the body and soul, and to constitute a function unique to humans.

There are several problems with this conception of the function of disgust. For one, as Josh Tybur and colleagues have pointed out, there are many analogies humans make to non-human animals that not only do not evoke disgust, but often evoke praise: smart as an owl; fast as a leopard; loyal as a dog; quiet as a mouse. And then there's busy as a bee; sly as a fox; cackling like a hyena; acting like a cougar; lazy as a sloth; like a dog with a bone. There are also many behaviors that humans and other animals engage in that do *not* elicit disgust: non-human animals eat, hunt, fight, mate, care for young, and drink water, and none of these appear to generate the existential threat suggested by the R-H animal-reminder disgust. Moreover, none of these elicit disgust in the same way that seeing maggots crawl out of a piece of meat does, or that seeing a large cockroach does (especially one that flies). There is a reason why our disgust narrows in on particular animals and particular behaviors. They threaten our existence only by virtue of threatening our health and ability to combat disease.

Another problem with animal-reminder disgust constituting a uniquely human response is that all of its elicitors—"inappropriate" sex, death, body envelope violations, and bad hygiene—represent threats to the health, viability, and reproduction of other animals, too. Other animals select mates and avoid selecting close genetic relatives. Other animals also face the same contamination threats posed by decomposing bodies, open wounds, and cues to disease in conspecifics. So elicitors of animal-reminder disgust elicitors are certainly not unique to humans. Indeed, over the past few chapters we've provided examples of how disgust or a similar system deploys in non-human animals. There are thus many conceptual problems with the notion that humans evolved an animal-reminder disgust.[5]

MAGIC?

Another facet of the R-H model of disgust is that to explain some of the features of disgust, it draws on the laws of sympathetic magic—a concept developed by social anthropologist James Frazer to explain magical beliefs in primitive cultures.[6] One law of sympathetic magic is the *law of contagion*. According to Jonathan Haidt and colleagues, "The law of contagion 'once in contact, always in contact', refers to the tendency to act *as if* brief contact causes a permanent transfer of properties from one object to another, even when there is no material substance transferred."[7] With respect to pathogen disgust and the transmission of disease-causing organisms, this description, from the vantage point of what can be seen with the human eye, appears accurate. When a cookie falls on the floor, one might not visibly see any change. However, the transfer of pathogens from object to object *really can* take place on a microscopic level. Furthermore, the longer the contact, the more likely the transfer of an infectious agent is to occur (an intuition that likely explains the origin of the three-second rule). The law of contagion thus reflects not magical thinking, but an adaptive way of thinking about disease-causing agents and contagion in general.

Another law of sympathetic magic is the *law of similarity*, which specifies that if one substance resembles another, it likely possesses similar properties. Rozin and colleagues have found that subjects tend to reject a glass of juice after a sterilized plastic cockroach had been dipped into it. Subjects continued to reject the juice even though the experimenters assured them that the plastic insect had been sanitized. Likewise, they have found that subjects avoid feces-shaped chocolate fudge.

Why won't people drink the juice or eat the fudge? We "know" it is OK, but social information from a trusted source does not seem to (easily) sway preferences—at least not in the direction from "bad to consume" to "good to consume." If the mind were a blank slate and blindly adopted rules about what counts as safe to consume, subjects should *not* show aversions, especially given their prior experience with sugars, and their complete *lack* of experience with eating strangely shaped fudge or drinking liquids containing plastic objects. Instead, despite the fact that both the cockroach and fudge posed little to no danger in terms of actual contamination, the human brain appears to take the cues to potential pathogen and toxin presence quite seriously, rejecting anything that resembles a possible threat. Subjects' avoidance behaviors suggest first and foremost that there is some kind of program in the head guiding aversions and that this program contains prior assumptions about the world. Two such assumptions: things that look like cockroaches are indeed cockroaches, and feces-shaped things are in fact feces. After all, we didn't evolve in environments in which palatable foods came in the same shape as dog poo, or where visual representations of cockroaches meant anything other than the presence of an actual cockroach.

Just stating that the plastic cockroach is similar to an actual cockroach or that feces-shaped fudge is similar to feces begs the question of similarity: What are the "relevant" dimensions that are supposed to shape our sense of similarity? There are almost infinite ways in which the pairs are similar. Feces and fudge are both not animate and not clear; they don't talk, aren't valid mate choices, aren't relatives, don't fly; both start with f and contain two vowels, etc. Intuitively, we of course know what is meant by "similarity," but we do so by virtue of circuitry calling out—screaming out—the dimensions that affected survival and reproduction in ancestral environments. The law of similarity takes advantage of our prepared pathogen-avoidance system to provide the dimensions along which similarity is relevant for consumption behaviors. Though we are prone to mistaking fudge for feces, we will rarely make the mistake in the opposite direction. All to say that in the disgust context, similar items are indeed similar because they exhibit similar cues indicative of pathogen presence.

From this vantage, the two laws of sympathetic magic do not constitute conceptually distinct aspects of disgust. Instead, they are easily re-interpreted as reflecting the operation of psychological mechanisms that evolved to make inferences regarding the likelihood of contamination by disease-causing agents using cues that were indicative of their presence in human ancestral environments. Erring on the side of caution when it came to assessing the presence of harms in potential foods would have been a fitness-promoting strategy, at least when all other systems were in balance. All else equal, the costs associated with forgoing a particular item of food (e.g., greater temporary hunger) pale in comparison to the costs of infection (e.g., energetic and metabolic investment in immune response, increased vulnerability to predators, and possibly death). In fact, rather than acting irrationally, one could say that evidence that subjects did not consume the juice and fudge reveals the operation of a system well honed for the ancestral environment. Learn what counts as poisonous or illness-causing and avoid anything that looks like it. Thus, we are likely biased to assume a possible threat of infection or poisoning in ambiguous situations. Disgust, though it might seem magical, and while it may produce substantively irrational results in the modern milieu, is, at least from an engineering standpoint, quite rational in the ecological niche for which it was designed.

MORALITY?

The R-H model posits a third type of disgust, sociomoral disgust, which is elicited by various sociomoral offenses. Indeed, subjects, when asked to nominate various disgusting acts, often include in their list acts such as theft, murder, rape, and cheating. There has been much written on "moral disgust"—theoretical justifications for such a concept, scales to measure it, and brain regions associated with it. But there might not actually be a *separate* psychological moral disgust program. There has been open debate regarding whether disgust regulates a definable moral "domain" in the same way it regulates sexual behavior, food consumption, and interpersonal contact. On the one hand, scholars such as David Pizarro and Paul Bloom suggest disgust is used only metaphorically in the moral domain. For instance, when someone says "politics makes me sick," Pizarro and Bloom would claim they likely don't *really* feel ill or disgusted, but instead use the language of disgust as hyperbole. On the other hand, others (including one of us) have suggested that morality is a bona fide separate domain of disgust. But given recent evidence and the sharp evolutionary insight of a handful of scholars, we suspect that Pizarro and Bloom are closer to the truth. We won't rule out the possibility that morality is a separate domain of disgust, but what seems to be emerging from the evidence is a moral psychology that instead capitalizes on disgust, utilizing it as one of a number of tools (a) to organize moral norms, (b) to express disapproval of violations and, possibly, (c) to distance oneself from targets of social condemnation.

In other words, rather than there being a separate "moral disgust," it seems more probable that disgust is both an input and output of moral systems. Levels of disgust serve as an input into systems surveying which moral norms to support; and disgust also functions as an output, signaling allegiance and motivating avoidance of those who might be targets of social condemnation. However, to make any inroads into how disgust operates in the moral domain, in either case, we need to understand the information-processing systems that evolved to support our moral intuitions. We turn now to morality and its many connections to disgust.

PART III

Morality

Disgust and Morality

What is the origin of our moral sense? To say much has been written on this topic would be an understatement of epic proportion. In this chapter, we'll attempt to contribute to this vast literature,[1] but we'll do so in the service of answering a more circumscribed question: How and why does disgust figure into our conception of right and wrong, good and bad? By the end of the chapter, we hope to have shed light on two distinct phenomena: the tendency—consciously or otherwise—to moralize acts that cause disgust (as in "Incest is gross and therefore wrong") and the tendency to use disgust to describe immoral acts (as in "Embezzling millions from poor people is disgusting").

As we explain, the traditional moral concepts of harm and fairness will only take us so far. In fact, adaptations for *promoting* cooperation, while typically center stage in evolutionary-inspired views of morality, are only half the story at best. We suggest that many proscriptions are enacted to promote exploitation and other outcomes residing at the ne*far*ious end of the cooperation continuum—and it is here that disgust does its dirtiest work. Our goal is to explain how and why. We are specifically interested in disgust's influence on (1) how we select candidate norms to moralize, (2) how individuals recruit support for campaigns to enact a particular norm, and (3) the expression of (often complete and unwavering) allegiance to norms endorsed by the majority.

Because morality is inherently social, our story begins, as a necessary first step, with a sketch of the procedures that evolved (conceivably) to guide decisions regarding when to cooperate or not, and we'll focus initially on dyadic interactions before scaling up to groups. By now it should come as no shock that functions can be detailed in terms of their information-processing procedures (yes, there is one last box-and-arrow model in this chapter). Recall from the first portion of this book, however, that the reason why particular behaviors increase in frequency over generations is not the same as our psychological motivation for engaging in them. We find the thought of sibling incest disgusting not because we understand the logic of why such reactions evolved; instead, we just feel repulsed at the thought of tongue-kissing a sibling. *How* programs move bodies through an environment and the feelings they generate is one thing; *why* they evolved and persist is another. Keeping in mind that selection is not synonymous with psychology, let's tackle a topic central to morality: why we care about the actions and well-being of other people.

SOCIAL VALUE AND WHY WE CARE

Evolutionary-minded psychologists have started to peel back the layers of intuition to reveal the programs guiding one-on-one social interactions. With each layer removed, the picture is becoming more and more clear: human psychology is rich with programs that appear well designed (a) to assign a "social value" to each person encountered, and (b) to track, and where possible increase, the social value others hold for the self. To put this more colloquially, we have a sense of how much we care (or not) for others, and a sense of both how much others *actually* care, as well as how much they *ought to* care, for us in return.[2] But what might such a social valuation system look like? Specifically, what variables contribute to our sense of care and, thus, decisions of how to treat another person? Here are five.

The first variable is *genetic relatedness*. As we've outlined in previous chapters, humans and other animals have psychological mechanisms that translate estimates of relatedness into social motivations to cooperate and compete.[3] And so kinship is one dimension that governs why we care. In several species, though, including humans, cooperation extends beyond relatives. Indeed, one category of non-relatives with whom we cooperate extensively is friends.

There is a logic for why the capacity to form friendships evolved. Evolutionary psychologists Leda Cosmides and John Tooby propose that having individuals beyond kin who cared about your welfare would have helped to protect against the vicissitudes of ancestral times.[4] People who cared about your existence and wanted to keep you around would have been extremely valuable as they could, for instance, nurse you back to health when sick, share food with you, take your side in a social skirmish, or help care for your child. In short, friendships would have increased the odds of survival and successful reproduction in ancestral environments, which were, by all modern Western measures, rough.

The existence of friendships suggests that systems regulating cooperation (and competition) take as input dimensions beyond genetic relatedness. To get a handle on what these dimensions might be, consider your own friendships. Why do you have as friends the people you do? If it is a good friendship, likely you get something out of the relationship, as do they. But the general sense that you just "like" each other and that you are "close" can be deconstructed into underlying information-processing procedures (after all, *something* is doing the work). Likely there is a system that estimates how much you mutually value one another. One possible design of a system that generates feelings of closeness includes procedures that assess (1) a person's 'association value' and (2) how that person socially values us in return.

Association value is the level of net benefits that associating with a particular person confers relative to others in the social world. We are talking about an overall assessment of how valuable that person is, not necessarily what he or she does for you in particular. When a person going about her own day does things for herself that happen to also benefit you, this registers as an elevated association value. Benefits come in many forms. The neighbor who picks up trash, the mate who can't stand piles of laundry, the driver who stops and looks both directions before proceeding, the physically formidable neighbor who sits on the front porch watching over the neighborhood, the hunter who kills large game or who spots snakes close to camp—by virtue of simply going about their day and behaving in ways that benefit themselves, they also happen to confer incidental benefits on you. Your sidewalk is now cleaner than before; your laundry gets done; you are less likely to get T-boned at an intersection; your neighborhood is a bit safer; you might get some pickings off the bone; and you are less likely to be bitten by a nearby snake.

On the other end of the association value scale are those whose actions tend to impose costs. The spouse who never picks up after himself or who gambles away the bank account, the reckless driver who runs a red light, a stranger who doesn't hold the door or who spits gum on the sidewalk, the roommate who listens to music way too loud—they all emit (depending on your taste in music) negative externalities. Their actions, intentionally or otherwise, impose costs by hindering goals, preferences, and behaviors leading to lower, and perhaps even negative, association values. All else equal, it would have paid, fitness-wise, to stay in the orbit of people who confer benefits (individuals with high association value) and to avoid those who impose costs (those with low association value). But assessing that a person holds high association value doesn't automatically buy you a close relationship. To the dismay of many stalkers, association value is just part of the story—how a person values the self is another.

By and large, we know how others feel about us. You know other people "like" you when they do nice things for you (e.g., they listen to your rants about your ex, they help you shop for clothing, they serve as your wingman out at the bar, they support you in faculty meetings). And you know other people don't like you when they are mean to you (e.g., they hit you, they tell other people you sleep around, they take your stuff, they tell people you're crazy). The frequency and magnitude of the benefits or costs a person specifically directs toward you serve as an indicator of the fitness consequences of interacting with that person in the future. Independent of how you might feel about them, it would have been profitable to stick near people who were motivated to deliver benefits to you and to avoid or eliminate those who aim to do you harm.

Together, the affordances another person offers (that is, their *association value*) and *how that person values the self* are factors beyond relatedness that would have shaped decisions regarding when to cooperate (care) or not. A high association value for another person *and* perceptions that the person values oneself are two ingredients, we claim, that cause feelings of closeness and help jump-start friendships.

The fourth variable that influences how we treat other people is *leverage*, a composite of the features that enable individuals to enforce their will upon others. Leverage depends on a variety of factors, including a person's physical formidability, health, mate value, skill set, and social allies in the form of kin, friends, and coalition members. One's own leverage is going to influence how valuable others are perceived to be, and thus influence motivations to cooperate on the one hand, or exploit on the other. High-leverage individuals, those with large amounts of power and the willingness to exert it (think the Emperor in the fictional Star Wars universe, or Kim Jong Un in the actual real-life universe), often hold low value and "use for" other people, even relatives. On the flip side, low leverage colors the world differently. When one is in a state of need, the value of any given individual capable of providing assistance will increase. When ill, socially excluded, friendless, pregnant, kinless, or physically disabled, one's ability to prevent exploitation would have been hampered in ancestral environments, putting a premium on social allies of any stripe. To wit, one tends to make a deal with the devil when in a position of relatively low, not high, leverage.

The fifth and final variable that contributes to why we care (or act as if we do) is the perceived likelihood of social condemnation. I might not be your kin or your friend, and I might hold more leverage than you (I am bigger), but to the extent I believe I will be socially condemned for not doing so, I may still (perhaps reluctantly) treat you fairly and with kindness. There is a growing literature from behavioral economics and psychology that shows that when you mask identity and remove the possibility of being punished, people tend to maximize personal gain. The threat of social condemnation by groups is a powerful force that shapes individual behaviors. This is a topic to which we'll return when we discuss one of disgust's links to morality.

Taken together, a person's *genetic relatedness, closeness (association value* plus the *value that person holds for the self)*, one's *leverage*, and one's perceptions of the *costs of social condemnation* are inputs to a system that computes an *expected social value*, the internal variable that regulates a person's willingness to trade off his or her own welfare for that of another individual (Fig. 8.1). The social value we hold for other people governs our desire and willingness to cooperate, remain indifferent, or exploit. When elevated, because a person is of high genetic relatedness, or a person has high association value *and* values the self in return (e.g., a spouse or close friend), expected social value motivates intense care. At extreme levels, a very positive social value might lead to self-sacrifice. At moderate levels, where the person neither confers benefits nor imposes any costs, social value might cause indifference. But when expected social values are extremely low, this can lead to behaviors at the other end of the spectrum: complete exploitation or elimination.

SOCIAL VALUE AND FIRST-ORDER MORAL GAMES

Expected social value as modeled here is one way natural selection could have fashioned programs that govern one-on-one interactions and intuitions about

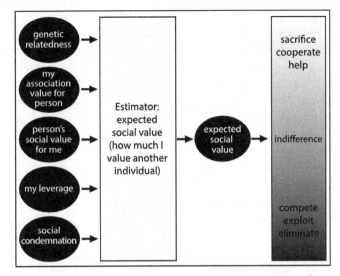

Figure 8.1. Information-processing structure of systems governing social interactions. Here we posit that the mind computes for each individual an *expected social value*, which governs all cooperative and exploitative motivations. At least five dimensions dictate expected social values. The first is genetic relatedness; all else equal, higher estimates of relatedness lead to higher expected social values and greater motivations to cooperate. The second and third inputs—one's association value for another person and perceptions of how that person values oneself—together contribute to our sense of liking and serve as the basis for the formation of friendships and non–kin-based cooperative interactions. When both are high, this is what generates our sense of closeness (I value you and you appear to value me). The fourth input is leverage: how I treat you (and vice versa) will be a function of how capable I am of getting my way (e.g., via physical dominance if male or sexual access if female). Last, how I treat you is also a function of how I might be condemned by the social group. I might not be your kin, I might not like you, and I might have decent leverage over you (I'm bigger), but to the extent I will be punished, I might still begrudgingly cooperate with you (in public). Together these five variables contribute to the critical internal regulatory variable controlling the extent to which one is willing to trade off one's welfare for that of another person, a dynamic value that can range from very low (willingness to exploit or kill) to very high (willingness to self-sacrifice).

how others ought to behave. My *expected social value* for you governs how I treat you, but I also have strong interests in how you treat me. The variable *person's social value for me* in Figure 8.1 is a potential locus of manipulation and conflict. This is because I likely have a different view than you do of how you should be spending your precious time and energy. Every person sits at the center of a unique web of relationships. From a given person's point of view, and all else being equal, it would pay to have each person in their social web devote all their time and energy to providing benefits to oneself, numero uno. But with multiple webs and multiple individuals each at the center of their own social world, this typically does not occur—not everyone can be Queen Bee (at least not without leverage).

But psychological systems that attempted (in a cost-effective manner) to tip the balance in one's own favor, when possible, would have often fared better in ancestral environments than those that did not. That is, under some if not most circumstances, it would have paid to get other people to increase the social value they held for you, thus increasing the likelihood that they would provide you with benefits and forgo harming you in any way. The strategies we evolved to improve our standing in others' minds are typically not consciously realized as such. Instead, we possess psychological programs that, when executed, tend to have *as a consequence* an increase in the manner other people trade off their welfare for ours. We, as proprietors of these programs, simply feel and act.

Take anger. Anger is an emotion that deploys in response to perceptions of social *under*valuation and functions to *increase* the manner in which another person values the self.[5] Recall the last time someone made you angry. Your friend didn't invite you to go wine tasting? Your husband didn't buy you a birthday present? Your wife cheated on you? Your boss gave a colleague a raise, but not you? These are all situations that reveal the person in question socially values you *less* than you think they ought to. What to do? Clearly the answer is to attempt to get the person to *increase* their social value for you. But how? We can't directly tinker with another person's neurons. Instead, the best evolution could do is to devise behavioral strategies that tended to have a similar effect. Anger is one such strategy.

Anger functions to strategically and self-interestedly recalibrate *upward* how much another person values you. Anger and the aggression it motivates are signals of one's willingness to inflict costs. But anger is best deployed strategically: only get angry if you appear willing and able to act. After all, if one threatens aggression but is then shown to be impotent, this could lead to future exploitation and harm. Aggressive threats require leverage. Consequently, one should expect anger to occur more often in individuals who believe themselves to hold higher leverage in a relationship and thus to be more capable of enforcing their will. Research by the psychologist Aaron Sell suggests this is so: physically dominant men and physically attractive women—two categories of people bearing ancestrally relevant qualities contributing to leverage—tend to get angry more easily and feel more justified in using anger to resolve conflicts. And not just conflict at the dyadic level: for men, fighting ability—that is, *physical* leverage—predicts support for military action.[6]

Anger isn't alone. Recent work within evolutionary psychology reveals that other emotions also target the social valuation others assign to the self, either attempting to push it higher after a perceived benefit has been delivered (e.g., gratitude) or halt its decline after a social misstep (e.g., shame and guilt).[7]

In addition to having strong interests in how we are treated by others, we also have interests in how friends and relatives are treated. When we perceive someone as having high social value, we care about them and do not want others to harm them or cheat them either. From *my* perspective, in an interaction between my sister and a store clerk, because I hold a relatively higher social value for my sister by virtue of her relatedness to me, I expect the store clerk to value my sister's welfare—to go out of his way to treat her kindly. And I will get angry to the extent that I perceive he has not valued my sister's welfare in the manner I expect him to. As a general matter, we tend to look kindly upon actions that benefit those for whom we hold elevated expected social values, and we tend to look disapprovingly upon actions that impose costs on such individuals. And the less we value third parties (because they are not kin, mates, or friends, because we are leverage positive, or because there is no threat of social condemnation), the less we tend to care about the outcomes of their social interactions.[8]

What we have sketched here depicts the never-ending psychological tug-of-war over levels of assigned social value. The strategic push and pull of inter-individual preferences creates dynamic interactions that Tooby and Cosmides call *first-order moral games*.[9] First-order moral games describe the 'games' individuals (nonconsciously) play in an attempt to get other individuals to value the self and those one cares for—family, friends, and associates—as highly as possible. At the inter-individual level, these welfare-based games give rise to *cooperative and competitive behaviors,* and they color our world in shades that reflect the costs and benefits of social interactions.

Disgust and Expected Social Value

Our main point so far is that the psychological systems responsible for generating estimates of social value—mine for you; yours for me, my kin, and associates— contribute to perceptions of what counts as beneficial versus costly and generate many of our social intuitions, particularly those relating to harm, care, and fairness. The social-value system explains why we wish to manage other people's behavior when it comes to dyadic interactions. And this leads us to the first way disgust is linked, albeit indirectly, to morality. Because the concept of social value is linked to concepts of harm and care, it is also linked to disgust: some acts that cause disgust are harmful.

As we discussed in Chapters 4 and 5, disgust is triggered in response to cues of pathogen presence that cause low expected values of consumption and contact. When someone sneezes on your son; when a doctor doesn't wash her hands after using the restroom; when a cook coughs into the pot of stew or picks his nose before handling cookie dough—these are all acts that potentially impose costs associated with pathogen transmission. They are acts marked by low values of contact and, by virtue of that contact, render foods as having low values of consumption.

The disgust felt in response to agents risking the spread of disease organisms works its way into the social-value system, we suggest, via assessments of *how another person values the self.* When another person directs their sneeze in your direction or wipes a booger on your seat cushion, it reveals disregard for your welfare (intentionally or otherwise). This has two downstream effects. First, to the extent that you believe the person ought to care more for your welfare (and you believe you carry some leverage in the situation), this will trip the anger system and you might say something to the person: "Hey, what are you thinking?" or "What's wrong with you—don't you have any manners?" Second, because that person revealed a low social value toward you, this will lead to a lower social value in your mind *toward him*. You will be less likely to cooperate and more likely to take advantage of an opportunity to exploit.[10]

A similar reaction can occur if we perceive someone to inflict costs on someone we value highly. You are likely to become angry if a person sneezes on your son or wipes a booger on your son's seat cushion. Generally speaking, individuals will tend to care about the actions of others as a function of the (relative) social value of the people affected. Don't sneeze on me or my son or my friends! Don't drop my food on the floor! Don't give my son contaminated cookies! Don't come near me with your odor of feces and urine! These things feel "wrong" because I want to prevent any chance of contracting a disease myself and I want to prevent such harms befalling those I hold high social value toward.

But when it comes to dyadic interactions, disgust also influences perceptions of right and wrong in the sexual domain. As we discussed in Chapter 6, estimates of *expected sexual value* regulate personal decisions about whom to pursue versus whom to avoid as a sexual partner. When low, expected sexual value triggers disgust and motivates sexual avoidance. When high, it triggers lust and sexual pursuit. In addition to guiding your own sexual motivations, expected sexual values serve as another input to the social-valuation system, again via estimates of how another person values you. For instance, from a woman's standpoint (and perhaps also a man's), to the extent that someone you don't want to have sex with is continually attempting to have sex with you despite your refusal, they are implicitly revealing they hold a lower social value for you than you think they ought to, perhaps because their own perceived leverage obviates the need to socially value you as highly as you might like. Regardless, they are not placing a high enough value on *your* preferences. And so repeated advances can turn flattery into harassment. The first advance might be met with an easy letdown, but a "no" nonetheless. Repeated advances will begin to incite anger: "No! What are you, deaf?" Again, perceptions of leverage will influence not only when a man might disregard another's wishes, but also a woman's response to situations in which a man is not valuing her welfare as highly as expected.[11]

Importantly, men and women will likely differ in how an offer of sex is translated into the perceived *value another holds for the self*. As we saw in the Hatfield and Clark study, when research confederates asked members of the opposite sex to have sex with them, most men said "yes" whereas all women said "no." The potential costs associated with a given sexual encounter differ for men and women and thus might color how "wrong" unwanted sexual attention is perceived to be. For a given woman, the sexual advances of a man assessed as having relatively low expected sexual values—perhaps because they are kin, unhealthy, of relatively lower socioeconomic status, or interested merely in short-term sex—are potentially costly (or, at least, not as beneficial as other opportunities) in terms of lifetime reproductive success. Advances by such individuals are thus more likely to be experienced as unwanted and wrong.

For men, the sexual advances of a (genetically unrelated) woman are typically interpreted quite differently—they could mean one is having a good day. The differences in evolved sexual psychologies outlined previously mean that men, who have a much smaller minimum investment in offspring, will view offers for sex differently than women, assigning higher association value to women offering sex than women will assign to men offering the same. This could lead to differences in what one considers harassment and therefore harmful and wrong. That is, although there might be strong agreement that certain types of physical/sexual contact and acts intended to restrict the freedom of movement or choice are wrong and condemnable, there is a considerable grey area regarding other less exploitative acts in which perceptions of wrongness will vary, not just between men and women, but potentially among women, among men, and even in the same person over time.[12]

To sum up, we suggest disgust influences perceptions of harm via the social-valuation system. That is, what causes disgust sometimes indexes harms related to pathogen transmission or personal sexual interests, and thus results in moral intuitions of these behaviors as being wrong or bad.

These Are Dyadic Interactions—What About Groups?

A person's expected value as a sexual partner and expected value of contact influence behaviors that bear on *my* personal interests. They help explain why I find incest wrong for myself and my kin, why I might not want to engage in sex with someone of the same sex, and why I find acts and people that transmit disease objectionable in my social environment. But this doesn't necessarily explain group-level norms. How do we get from personal preferences to group-wide norms, norms that people often incur costs to enforce? To wit, we pay taxes to adjudicate and sometimes jail people who engage in behaviors that do no obvious harm to us personally (e.g., cases of consensual, adult incest). While it might pay for me to incur costs to attempt to change your future behavior when your behavior affects me and my own, why would I ever expend precious time and resources to regulate the behavior of people I will never interact with?

Preventing harm and promoting cooperation do not seem to always explain such desires to punish third-party behavior. For instance, concepts of harm and fairness do not go far in explaining norms proscribing homosexuality. For the most part, same-sex activities have nothing to do with heterosexuals. In fact, from an evolutionary perspective, heterosexuals—particularly heterosexual men—should ostensibly be in favor of male homosexuality. Strategically speaking, male homosexuality removes competition for mates and, with no offspring produced from homosexual unions, decreases competition for food and other resources. Why isn't this considered a highly desirable outcome—a truly positive affordance to be praised by heterosexual men? One could imagine moral campaigns attempting to turn heterosexual men into homosexuals! But the world over, this tends not to be what we see.

Certainly, belief systems might account, in part, for attitudes regarding homosexuality. But religious ideals derived, at some point in time, from the psychology of humans (most commonly, from men). If we agree on this point, then claiming religion is the reason why we observe laws against homosexuality simply regresses the question to why men selected homosexuality as a behavior to proscribe in religious texts in the first place. Beyond homosexuality, there are many other issues people find immoral that have little to do with overt harms or fairness. Consensual adult sexual relationships such as incest, polygamy, and prostitution, gender "switching," contact with lower social castes, food taboos, genetic engineering, taking drugs, pornography, curse words, and other "offensive" speech are all often moralized, even when the behavior has no material impact on the lives of those doing the moralizing. Why do we care so passionately about the behavior of strangers when the behaviors in question are often not coercive or antagonistic?

Proscriptions against behaviors with no clear conflict of interest suggest that humans develop and enforce norms and laws that sometimes have little to do with harm, fairness, or overt conflict. After all, Mark and Julie, the incestuous siblings we've encountered in previous chapters, do no harm to each other—or anyone else for that matter—yet most subjects maintain their actions were wrong. How can we explain this pattern? To answer that, and to show why disgust plays a role in this process, we have to start by exploring the formation of human alliances.

ALLIANCE FORMATION AND THE SOCIAL VALUE SYSTEM

Our ability to categorize others based on their social value to us gives rise to a set of conditions for social games on a grander scale, at the level of groups. The jump from individual (1:1) to multi-individual (e.g., 2:1; 3:1; 5:2) interactions, however, requires additional mental machinery that extends beyond systems for detecting the social value of another person and for motivating cooperation, competition, or indifference toward that person. To form a group requires systems facilitating coordination—the mental and physical coordination of two or more individuals in the pursuit of a common goal. In very broad strokes, joining forces with another person requires the ability for one to identify a desirable goal oneself, assess the degree of mental alignment between oneself and another person, coordinate movements to achieve the desired goal, and determine how the benefits/costs are to be divvied up between participants. Humans possess these abilities, and some components are shared with a handful of non-human primates and aquatic mammals as well.[13]

Coordination launches social behavior to an entirely new level of complexity. At this level, individuals can further attempt to transform the world into a place that promotes one's interests by utilizing the power of alliances. These, according to Tooby and Cosmides, are *second-order moral games*.[14] Second-order moral games change the calculus of social valuation by changing perceptions of leverage. In many relationships—for instance, parent–child relationships, friendships, or romantic relationships—leverage might be balanced in such a way that the parties are, generally speaking, equals. But in other relationships, for instance those in which there are larger power or status asymmetries, one of the parties might be unable to impose his own will, producing conditions that could potentially lead to exploitation. In a social species such as our own, low-leverage positions in which individuals were in a constant state of "social checkmate" and thus open to repeated exploitation at the hands of more powerful individuals would have put a premium on the evolution of psychological mechanisms that enabled individuals to move from positions of low bargaining power to positions of higher bargaining power.

One solution? Recruit a third party—someone who tips the balance of power in your favor. Third-party recruitment transforms disputes between two individuals into multi-individual coordinated interactions aimed to shift the manner in which one or many regard the welfare of others. This is psychological tug-of-war on a grander scale. Psychological mechanisms that facilitated third-party recruitment to help change a particular individual's undesirable (exploitative or merely indifferent) behavior would have fared better in ancestral environments than mechanisms blind to the benefits alliances afford. In situations where one cannot on one's own transform the world in ways that are beneficial, other people can be recruited to the project. Bandits stealing your cattle? Convince other ranchers they could be targeted too and coordinate efforts to catch them bandits. Your child hit by a drunk driver? Get other moms angry and begin a campaign so that it doesn't happen to you or loved ones again. Think our tax laws are unfair? Recruit voters who would benefit from a different system of taxation. Disgusted by a chef handling your food with dirty hands? Recruit germaphobes to enact glove and hairnet legislation.

In humans, alliance formation is a well-developed art. A common occurrence throughout history has been the banding together of individuals to strengthen their defensive and offensive positions and to increase their bargaining power against individuals and groups inflicting harms. Many examples of alliance formation, such as the examples above, however, concern an overt conflict involving cheating, physical harm, or fairness. The question is, how do we get from moral campaigns such as "drunk driving is wrong" to moral campaigns such as "eating meat is wrong," "incest is wrong," or "homosexuality is wrong"? Preventing you from driving drunk clearly benefits me, my family, ME, my friends, and *ME*. But preventing homosexuals from having sex doesn't, at least on the surface, do much to help a heterosexual stranger. What is the conceptual bridge that gets us from moral proscriptions with clear roots in concepts related to harm and fairness to moral proscriptions without such foundations?

THE MISSING INGREDIENT: RESOURCE COMPETITION

A stable feature of hunter-gatherer ancestral life was resource variability. Herds migrated, waterholes dried up, and fruits, nuts, and tubers varied seasonally. A psychology forged in environments characterized by extreme swings in fortune is a very different psychology than what would have evolved if essential survival resources were unlimited, as they are, or at least appear to be, for many today. One big difference is, or would be, the motivation to marginalize or eliminate resource competitors. When resources recurrently vary, as they did throughout human evolution, motivations to secure and protect them would have had large consequences on survival and subsequent reproduction. (It is even possible that motivations to sequester local resources might *still* have evolved under conditions of repeated surplus, but no need to cast an even darker shadow right now.) Resources include many things, but evolutionary scientists tend to boil resources down to food, mates, and territory (physical locations where food and mates might also be present). In ancestral environments, humans—like many non-human animals—were in competition for access to valuable resources, and this repeated state refined mental systems to be sensitive to the presence of competitors.

The depletion of local resources—waterholes, flowering plants, migrating herds—meant that the mere existence of other people potentially jeopardized one's own survival. This runs contrary to the idea of humans as inherently social, requiring large numbers of other people to gather food, ward off predators, and otherwise survive. But as we've stressed, context matters. When resources are plentiful, others can be more or less tolerated. But when food is scarce, (unrelated) mouths to feed become a liability. What's more, ancestrally, even when food *was* present, famine could have been right around the corner. Ethnographic evidence suggests that resource availability is one factor that governs the fusion and fission patterns of hunter-gatherer groups. During rainy seasons, resources are more abundant and groups coalesce; during dry seasons, resources are scarcer and groups splinter.[15]

What does this mean psychologically? For one, our psychology might be biased to expect resource variability, causing us to keep a wary eye on the number of people drawing on available goods. Even today, in a period during which food—and basically everything in the Western world—is produced in abundance, our psychology likely still reflects the resource-limited environment to which it is adapted. Other people, to our hunter-gatherer minds, still pose threats as potential resource competitors. Individuals who identified groups competing over similar pools of resources and prevented them from competing would have fared better during times of dire need than individuals who surrendered, or sacrificed, to give resources to others. All to say, we did not descend from individuals who were indifferent to resource availability nor from individuals who preferred to forgo available resources for the good of others. We descended from individuals who strategically traded off the benefits of sharing with the benefits of individual survival.

ALLIANCE FORMATION PLUS RESOURCE COMPETITION EQUALS TROUBLE

The psychological equipment that enables the ability to recruit third parties and build leverage-increasing alliances for interpersonal disputes, when combined with a psychology sensitive to resource availability, leads to coalitions with the common goal of marginalizing and eliminating potential and actual resource

competitors. Put simply, under certain conditions, we gang up on groups to con-
trol/limit/prevent their access to resources, even where "resource availability"
never consciously registers as our reason for doing so.

Humans are not unique in this respect. The roots of coalitional actions with
the goal of protecting resources are shared with some of our closest living relatives.[16] A stable feature of male chimpanzee life is the formation of parties
to monitor the boundaries shared with neighboring troops. In addition to
patrolling home territories, males also form parties to *initiate* conflict with
neighboring troops. The biologist Richard Wrangham has conducted extensive
research on non-human primates and suggests that male chimpanzees possess
a particular appetite for conflict with neighboring troops, engaging in what
he terms lethal raiding, the *unprovoked* attack of one coalition on another.[17]
Wrangham points out several interesting features of chimp lethal raiding. One
in particular relates to group size. Specifically, the number of males present in
a coalition determines whether the troop advances or retreats from a contest.
The more males present relative to a rival gang, the more likely an aggressive
encounter will take place. Jane Goodall reports similar patterns with patrol parties of unequal size.[18] By contrast, when numbers of males are equal between
groups, chimps tend to stand their ground and generate vocal displays, presumably functioning to signal their formidability.

What is interesting about the dynamics of lethal raiding and coalitional aggression is that somehow chimps must know their numbers. Males appear to know
when they are outmatched and need to retreat to areas of safety, as well as when
they have the upper hand and can advance into enemy territory. Research supports
this idea. In one experiment, an audio recording of a lone foreign male making
a pant-grunt was played to groups of varying sizes and compositions.[19] The researchers wanted to know when chimps decide to engage, hold steady, or retreat.
They found that all 13 groups that contained at least 3 males closed the distance
to the "lone male" (but only 12 out of 13 parties met the 50-meter criterion for
"an approach"). Groups with one or two males approached only about 50% of the
time, and all-female groups never approached the speaker—if anything, female
groups withdrew. The greater the imbalance of males, the greater the number of
loud calls made by the attacking party, the faster the attacking party sweeps in to
fight, and, in actual aggressive encounters, the greater the chance of success.

Wrangham, building on the work of Goodall, offers an explanation for why
male coordinated aggression, such as lethal raiding, evolved. He calls it the
imbalance-of-power hypothesis:

> The imbalance-of-power hypothesis proposes that the function of unpro-
> voked intercommunity aggression (i.e., deep incursions and coalitionary
> attacks) is intercommunity dominance. By wounding or killing members of
> the neighboring community, males from one community increase their rel-
> ative dominance over the neighbors. According to the imbalance-of-power
> hypothesis, the proximate benefit is an increased probability of winning
> intercommunity dominance contests (nonlethal battles); this tends to lead to

increased fitness of the killers through improved *access to resources* such as food, females, or safety. (emphasis added)[20]

In chimpanzees, the motivation to protect resources, the fact that other individuals and groups represent resource competitors, and the ability to form coordinated groups around a common goal create the conditions of intergroup conflict. Numbers dictate success, and chimps appear to use numbers to assess relative formidability in a given contest. Humans too are sensitive to numbers. The existence of other people—people who are unrelated, people with whom one does not trade, or, more generally, people who do not emit positive externalities—serves as input to systems that activate behavioral strategies for monitoring, suppressing, marginalizing, or eliminating. That is, human coalitional psychology doesn't just resemble chimp coalitional psychology; it has taken it to new heights (or depths, depending on your viewpoint). Human coalitional psychology reveals an appetite for identifying smaller groups, evaluating whether their existence yields a net positive or net negative on one's own fitness interests, and, if negative, recruiting allies to strategically marginalize them.

Because the business of resource acquisition and defense tends to be a facet of male mating psychology, "we" refers primarily to men. This is not to say that women don't compete for resources—they do. But, across many species, including our own, the ability to defend resources, including food supplies, had a far greater impact on male reproductive success than female reproductive success—a topic we addressed in the chapter on mating psychology. Across the animal kingdom, males with access to resources tend to attract, retain, and mate with females who, in turn, require the resources to produce offspring. Resources are thus a critical feature dictating male reproductive success.

So men compete for resources. No big surprise there. But what might be jarring is the notion that aspects of our moral psychology—the systems that color certain behaviors as "right" or "wrong"—might be, in part, a direct outgrowth of an evolved psychology aimed at resource defense. Motivations to dominate are sometimes cloaked in the language of morality. Some moral "projects" take aim explicitly or implicitly at groups perceived to hold low leverage (because of their small numbers, low political power, or other attributes) in an effort to neutralize or regulate their access to valued resources simply because they hold less leverage and can be more easily targeted. This, we claim, helps to explain many moral stances against behavior that appears to cause no obvious harm to the group taking the moral stance. It also helps to explain many past and ongoing campaigns against minority ethnic groups and, more generally, groups that tend to hold any minority viewpoint, no matter the content.[21]

As we'll discuss in greater detail shortly, both deep and recent history demonstrate how the imbalance of power can have devastating effects. By and large, minority groups tend to suffer at the hands of the majority for the simple reason that they are minority groups and represent resource competitors. The Jews, gypsies, and homosexuals of Nazi Germany were all minorities, in the broadest sense of the term, and many also controlled valued resources. The propensity of minority groups in Germany, such as the Jews, to prefer trade with in-group members may have also contributed. Jews didn't just possess valuable resources; they were perceived by outsiders as not sharing them.

What the Nazis did to minority groups was overt, as was the ethnic cleansing campaign of the Bosnian Serbs against Bosnian Muslims and Croats, the campaign of Sunni Muslims against ethnic Kurds and Shiite Muslims, the Hutu massacre of the Tutsis, Stalin's famine within a famine targeting Ukrainians, the ongoing campaign in Myanmar against Rohingya Muslims, the current-day imprisonment of homosexuals in Chechnya, and the historical campaign of white Americans against blacks. But majority aims to rid minority groups can also be done covertly. The recent banning of eggs from school lunches in India might be because eggs are not vegetarian and, like many Hindus, the state chief minister who banned eggs is also vegetarian. It might, however, also be because the Muslim immigrant population is increasing in various Indian provinces and Muslims, unlike Hindus, are not vegetarian. Muslim children eat eggs.[22]

Knowledge of an evolved psychology that sifts the world for potential resource competitors starts to bring into focus why moral norms and laws exist to proscribe particular behaviors. Individuals who eat foods not commonly eaten in the local community; individuals who engage in atypical sexual acts; and individuals who, as a general rule, speak, dress, or act in a manner that is different from the local majority (or the powerful) constitute relative minorities. Behaviors such as these trip wiring in the human (particularly male) brain that sifts the world for groups of lower leverage and motivates behaviors to suppress, deny, and eliminate—for no other reason than because in ancestral environments, male psychologies that strategically motivated the elimination of competitors for food, women, and territory when perceived success was likely would have outcompeted and thus increased in frequency over psychologies blind to the fitness outcomes such actions afforded.

This is why in humans, as in other non-human primate species, minority and out-group status is so precarious. Conditions in which one is significantly out-leveraged by groups of individuals evincing a degree of coordination increase the likelihood of exploitation. It is no wonder minorities tend to suffer greater rates of mental health issues such as anxiety and depression—enduring states of hypervigilance and low perceived social value can take their toll.

DISGUST, SOCIAL VALUE, AND EXPLOITATION

When it comes to marginalizing minorities, disgust is a common theme. Here we discuss three ways disgust is linked to morality and social norms whose ultimate goal is not harm prevention, equality promotion, or cooperation, but instead exploitation, marginalization, and elimination.

Disgust as Moral Spotlight

The psychological systems that evolved to guide food consumption, physical contact, and sexual reproduction produce estimates of *personal* value. They guide *personal* behaviors and, as we saw, they influence perceptions of harm via the social
value system—harm directed toward oneself or those for whom one holds high
social value (like kin, or close friends). But disgust, once activated, can also serve
as a rallying point used by systems for alliance coordination. That is, the disgust
felt in response to low expected values of contact (which could occur because
people eat items perceived to hold low expected values of consumption) and low
expected sexual values shines a spotlight on undesirable acts now visible to systems on the lookout for opportunities to marginalize or exploit other people.

These internal variables might be taken as input directly or, because they shape
perceptions of expected social value (as we discussed above), they might exert
their effects on alliance-coordination systems via estimates of social valuation.
That is, disgust may be working to identify a person who poses a direct, proximate
harm (for example, disease) to you or your loved ones, or it might be working to
identify a potential person (for example, one who has atypical sexual tendencies)
who—by virtue of engaging in a behavior that you and your neighbors might find
aversive—makes for a potential target for exploitation. Either way, low values of
consumption, contact and sex occur in response to behaviors one is *not* inclined
to engage in and potentially push down the social values of others engaging in
those acts. A mechanism sifting the world to identify possible fitness opportunities might target groups that register low on any of these indices. This is because,
all else equal, it would be more costly fitness-wise to exploit individuals of high
social value (e.g., potential friends and mates) than individuals of low social value
(non-mates, non-cooperators, disease-spreaders).[23] A system that identified the
lowest-valued behaviors and lowest-valued individuals on the totem pole—as well
as the smallest and weakest groups of such individuals—and motivated a campaign against them would have had the result of removing groups of resource
competitors for whom one had relatively little value. Brutal.

Disgust, in addition to identifying behaviors and people one tends to value less
for the purpose of initiating moral campaigns, might also function as a gauge
for how beneficial or costly it would be to join a campaign already in motion.
As psychologists Peter DeScioli and Rob Kurzban have suggested, disgust might
simply indicate which of the available candidate norms would serve one's own
interest.[24] All else equal, norms that did not infringe on one's own preferences
would have been more favorable than those that proscribed behaviors one tended
to enjoy. Disgust identifies the former. Behaviors that trip disgust wiring and belong to the category of actions that one does *not* prefer to do oneself are the kinds
of behaviors that one might back as candidates for proscription.

But no matter whether disgust generates novel ideas in the head of an individual regarding personal fitness opportunities or whether disgust serves to gauge
the utility of a particular norm, a question remains: How do moral campaigns take
flight? We suggest that the mere sharing of a negative evaluation (which indexes

a low magnitude of value in *some* domain) primes systems for alliance formation and provides lift to particular moral campaigns.

It seems strange that merely sharing a preference or sharing an aversion would be the spark that ignites a fledgling moral campaign. Yet in social psychology, one of the most reliable and robust effects (that is shockingly easy to demonstrate) is called the *minimal group effect*, which refers to the propensity of individuals to form coalitions. It doesn't take much. All you have to do is toss a coin and assign some people to "heads" and some to "tails" for coalitional psychology to emerge. Suddenly people have strong preferences for exclusively sharing resources with members of their own group and for discriminating against those of the out-group, all determined by the random flip of a coin.[25] Marginal, yes; trivial, no.

UNIVERSAL PSYCHOLOGIES, COMMON PROSCRIPTIONS

Because humans by and large share a common evolved psychology, tuned in similar ways, individuals will tend to agree on the kinds of acts that bring about low expected values of consumption, contact, and sex—that is, there will be general agreement on the kinds of behaviors that are disgusting and thus the kinds of behaviors that tend to populate moral norms—not with *exact* agreement over time and space, but numerous points of commonality. Everyone, for instance, has a psychology of food, and so most people see consuming feces, drinking urine, and eating vomit as usually highly disgusting. Every person has a mating psychology tuned to find particular attributes attractive and other attributes unattractive. Most people tend to agree that sex with very young children, extremely close family members, and other animals is highly undesirable. But as you back away from sexual partners for whom most people hold low sexual value, there might be more disagreement. Behaviors toward the extreme ends of the spectrum will provoke greater moralization because extremes tend to be where the majority of minds coalesce. Disgust happens to be one of the emotions that identifies extremely low values across a variety of domains (though, of course, not all behaviors at the extremes become moralized).

Disgust, however, does not have a monopoly on this effect. Anger operates in a similar manner, and so does fear. Someone who commits an act inciting anger, or that frightens us or threatens our safety or overall well-being also runs the risk of being a target of exploitation and condemnation. But disgust is different than anger and fear. The evolved targets of disgust are, in most cases, disease-causing organisms. We don't attempt to increase the value bacteria hold for us by getting angry at them, and we're more than just scared of them—we want them expelled from our bodies. Something that is a source of contamination is to be avoided and removed, not rehabilitated. Furthermore, it would have been a rare occurrence for particular acts to transition from low contact/sexual values to high contact/sexual values. One's opposite-sex sibling is mentally tagged with a low sexual value causing extreme sexual disgust when the act is imagined. Likewise, spoiled milk or rotten meat is mentally tagged with low consumption value (causing disgust) when such foods are brought into close proximity. It is unlikely (though not impossible) that one's sibling will ever be removed from the category of "undesirable sexual partner" to "highly desirable" or that rotten maggot-ridden meat will appear on the menu of five-star restaurants (again, not impossible). The reason for this relative immutability is due to the dire effects on survival and reproduction inbreeding and contamination had over evolutionary time.

Contrast this with anger. The function of anger is to strategically change the behavior of an individual for one's own gain—when this occurs, anger typically subsides. An enemy today could be a friend tomorrow. Given the constantly shifting chessboard of social value, where alliances and allegiances can change rapidly, anger can dissipate into liking. Not so with disgust: disgust rarely dissipates into appeal—disgust sticks. This could be why disgust is often recruited to convey moral issues.

SEXUALITIES, MAJORITIES, AND INCREASING MINORITIES

Our main point regarding the first way disgust interacts with the "moral" system is that disgust *shines a spotlight* on particular behaviors that generate low personal value and thus constitute viable options (in the mind of a given individual) for proscription. But others need to agree for moral projects to take flight and reach cruising altitude. The more people on board, the stronger the moral project. Depending on the social milieu, the particular individuals in power, and their particular attitudes, moral projects can flare up. Under favorable (high-leverage) conditions, ideas and proscriptions will spread; in unfavorable (low-leverage) conditions, the volume of moral campaigns gets dialed back.[26]

At the time this book is being written, there are still many states in the United States (speak nothing of other countries) that deny, or are attempting to deny, rights to gay men, lesbians, and transgender individuals. When the "moral" majority comprises heterosexual men, the disgust alarm sounds in response to male homosexuals, making gay men a potential target for exploitation. One reason why gay men are targeted more than lesbians might be because gay men have two strikes against them: not only do they cause disgust in heterosexual men due to low contact or sexual value, but the mere association of multiple males (already tagged as having low value) has the potential to trip coalitional circuitry. Men in the seat of power are no doubt very sensitive to the association of other junior males; coalitions at the junior ranks have the ability to dethrone alpha males. And, as the aggressive coalitional attacks in chimps suggest, at least ancestrally, coalitions comprising (more) males are perceived as more physically formidable than coalitions comprising (more) females.

In any case, the historical targeting of homosexual men (a history we will explore in greater detail in the next section) led to the withholding of various resources and rights enjoyed by heterosexual men, to speak nothing of the public aggression, torture, and bullying homosexuals have endured. But perceptions have started to change. Perhaps there has been a shift in perceptions of leverage that has quelled motivations to exploit gay men and lesbians in such overt manners. Modern media, for all its drawbacks, might have served an important function in the steps toward equal treatment for individuals identifying as homosexual. Perceptions of the vast numbers of individuals who identify as homosexual, propagated in large part by social media streams, has caused a rapid reduction in the strength of "moral" projects targeting homosexuality. Where numbers are perceived to be large and growing, mainly in the coastal states, laws against homosexuality have flipped virtually overnight from being an act causing outrage to an act viewed as blasé. When groups previously seen as minorities grow in number to achieve levels of formidability and leverage (particularly economic and political leverage), existing majorities no longer enjoy the same level or ease of power they once relied on to support their moral campaign. Someone who was in a former majority or in a position of strong leverage might now find himself at the business end of the barrel.

It's worth taking a moment here to point out that the face of America is rapidly changing. By 2065 it is projected that whites will make up 46 percent of the population, down from over 65 percent today; blacks will make up 13 percent; Hispanics 24 percent; Asians 14 percent.[27] Likewise, religious affiliations are changing. An April 6, 2017, article from pew.com explains:

> In the next half century or so, Christianity's long reign as the world's largest religion may come to an end, according to a just-released report that builds on Pew Research Center's original population growth projections for religious groups. Indeed, Muslims will grow more than twice as fast as the overall world population between 2015 and 2060 and, in the second half of this century, will likely surpass Christians as the world's largest religious group. While the world's population is projected to grow 32% in the coming decades, the number of Muslims is expected to increase by 70%—from 1.8 billion in 2015 to nearly 3 billion in 2060. In 2015, Muslims made up 24.1% of the global population. Forty-five years later, they are expected to make up more than three-in-ten of the world's people (31.1%).[28]

Whites in America, and Christians worldwide, who today might hold a majority, might one day not remain in such position. If male psychology is indeed one laden with motivations to eliminate groups identified as competitors and if numbers are one way men assess their formidability, the future could hold substantial changes in fortune for many groups. Seats of power change. One idea as we move forward is that self-preservation tomorrow might be achieved via greater mutual social valuation today.

EVIDENCE THAT DISGUST PUSHES MORAL JUDGMENTS

Evidence that disgust increases the visibility of particular acts to a "moral" system comes from a wide range of studies. Some studies even suggest that "incidental" disgust—disgust that has nothing to do with the object being morally evaluated—can nonetheless influence those decisions. David Pizarro, a professor at Cornell University, found that subjects exposed to a noxious smell—fart spray—rate many behaviors, including homosexuality, as more morally wrong than subjects who were not olfactorily abused.[29] A study conducted by

Jonathan Haidt and colleagues found that as compared to subjects seated at a clean desk, subjects seated at a dirty desk doled out more harsh judgments in response to minor infractions.[30] Likewise, subjects asked to put their hands in imitation vomit reported greater immorality of offenses, particularly those that evoke disgust.[31] (We should note that recent analyses have questioned, with good reason, the robustness of the results from these incidental-disgust studies, but the original researchers maintain that their conclusions as to the effects were valid.[32])

In another study, Thalia Wheatley and Jonathan Haidt showed that the disgust felt toward a particular concept need not derive from consciously available probes—it can also be supplied hypnotically.[33] Wheatley and Haidt hypnotized subjects to feel disgust toward an arbitrary word, in this case the words "often" or "take." When brought out of the hypnotic trance, subjects read various vignettes, some of which included the target word while others did not. These vignettes depicted events like sex between cousins, eating one's dog, shoplifting, and bribery. By and large, subjects rated vignettes that contained the target word not only as more disgusting but also as more morally wrong than vignettes that did not contain the target word. It appears that a twinge of disgust, subconsciously implanted, renders actions more morally wrong. Also, a fun aside, before they hypnotically induced subjects a second time to remove the disgust tag on the target word, they asked subjects, "Would you like to *take* a cookie?" and told them to "*Take* as many as you want." They found that subjects hypnotized to feel disgust toward the word "take" took on average half as many cookies than subjects hypnotized to feel disgust toward the word "often." (Subliminal disgust as diet control? Hmmm.) What we take from this study is that changing the internal dial on how disgusting a particular act/concept is perceived to be influences one's views on the publicly expressed "rightness" and "wrongness" of the act/concept.

A last study we mention is on moral attitudes regarding sibling incest. Humans possess an inbreeding-avoidance system that uses ancestrally relevant cues to kinship to categorize another person as a particular type of kin. For siblings, we use information about co-residence duration—the longer two individuals lived together starting from early childhood, the greater the probability they are siblings. Earlier in the book we discussed how longer periods of childhood co-residence predict greater sexual aversions later during adulthood. But if disgust is an input for moral-project candidacy, then in the mind of a subject, the more intense the sexual aversions felt toward one's own siblings, the more morally wrong sibling incest in general will be. And this is what has been found: by and large, the more time one lived with one's opposite-sex siblings throughout childhood, the greater the disgust and the more morally wrong one ranked brother–sister sex and marriage.[34]

In sum, disgust acts as a spotlight identifying behaviors that might serve as a rallying point to coordinate coalitions for the purpose of exploiting and marginalizing groups of people.

Disgust as Moral Signal

Related to the idea that disgust shines a spotlight on people and actions perceived as holding low consumption, contact, or sexual value is the idea that disgust serves a signaling function for alliance formation. Alliance coordination is facilitated to the extent there is a signal relaying individual preferences and desired goals. Moral projects require coordination, and disgust, with its universally recognizable facial expression,[35] could be used to signal one's position with respect to a moral project and to identify others' positions as well. This means that when people display disgust, by uttering "eww" or wrinkling their nose, it could be because they genuinely feel disgusted. Their brain computed a low sexual or a low contact value and produced as output the disgust-avoidance response. But it could also be that the person is using the language of disgust as a strategy to assess or sway allegiance to a particular moral project, an idea suggested by David Pizarro and Paul Bloom.[36]

"It is *disgusting* that CEOs get such huge bonuses." "It makes me *sick* that our country drops bombs on innocent children." "If I hear another word about the elections I will *vomit*." Why do we use disgust in this way? We don't actually vomit or get sick. One way to think about this is that applying disgust to non-pathogen or nonsexual acts is similar to when we "lust" for a sports car. We don't actually plan to have sex with the car; lust, like disgust, is instead being used to communicate something else. As Bloom suggests, "To say that something is disgusting is to imply, 'If you were to see it, you would find it disgusting too.' (If you don't, there is something wrong *with you*.) There is no response to the language of disgust. It is a conversation stopper."[37]

We mostly agree with this sentiment, but add the following. First, as the fart-spray and dirty-desk studies seem to show, simply turning up the disgust dial—regardless of the source of the heightened disgust—can often turn up the dial on moral wrongness. To the extent that this disgust-as-communicative-tool *actually* elicits disgust, or any of the psychological penumbrae of disgust, it could also have downstream effects on moral judgments.

Second, disgust can project one's allegiance to a particular moral campaign. It can be used to sway others' opinions or merely to gauge other people's temperature on the viability of a particular view. Of course, sticking your neck out and publicly identifying with one side versus another could be a dangerous move depending on the audience. Imagine hearing someone proclaim, "it is disgusting how guns are ruining society." Now imagine such a statement falls on deaf ears. No one says a word back; no heads nod in agreement. Just crickets. Awkward! That campaign is dead in the water. But what if a chorus of people agreed with the disgust sentiment, slinging additional disgust metaphors into the mix: "they're scum" and "those dirty bastards will kill us all!" Now we're off to the races. Disgust might not be a conversation stopper in all situations; in some cases, it could be used to assess agreement and rally the troops.

The notion that disgust serves a signaling function to others is supported by a variety of research.[38] For instance, subjects are more likely to make a facial expression of disgust in response to non-pathogen and nonsexual acts when in the presence of another person than when alone.[39] If disgust faces serve to reveal one's allegiance, then it only makes sense to display it when there is someone to display it to. Interestingly, the usage of disgust to describe moral violations occurs quite young. Bloom has found that children as young as six years old use the term *disgust* and display disgust facial expressions in response to moral violations like theft and harm.[40]

Disgust as Moral Shield

Once it is clear which side those in power are on with respect to a particular behavior, disgust could also be used to signal allegiance to moral norms for the purpose of avoiding condemnation. In a world in which third parties can be recruited to form alliances, a single individual has quite a minefield to navigate. Ancestrally, the costs of being targeted by a majority could have been severe, and often could have resulted in ostracism or even death. How might evolution have equipped us to protect ourselves against being targeted by a given coalition advancing a particular moral project? What would have been an effective mechanism that prevented condemnation by locally powerful alliances?

One mechanism is avoidance. Disgust, as one of the emotions governing avoidance motivations (another being fear), might be used to steer us clear of individuals who violate the majority (or powerful) opinion. This prevents us from being painted with the same brush and thus "contaminated" by such an affiliation. In a series of classic disgust studies, Paul Rozin and colleagues asked U.S. college subjects if they would wear (expected value of contact) clothing worn by evil people, such as a murderer or Adolf Hitler. Most said "no." With respect to the sweater, subjects said "no" even if the sweater had been unraveled and reknitted![41]

One might think that this avoidance could be attributed to actual germ contagion. But one recent study suggests that, instead, this avoidance is geared toward evading reputational damage, which functions to reduce the threat of condemnation. Tom Kupfer and Roger Giner-Sorolla asked subjects who were participating in a study on historical clothing to wear a Nazi armband, but the subjects were given a choice of how to wear it: either under a jacket, but against the skin, or over the jacket and visible. They found that the majority of subjects opted to wear the armband underneath the jacket, touching their body, an effect that was much greater if the subjects knew others were going to see them.[42] This finding suggests that we are sensitive to reputational damage, not the transfer of some contagious immoral essence. In sum, humans appear to be quite sensitive to interacting with individuals condemned by the majority or those in power.

The idea that disgust and avoidance behaviors are used strategically to avoid social condemnation is perhaps nothing shocking or new. But the notion that our moral conscience evolved to protect us from the costs imposed by more powerful coalitions might be. DeScioli and Kurzban make the provocative claim that one's moral conscience—the subjective feeling that taking a particular action would be "right" or "wrong"—serves to regulate personal actions in an effort to minimize condemnation by those in power. That is, perception of what one might be condemned for in the local environment influences personal motivations to act "appropriately" as well as personal judgments and public communications of the "rightness" and "wrongness" of particular actions.[43]

If you recall from our discussion of moral dumbfounding, subjects maintained that the incestuous acts engaged in by siblings Mark and Julie were wrong even after every contingency had been addressed. Why were subjects so stubborn in their allegiance? One possibility is that because in the current social environment sibling incest is indeed condemned, out of fear of condemnation, moral conscience reinforces the "wrongness" of the act. However, some scholars maintain that subjects are still concerned about harm even after being told that the incestuous siblings enjoy the act, they use protection, and promise to keep it a secret.[44] We agree that subjects are indeed concerned about harm, but not harm to the siblings in the hypothetical, but rather a type of perceived harm—condemnation—that would result if the *subjects* disagreed with a widely held social norm. What is noteworthy is that subjects can't explain their reasons for why Mark and Julie's actions are wrong. This is a hallmark of total allegiance: maintaining the party line is an important feature of our moral psychology.

SOCIAL VALUE VERSUS MORAL ALLEGIANCE

In the beginning of the chapter we argued that personal interests, leverage, and perceptions of the costs of condemnation influence in a graded manner how we treat other people via the computation of a variable labeled *social value*. Here we are talking about allegiance to established, currently condemned, proscribed behaviors, which seems to be more black and white. Indeed, there are two different systems at work. How you treat another person in a dyadic interaction is one thing. Your signaling of allegiance to a particular moral norm is another. A study by Deb Lieberman and Lance Linke nicely illustrates the difference.[45] In the study, subjects were asked to mete out punishments and assess the moral "wrongness" of hypothetical crimes of theft. In one version, they varied the identity of the victim of the theft, who was described as being a family member, a schoolmate, or a stranger; in the other version, they varied the identity of the perpetrator, again described as being a family member, a schoolmate, or a stranger. Subjects meted out punishments based on how close the subjects were to the victims: crimes against a family member were punished most severely, followed by crimes against a schoolmate, then crimes against a stranger. And when the perpetrator of a theft was identified as a family member, subjects doled out lighter fines and jail times than when the perpetrator was identified as a schoolmate, which in turn were less than what was assigned to a stranger. Social valuation clearly guides personal motivations to punish. But, in this case, social valuation did *not* influence moral judgments. Regardless of the scenario—that is, whether a perpetrator targeted a family member, a schoolmate, or a stranger, or whether one's own kin or one's own schoolmate committed the crime—subjects rated the crimes equally immoral.

So do moral judgments have *nothing* to do with social valuation? Not so fast. The process by which certain acts rise up to *become* cultural norms is not the same as reactions to these acts once they are *established* as culturally proscribed behaviors. Personal social valuation gets the ball rolling and guides personal motivations to initiate or back campaigns to proscribe a particular behavior. But the fact that what subjects do (punish) differs from what they say (claim as immoral) suggests that more is going on than just social valuation. That something, we suggest, often involves the specter of group condemnation. We should expect to see agreement in expressed moral attitudes in response to acts universally condemned in one's own group. Claiming allegiance to a particular norm by using the language of morality shields you from negative social evaluation and group condemnation. It might not feel like you are surreptitiously avoiding group condemnation when you say "Theft is highly immoral regardless of who does it," but we suggest you are (at least in part), in a similar manner as it might not feel like you're furthering your reproductive interests when you tell your mate "I love you."

And it isn't just *moral* judgments that appear to be sensitive to group condemnation: all public judgments might fall into this category. In general, individual judgments are sensitive to the prospect of condemnation, whether by groups or by individuals perceived to hold powerful positions. Two landmark psychological studies, one by Solomon Asch and the other by his student, Stanley Milgram, reveal just how sensitive people are to condemnation. Asch, a Polish immigrant, and Milgram, a first-generation American, were both Jews who were deeply affected by the genocide perpetrated by the Germans during World War II. They each spent a significant portion of their career trying to understand the factors that contribute to group conformity and obedience.

One of Asch's famous studies examined the tendency for people to conform to group behavior.[46] Asch sat subjects at a table with other people who also appeared to be subjects but in fact were merely confederates in the experiment. Asch presented the group with a single test line drawn on a board. He then asked all subjects—the real subject and the confederates—to select which line from a set of three was closest in length to the test line. Easy enough; any child could do this and get it correct. Asch went around the table and asked each subject to state out loud which line they selected. When asked to select first, the real subjects selected the correct line. But when the subject was one of the last to select, things got more interesting. This is because Asch manipulated which line the confederates selected. When the confederates selected a line that was, from all viewpoints, clearly *not* the line identical to the test line, subjects tended to follow suit. That is, subjects went against their own perception and publicly endorsed the line selected by the majority. Milgram in similar fashion found that subjects will administer increasingly painful shocks to another person when told to do so by an authoritative figure despite subjects' preferences to the contrary. The presence of majorities or individuals with power can change behavior in ways that might contradict personal preferences. Costs of group condemnation foster conformity and compliance, sometimes in strange and dangerous ways.

SUMMARY

In this chapter, we've identified four ways in which disgust relates to morality: (1) as a way of identifying particular behaviors that might pose a pathogen or sexually related threat of harm to an individual; (2) as an internal spotlight that identifies acts of low value, thus informing the kinds of moral norms to initiate and back as part of a moral campaign; (3) as a public signal of what people condemn or as a communicative tool to persuade others to take a particular moral stance; and (4) as a way to avoid condemnation and being associated with those who violate social norms. Disgust, by virtue of indexing expected values of consumption, contact, and sex, is hijacked by moral systems looking for reasons to target and exploit minority groups. The morality we are talking about relates to humans' evolved thirst to coordinate, defend, and exploit. In this view, a darker side of human nature manifests itself as moral cognition—the identification and exploitation of groups perceived as less formidable.

This view of morality differs from many previous treatments of morality in one important way: it extends beyond the bounds of harm prevention and cooperation promotion to the underworld of exploitation. This darker side of human nature has, by and large, been greatly underappreciated by scholars, but perhaps for obvious reasons: the person positing such theory could (erroneously!) be seen as championing these views. In an academic world where cooperation promotion has been the party line when it comes to morality, any view that departs from this majority comes with the risk of condemnation. (It is good to look good.)

Though some moral psychologists have indeed acknowledged that morality extends beyond harm and fairness, it is still a common theme to see morality as a mechanism that binds and builds.[47] We agree with this notion in the sense that humans evolved mechanisms to strategically build relationships and bind people together in ways that benefit themselves—on both the dyadic and group levels. But the term "morality" is often used as a façade—it offers cover, sometimes for nefarious ends. In much the same way as when we say "gross, eww, disgusting" we are expressing adaptations that evolved to protect us against contamination, when we say "wrong, bad, immoral" we are expressing adaptations to extract benefits by, among other things, bending others to our will and protecting against the costs of group condemnation.

The relationship between disgust and morality is perilous and carries high stakes. Because of its access to our systems for generating moral norms, disgust, long viewed as an emotion meant to cause aversion, can instead instigate and incite conflict. As we'll show in the coming chapters, this can be especially problematic when those relying on disgust hold the institutional power of the state, and the leverage to impose their will. By understanding how disgust infiltrates moral psychology, we now have a clearer framework for taking a second look at legal rules that emanate from this dynamic, and for showing why, in our opinion, disgust should be viewed as suspect when it comes to the process of making and deciding law.

PART IV

From Intuitions to Institutions

Don't Eat, Don't Touch, Don't Mate

Every summer, cities across the United States host festivals that cater specifically to dogs and their owners. There's the Pup Crawl in Atlanta, Woof-Stock in Toronto, PawktoberFest in Colorado Springs, the Bow Wow Meow Luau in Redmond, the Yappy Hour Summer Series in Cleveland, and more "Barks in the Park" than you can (ahem) shake a stick at. Designed to celebrate the bond between man and his best friend, these gatherings tend to revolve around the type of activities that you might expect: walks, races, Frisbee tosses, costume contests, trick competitions, parades, that sort of thing. Many also encourage the adoption of dogs from shelters and rescues, and promote the support of organizations, like the Humane Society, that are dedicated to the care and safety of pups.

Halfway around the world, the southern Chinese city of Yulin also hosts an annual summer festival dedicated to dogs. In Yulin, however, the festivalgoers travel from far and wide not to enjoy the company of dogs, but instead to enjoy the taste of them. An estimated 10,000 dogs are killed and eaten each year at the Yulin Lychee and Dog Meat Festival, a gathering that has drawn global ire from animal-rights organizations, Hollywood celebrities, and the various social-justice contingents of Twitter, Facebook, and Instagram. In spite of the protests, however, the festival persists: in the Dongkou meat markets of the city, rows of vendors continue to hang roasted dog carcasses from meat hooks, chopping them into individual cuts on open-air tables as customers place orders. In the produce markets downtown, in a scene that evokes a strange combination of PetSmart and a livestock market, people are still able to buy live dogs from the crammed kennels that line the streets for use in their own home cooking. And in restaurants and food stalls, diners can still readily find a range of dishes featuring dog meat as the central ingredient (the traditional offering: stewed dog with ginger, garlic, orange peel, bay leaves, and fennel).[1]

To Westerners, the thought (and images, if you wish—they're widely available online) of dogs being slaughtered, skinned, cooked, and eaten at the festival are likely to turn stomachs and spur feelings of moral objection. To the festivalgoers, on the other hand, the revulsion and moral objections of the West are merely cultural ethnocentrism. Indeed, setting aside the abhorrent conditions in which the dogs are kept at the Yulin festival, the actual butchering, cooking, and eating are little different than what a typical Westerner might encounter with respect to other animals at their local butcher, or at one of the many barbecue festivals that dot the American landscape every summer.

According to animal-rights groups, as many as 10 million dogs are consumed in China each year, with another 5 million consumed in Vietnam.[2] Studies place the number eaten annually in South Korea at around 2 million.[3] This is an incredible contrast to the United States, where the practice is virtually nonexistent and dogs are often treated as members of the family. Like incest, eating dog is a practice that many (probably most) Americans think of as both disgusting and morally wrong. In one study, participants objected to a family eating their dog for dinner even when the dog had been accidentally killed by a car in front of their house.[4] But *why* do many Americans find the thought of eating dog disgusting while many Chinese, Vietnamese, and South Koreans do not? Does dog meat really pose the type of pathogen and toxin threats we usually associate with disgust toward food? If so, then why aren't other cultures disgusted? If not, then why are we? And why the strong moral objections to dog as a potential food but not other foods that pose potential threats to our health, like rotten milk? And, if so many Americans hold such deep moral objections to eating dog, why isn't it illegal in every state?[5]

At this point, if we've done our job, you should have an understanding of both (a) the psychological scaffolding responsible for conscripting disgust into moral judgments and (b) the evolutionary explanations for why our psychology has developed along this trajectory. That is, you should have at least a loose grasp of both *why* and *how* we tend to make the leap from "gross" to "wrong." The generalized review: disgust originally evolved as a way to keep pathogens, toxins, and other harmful substances from entering our bodies. As happens so often in evolution, this mechanism was recruited for a secondary task—to discourage sexual behavior that might result in fitness-negative (or, at least, suboptimal) reproductive outcomes. Finally, once these mechanisms were in place, they were then "available" to be used in the service of the various norm generators, norm enforcers, and alliance-recruiting devices of our moral psychology.

From here on out, this book is about answering the question of *so what?* Specifically, the rest of the book is concerned with establishing a through-line that connects the judgments facilitated via these pathways to actual norms, taboos, and rules; in other words, to show that these disgust-linked moral intuitions do indeed manifest themselves in the law.

Now, there is nothing simple or tidy about how laws are made. The institutional process of generating and codifying rules, much like the psychological process of generating thoughts and feelings, is a messy compromise of interests. Traditional values are balanced against evolving mores. A fealty to precedent is balanced against a need to keep up with a changing world. The wishes of the voting majority are balanced against the Constitutional protections granted to those with less political power. Deference to lower courts is balanced against the need for appellate courts to get it right. Voters, legislators, judges, and other lawmakers may base their decisions on careful reflection and years of experience, but they may also be influenced by extraneous factors, such as how long it's been since their last meal.[6] In law, as in psychology, understanding causation is rarely as simple as a one-to-one mapping, or a first-this-then-that trajectory.

This is as true in our area of focus as it is with any other. It isn't always as easy as simply tracing "disgusting" to "wrong" to "illegal." We humans find lots of things disgusting—such as nose picking—that we don't necessarily perceive as morally wrong. We also moralize many things, such as drunk driving, that we don't find gross. Likewise, we consider numerous behaviors to be morally objectionable, such as infidelity, that are freely allowed by the law, whereas many legal rules—such as the prescription to drive on the right side of the road, as opposed to the left—are administrative in nature, not moral. Disgust doesn't always translate into moral objection, and moral objection doesn't always translate into law.

But sometimes they do. And when they do, the stakes can be quite high. To find examples, we needn't look far or constrain ourselves to obscure corners of the legal world. Instead, we can find evidence in several areas of high-profile jurisprudence, including obscenity law and other First Amendment issues, defamation law, evidence law, criminal law, criminal procedure, and Fourteenth Amendment issues revolving around privacy and equal-protection rights. As we'll see, the law is replete with proscriptions derived from low estimated values of consumption, contact, and sex: don't eat, don't touch, don't mate. But disgust's impact often extends well beyond these direct proscriptions, too, influencing which words and images we find offensive; affecting jurors' decisions of guilt and punishment; and feeding into the moralization tactics used in both social activism and acts of discrimination.

We will explore each in turn, but before we get there, we want to emphasize upfront that the many conflations of disgust and law that we will examine do not emanate from a single shared mechanism—psychological or legal. Instead, a multitude of combinations might produce the various laws and customs that we observe. Someone might, for example, wish to proscribe something that disgusts them because that something poses a direct threat of harm to that individual. People endorse sanitation codes that require restaurants to maintain certain levels of cleanliness and public defecation laws that prevent people from evacuating themselves on the street for obvious reasons: they don't want to risk getting sick while out to eat, or encountering excrement on their walk home. (California even went so far as to pass—and subsequently repeal—a law requiring bartenders to wear gloves.[7])

But people might also object to certain activities because, ancestrally, those activities posed an *indirect* threat of harm. To the extent that sex with an animal correlated with increased pathogen risks in the ancestral environment, preventing or discouraging an acquaintance within the group from engaging in such an act may have lessened the risk of illness or disease for you, too. As you'll see, many of the laws that have historically targeted homosexual behavior have also been extended to punish certain types of sexual activity between heterosexuals—for example, anal sex—that may have created an elevated pathogen risk or risk of contagion.

Along the same lines, for parents with children (or other genetic relatives), endorsing certain viewpoints and rules may have served to protect not just one's direct or indirect fitness, but one's inclusive fitness as well. To the extent that an objection to the handling of corpses was correlated with a decreased chance of your kin doing so (and, therefore, also correlated with their health), there is reason to expect such an inclination to flourish. To the extent that denouncing homosexual behavior was correlated with an increased chance of your children reproducing, there may have been incentive to select for such a stance.[8]

Further, some links between disgust and morality have nothing to do with preventing harm and everything to do with inflicting it. As we discussed, individuals might object to certain disgust-inducing practices—including those just listed, and even when they are not connected to you or to anyone in your social circle—because they serve as a coalitional signal, a way of catalyzing opposition toward an outside group, or of distancing you from that group. If I'm not gay, and neither are my relatives, and for that matter neither are my friends or allies, we now have a common aversion around which we can rally, and which we can use as an identifying characteristic for out-grouping, marginalization, and exploitation.

As we've outlined, disgust can work through social-value concepts of harm and care, through systems that index the desirability of certain persons or behaviors, and through moral-signaling mechanisms designed to both condemn and avoid condemnation. Laws, taboos, and moral choices might rely on any one of these mechanisms, none of them, or all of them. There are a host of ways in which we are predisposed to equate "gross" with "wrong" and along with them a host of avenues for those intuitions to exert influence over the process of making, deciding, and implementing law. Indeed, just as there are numerous ways in which disgust and morality can intertwine, there are also a variety of avenues by which the disgust–morality linkages can interact with the legal system. A voter might endorse a certain rule or, more commonly, a certain political representative who endorses a rule, that emanates from one of these linkages. A legislator might listen to their own disgust-tinged moral compass, or they might appeal to the intuitions of his base in order to get or retain their position. When a juror is deciding a case, or a judge is making law via judicial opinion, they too might be—subtly or obviously, consciously or unconsciously—influenced by any one or more of the psychological pathways by which "gross" becomes "wrong."

The chief point to glean is that, rather than a one-size-fits-all heuristic, there are instead a variety of psychological-condemnation devices that intermingle with disgust and that might influence, in a number of different ways, the various actors involved in the legal process. As we work our way through the avenues by which these devices become institutionalized, keep in mind that what you are seeing is not a singular dynamic, but rather a complex series of interactions between psychological processes with other psychological processes, between psychological processes and the various components of the legal apparatus, and among those legal components themselves.

Food taboos, at first glance, might seem a relatively straightforward application of the framework we've outlined. The logic of the application might go something like this: we have an evolved predisposition to avoid certain foods, or types of foods, that reliably posed threats in the ancestral milieu (in the technical sense, held low estimated values of consumption). Those foods, once disgusted, then became moralized—it was considered not just "gross" but also "wrong" to eat them. Such an intuition might not have been necessary for us to personally avoid eating those foods, but it may have helped friends and genetic relatives (who, for whatever reason, lacked the typical inclination) avoid them, and it might also have prevented other group members from getting sick (and, as a result, decreased the chances that we would be exposed to illness or disease). Moreover, to the extent that other groups, or individuals within the group, participated in eating these pathogen or toxin-rich foods, the disgust generated in response to their actions could have formed a rallying point to coordinate the marginalization of that group. As a consequence, because these moral intuitions would have been universal and widespread, it was only a short leap to their institutionalization in the form of a cultural or religious proscription.

And this rubric does indeed go far in explaining many of the food aversions that we observe across cultures. It aligns with the traditional explanation for why several cultures—and their incumbent religions—consider it taboo to eat pork, for example, which can harbor trichinosis and other masses of sickness-causing parasites.[9] It also helps explain why we find it socially unacceptable for children to drink alcohol, or for people to eat rancid food or their own excrement. There are subtler examples, too, such as the prohibitions many cultures have for eating uncooked food, or the taboos of Amazonian and coastal communities that prohibit eating piscivorous fish, which, because of their place high in the food pyramid, can be rich in contaminants and toxins.[10] In addition to the taboo of young children drinking alcohol, this explanation helps account for the moralization of other toxin-rich narcotics, such as cocaine and heroin,[11] a moralization that is not only used to stigmatize addicts but is also frequently marshalled in favor of antidrug policies and the criminalization of drugs.[12]

However, as encompassing as this disgust-to-morality-to-policy pathway is, it still cannot account for the vast array of food aversions that we observe around the globe. To begin with, many taboos focus on foods that have, all things considered, relatively *high* estimated values of consumption and that would be vital sources of nutrition for the societies that reject them. In fact, while humans tend to universally avoid some potential foods, such as excrement or rancid meat, many of the foods that are taboo in one culture are often embraced in many others. As the anthropologists Dan Fessler and Carlos Navarrete note with respect to the aversion toward pork, "it is not clear that the benefits [of avoiding potential pathogens/ toxins] outweigh the costs—if pork consumption is more harmful than helpful, why is it so common cross-culturally?"[13]

Indeed, Jews avoid pork but eat beef, Hindus avoid beef but eat chicken, the Matsigenka avoid chicken but eat fish, Somali clans avoid fish but drink milk, the Chinese avoid milk but eat dog, and so on.[14] If low consumption value were the *only* driving factor in food taboos, then we wouldn't expect to see the amount of variation, and apparent arbitrariness, between cultures that we some-times observe.

But the number of moving parts involved—both psychologically and societally—almost guarantees that we will see variations and exceptions to the pattern. Consider that exposure plays a large role in food aversions; studies show that we tend to avoid foods that other people within our group avoid, and there is a demonstrable link between disgust and novel (particularly novel *animal*) food products.[15] Consider in turn that there might be a host of reasons that certain groups are not exposed to foods. For the African pastoral herdsman that have taboos against eating fish (a Somali goat-herder insult: "speak not to me with a fish-eating mouth"), the lack of exposure to eating fish might be attributable to a simple lack of availability.[16] For Westerners who balk at the thought of eating dog, the lack of exposure to dog as a food is more likely due to the dog's traditional status as the family pet and, relatedly, the availability of other sources of meat.

Moreover, one group might initially prohibit a food commonly consumed by a rival group (e.g., a rival clan in traditional societies, or a competing religion in more contemporary societies) as a way of marking coalitional boundaries and emphasizing the "out-group" status of their rival—regardless of the particular food's consumption value. Once determined to be a marker of out-group status, people will uphold the immorality of consuming the particular food so as not to be associated with the out-group and thus shielding themselves from condemna-tion. Moreover, the effects of that prohibition now have the potential to cascade into our systems for aversion: a prohibition against a particular food item, for example, generally means less exposure, which in turn means an increased likeli-hood of experiencing disgust toward the food, which only strengthens the force of the prohibition and the disgust directed at the rival group. To wit, when asked why they consider certain foods taboo, many societies will—in a way reminiscent of Haidt's incest study—reply first that it is forbidden, then point to some feature of cuisine they find repugnant (such as the eating habits of the animal).[17] As Fessler and Navarrete note, "it appears that informants' initial explanations as to why some animal is not eaten is often simply 'It's disgusting!' "[18]

The point, which we will make here and will echo throughout the coming chap-ters, is that disgust plays an influential role in moral and legal affairs, but it does not do so in a uniform manner. For a bevy of reasons, people won't always agree on which things are disgusting, and even in the numerous cases when we do, there's no *guarantee* that those things become illegal. After all, despite the ubiquity of the dog meat taboo in America, it is legal to eat dog in all but a handful of states (though you can see how it easily could become illegal, given the right catalyst). Eating feces—a stronger and more ubiquitous taboo—is even less regulated.

Continuing the point, while food taboos are a widespread feature of human cul-tures, it is exceedingly rare for them to actually become codified law and receive the force of the state. Even where moral judgments are strong and unified, they often still play second fiddle to other interests, such as the strong American proclivity for autonomy (or, as Samuel Warren and Louis Brandeis phrased it, "the right to be let alone").[19] But variation does not equal randomness, and as you will see, the lack of procedural uniformity belies a consistent underlying phenomenon: disgust, through a range of interconnected and overlapping channels, exerts a powerful moral sway that constantly and pervasively materializes in legal affairs.

Obscenity

Near the beginning of his famous "Seven Dirty Words" routine, the comedian George Carlin proclaims that "no one has ever gone to jail for screaming 'topography.'"[1] Which appears to be true—we looked, and though we would have loved to have been able to report that someone had gone to jail for screaming "topography," we came up empty. But *some* words can get you thrown into jail, or arrested, or fined. In the United States, for example, the Federal Communications Commission (FCC) has issued millions of dollars of fines to radio and television broadcasters for airing indecent content (before Howard Stern moved to satellite radio, his show alone amassed more than $2 million in FCC fines to radio licensees),[2] and performers from Lenny Bruce, to 2 Live Crew, to Mae West and Jim Morrison have all been arrested for the language they've used. The First Amendment of the Constitution guarantees the right to free speech, but it does not guarantee the right to *all* speech—there are exceptions to the rule, instances in which the government can limit what you can say (or write, or display, or any of the many communicative media considered "speech" under the First Amendment). The government may prohibit, for example, defamatory speech, or speech that has the capacity to incite an imminent violent response. Likewise, the First Amendment offers no quarter for speech or expression that is considered "obscenity."

The difficult part, of course, comes in delineating exactly what is considered obscenity. For decades the Supreme Court wrestled with pinning down a clear definition. Justice Potter Stewart characterized the task as attempting to "define what may be indefinable"[3] and Justice Hugo Black similarly objected to "saddling this Court with the irksome and inevitably unpopular and unwholesome task of finally deciding by a case-by-case, sight-by-sight personal judgment of the members of this Court what . . . is too hard core for people to see or read."[4] But in 1973 the Court, in *Miller v. California*, settled on a standard that, more or less, remains the applicable standard today. The *Miller* Court established a set of three criteria for determining whether or not something is obscene: (a) whether the average person, applying contemporary community standards, would find that the work, taken as a whole, appeals to the prurient interest, (b) whether the work depicts or describes, in a patently offensive way, sexual conduct specifically defined by the applicable state law, and (c) whether the work, taken as a whole, lacks serious literary, artistic, political, or scientific value.[5]

What do these criteria mean, beyond their plain language? Well, some of them come with further guidance. The Supreme Court, in a previous case, defined the word "prurient" in a footnote as "material having a tendency to excite lustful thoughts." The footnote went on to specify that the dictionary definition of prurient included "Itching; longing; uneasy with desire or longing; of persons, having itching morbid or lascivious longings; of desire, curiosity, or propensity, lewd."[6] Luther Campbell, the lead singer of the rap group 2 Live Crew and a fixture of obscenity jurisprudence, paraphrased the test of prurience as simply asking "does it turn you on?"—which isn't that far off.[7] But in 1985 the Supreme Court clarified that prurient is not simply material meant to excite *lustful* thoughts, but rather "that which appeals to a shameful or morbid interest in sex."[8]

The "contemporary community standards" component is generally applied at a local (as opposed to national) level. This means that the court or the jury is tasked with first defining the relevant local community—which can be as small as a rural community in South Dakota, or as large as a state such as California or Texas—and then asking whether the average person in such community would find that the material both applies to the prurient interest *and* does so by depicting sexual conduct in a patently offensive way.

What, then, does it mean to depict sexual conduct in a "patently offensive way"? In *Miller*, the Court did not require states to use a uniform definition of "patently offensive," but the Justices did offer that this requirement could be satisfied by, for example, "[p]atently offensive representations or descriptions" of two different types of conduct: (a) ultimate sexual acts, normal or perverted, actual or simulated, or (b) masturbation, excretory functions, and lewd exhibition of the genitals.[9] Several states have included other sexual acts not specifically mentioned by the *Miller* Court, such as sadomasochism and bestiality, in the category of "patently offensive" behavior as well.[10]

Speech that falls under these definitions and satisfies all three criteria of the *Miller* obscenity standard is essentially fair game for restriction; the First Amendment offers no protection for obscenity, and so government regulatory bodies can ban the sale and distribution of obscene materials outright. This reaches books, music, movies, magazines, television, dancing or other performances, standup comedy, and paintings or other artwork. Whereas early obscenity trials typically involved magazines such as *American Aphrodite* ("A Quarterly for the Fancy Free") or books such as *Ulysses* or *Lady Chatterley's Lover*, the archetypal modern federal case revolves around deciding whether or not a web-based pornographic movie is hard-core enough to amount to the level of obscene.

But obscenity is not the only type of offensive speech that governmental authorities have the authority to curb. The FCC also has the authority to regulate the broadcast of speech considered "indecency" and "profanity." Unlike obscenity, which can be banned completely, indecency and profanity are entitled to *some* protection by the First Amendment: they may only be restricted on broadcast radio and television during daytime hours—6 a.m. to 10 p.m. The rationale here is, generally, that while indecency and profanity are not as bad as obscenity, they may still be restricted from being broadcast into people's homes and onto public airwaves during certain hours when children might be exposed to them. Profanity is defined by the FCC as "language so grossly offensive to members of the public who actually hear it as to amount to a nuisance." Indecency is defined as "material that, in context, depicts or describes sexual or excretory activities or organs in terms patently offensive as measured by contemporary community standards for the broadcast medium."[11]

Looking at these different definitions in the aggregate allows us to illustrate two points that are central to our overall argument. The first point is that, by and large, obscenity, indecency, and profanity are, on a case-by-case basis, determined using instinct and intuition. Though state statutes and subsequent case law have helped to flesh out some of the different standards for restricted speech, judges and jurors are generally left to supply their own meanings of *shameful, morbid, average person, contemporary community standards,* of what might *excite lustful thoughts,* and of what might reach the level of *prurient* or *patently offensive.* In other words, the criterion for identifying a *patently offensive representation* is often simply whether the representation patently offends.

This is important because it illustrates a portal by which moral intuitions are shepherded into a legal standard. That is, a psychological instinct becomes *nested* within a legal rule, so that when the judge or jury is trying to evaluate whether a particular legal rule is satisfied, what they are ultimately doing is consulting an intuition, and often a subconsciously generated one at that. As a result, explaining and predicting what type of material or conduct falls within the purview of a legal rule—here, explaining why certain material might be considered shameful or prurient or patently offensive and, hence, obscene—requires an investigation into and understanding of the psychological machinery that is generating those ultimate intuitions.

Which brings us to the second point illustrated by these various definitions. One might think that a legal rule that regresses to individual intuitions of offensiveness could produce widely variant interpretations of obscenity, echoing Justice Harlan's famous assertion that "one man's vulgarity is another's lyric."[12] And while it is true that different schools of thought might differ over what speech, in general, should be curbed by the law, that question is a different question—a much broader and more complicated question—than the question that the Court has ultimately hinged the determination of obscenity on, which is whether or not certain content *offends*. And to that end, there is a large body of ethnographic evidence that demonstrates a surprising consistency—both within and between cultures—as to what types of words and images we find deeply offensive: they often overlap with the objects we find disgusting.

By surveying the Court's definitions of obscenity, indecency, and profanity, we can see that the content that our legal system has specifically singled out for proscription falls into one of two general categories: excretion or sex. But not *just* sex: the words used by the different standards suggest a bias against nontraditional, non-reproductive sexual content—*shameful, morbid, prurient, patently offensive, lewd.* Not coincidentally, excretion and nontraditional sexual conduct are disgust-survey staples and also happen to overlap with our two facets of disgust—excretion being a primary elicitor of contact/consumption-based disgust, and many of the triggers of sexual disgust being commonly slotted into a category of prurient, patently offensive, lewd, shameful, or morbid.

We'll get to some more specific examples shortly, but the major idea to grasp at the outset is that prohibited speech provides a nice window onto how disgust feeds into systems of norm generation: the words or images that reference objects we have evolved to feel disgust toward often overlap with the words or images that become socially taboo and, as a result, the words or images that tend to become legally proscribed. And, as the various legal standards outlined above show, this phenomenon is permitted and maintained by two forces: (1) via judges and lawmakers who single out disgust-eliciting content (excretion and nontraditional sexual conduct) for proscription, and (2) via an infrastructure set up to institutionalize individual and community intuitions of offensive speech—speech that frequently overlaps with intuitions derived from psychological adaptations governing social value and what to eat, what to touch, and whom to fornicate with. In other words, the speech we find disgusting.

We don't want to overstate our case; speech might be considered obscene or offensive but not necessarily disgusting. In fact the most high-profile incident of indecency—the FCC's attempt to fine CBS for Janet Jackson's baring of her breast during the Super Bowl halftime show—concerns conduct that might be considered inappropriate for a number of reasons, but not necessarily because it is disgusting. Likewise, not all words or images that people find disgusting would they also think obscene or offensive. The word "moist" (which might conjure pathogen or sexual associations, or both) routinely tops lists of the most disgusting words, but it isn't likely to engender an FCC fine anytime soon.[13] Still, speech showcasing or referring to the things we find disgusting tends to make up a noteworthy proportion of the things that come to be deemed obscene, indecent, or profane.

THE WORDS YOU CAN'T SAY ON TELEVISION

To make these abstract claims more concrete, let's take a look at one high-profile example of how disgust, moral norms, and laws regulating speech intertwine: taboo language. And George Carlin's famous list of the seven words you can't say on television is as good a place to start as any, as this list was the impetus for *Federal Communications Commission v. Pacifica Foundation*, the 1978 Supreme Court case establishing the regulation of indecency in broadcasting.[14] We should note upfront that his list is not black-letter law; the actual standards for what you can say on broadcast television depend, on a case-by-case basis, on whether the use of the word rises to the level of indecent or obscene. That being said, most of the terms included in Carlin's inventory still probably constitute indecency, and some even obscenity, and they nicely illustrate how words make the journey from disgusting to taboo to legally proscribed.

In one version of his routine, Carlin begins by musing about the mysteriousness of taboo words: "They are just words that we have decided, sort of decided, not to use all the time. That's about the only thing you can say about them for sure."[15] And the nature of taboo words, at first glance, does seem arbitrary. After all, they're just words. So why this one and not that one? Why one version of a word but not another? We think that one of the keys (but certainly not the only key) to finding some pattern in the words we won't say can be found in the objects to which those words refer.

To wit, according to Carlin, the seven words you can't say on television are: shit, piss, fuck, cunt, cocksucker, motherfucker, and tits. Of the seven words, all are either sexual or excretory in nature. Two refer directly to excretion, two to sexual organs, one to the act of sex, one to incest, and the last to sodomy. All refer to items that have documented disgust-eliciting properties: either pathogen presence (in the case of "shit," "piss," and "cunt") or disgust-eliciting sexual behaviors (in the case of the sodomitic "cocksucker," the incest-referencing "motherfucker," or the callously indifferent "fuck"). "Tits" doesn't fit quite as nicely, at least on first appearance, though, much like "fuck" and perhaps "cunt," "tits" evokes the notion that the person to which they are attached is of low social value.

By way of example, rare is the case when someone will use the word "fuck" to refer to a mutually enjoyable, reproductively aimed act of tender love performed by a husband and wife. Usually, when referring to the act, "fuck" carries with it the implication that *at least one* of these elements is missing. For example, "fuck" may refer to sex with a committed, exclusive partner, but with a licentious undertone suggesting a particularly carnal or deviant episode. Or, it might refer to regular sexual intercourse, but in a casual or illicit context, such as with a stranger, for a one-night stand, or with a nonexclusive partner in an affair. "Fuck" is also sometimes used with a suggestion of callousness, or of extracting pleasure without regard to the happiness—or social value—of the other participant. In common parlance, people say *we* had sex, or *we* slept together, or *we* made love, for example, indicating a joint endeavor, but conversely might more often say something like *I* fucked him, or *he* fucked her, suggesting the act as something one does *to* another person. It is a rare thing indeed for a fellow, having taken a newly acquainted female companion home the previous night, to have a confidant inquire of him the next day: "So, did you make love to her?"

In the same way, "tits" and "cunt" are crass suggestions of low or unimportant social value. It's also likely that sex differences exist in the level of disgust evoked by these words, or that men and women might find them disgusting or offensive for different reasons. This difference in opinion is to be expected precisely because of the different male and female psychologies associated with casual sex. Women might find "fuck," "cunt," and "tits" more disgusting than men because they suggest callousness or one-time use—a lease, not a mortgage. Carlin (a man), on the other hand, dismisses "tits" as lightweight fare: "you know it doesn't belong on that list. I mean, it really doesn't belong with that heavyweight filth."[16] And the psychologist Steven Pinker offers, from a male point of view, that the disgust associated with the word "cunt" is less about its derogatory undertones and instead "becomes less mysterious if one imagines the connotations in an age before tampons, toilet paper, regular bathing, and antifungal drugs."[17]

Indeed, in his own chapter on dirty words, Pinker points to the research of Valerie Curtis and Adam Biran, as well as the research of linguists Keith Allan and Kate Burridge, in noting the three-way correlation between the effluvial substances we find disgusting, their capacity for causing disease, and the offensiveness of the words describing them.[18] Generally, the greater the capacity for disease, the more disgusting we find the substance, and the more offensive we find the word referring to the substance: shit is worse than piss, which is worse than fart, which is worse than snot, which is worse than spit.

Our contentions become even more persuasive when we compare the words we proscribe and find taboo against the words proscribed in different cultures. Across the globe, words referring to these same objects of disgust repeatedly crop up in lists of taboo or prohibited speech. Though the actual words may differ, the objects to which they refer frequently include (a) words referencing pathogen indicators (feces, urine, blood, pus, disease), and (b) words referencing non-reproductive or fitness-reducing sexual partners or acts (prostitution, incest, sodomy). Recently, for example, Vladimir Putin signed legislation banning the words *khuy* (cock), *pizda* (cunt), *ebat'* (to fuck), and *blyad* (whore) from use in movies, television, theaters, and the media,[19] and the Central Board of Film Certification of India circulated a list of banned words (later withdrawn under protest) that included Hindi versions of English curses, such as *madarchod* (motherfucker) and *raand* (slut), as well as the novel-but-congruous *bhenchod* (sisterfucker) and *chutia* (slang from *chutiya*, meaning "one who lives on the earnings of his wife's prostitution").[20]

Though we Americans seem to single out references to sexually related pathogen carriers, many cultures place taboos on words referencing other pathogen outlets, such as the British *bloody* or the Colombian *chucha* (referring to an offensive body odor). The language writer James Harbeck has pointed out that several cultures have a special aversion to words referencing disease.[21] The Polish, Dutch, and Thai each have swearwords relating to cholera, and the Dutch also consider it an extreme insult to wish cancer on someone. Similarly, there is a taboo phrase in the Nigerian Igbo for wishing leprosy on a person.[22] Going one step further, many cultures have bred particularly potent insults by fusing a sexual act or organ (most commonly a vagina) with a pathogen- or disease-connoting property, such as the Finnish *vittu tätä paskaa* (fuck this shit), the Hindi *bhosdike* (born from a rotten vagina), the Dutch *kankerkut* (cancer vagina), the Hokkien insult *kàn ni na* (fuck your mother's smelly cunt), or the Cuban insult *me cago en el coño de tu madre* (I shit in your mother's cunt).

Again, it is neither necessary nor sufficient for a word to elicit disgust in order to become taboo. Like all of the areas of law we will discuss, disgust often plays a significant role in shaping norms, taboos, and laws, but it certainly does not hold a monopoly on the practice. There are many individual psychological mechanisms and group-level cultural processes that contribute to the formation of language taboos, and many of the words that become verboten—such as, for instance, religious curses and blasphemous exclamations (e.g., *to hell with you, go to hell, damn you, God damn it*) have nothing to do with either prurient sex or excretion. (Though, once a group, such as the church, is in power and has a firm grasp on the moral majority, the acts the group condemns can then pattern individual moral consciences: to the extent you can be punished, exploited, or ostracized for something you say, the more likely you will find, or at least profess to find, such speech morally wrong. And the fact that a particular behavior is now tagged as morally wrong makes it more likely that the rhetoric of disgust will be recruited to signal one's allegiance to the rule. So utterances that do not in and of themselves cue low values of consumption, contact, or sex might still be rendered disgusting via a back door.[23])

Other mysteries prevail, such as the processes by which our linguistic and moral faculties draw lines between different words that refer to the same object, some of which offend and disgust, others of which do not (e.g., *cock* vs. *penis*, or *piss* vs. *urine*). And words fall in and out of moral favor over time and might be considered disgusting or offensive within one group and relatively tame within another—the relative ease of use of *cunt* in England would probably be jarring to an unwary American, for example. The point is simply that disgust plays a recurrent, meaningful role in these processes and very often serves as a psychological lodestar in the formation of these taboos.

The patterns we observe with taboo language and its overlap with elicitors of disgust are also easily extended to the realm of images and movies. Take, for example, the photograph titled *Immersion*, or *Piss Christ*, by Andres Serrano (Fig. 10.1), which depicts a crucifix submerged in Serrano's urine (and highlighting key colors in disgust's palette). While never ruled "obscene," this image was nonetheless a hugely controversial piece both in the United States and abroad. In the dismissal of a suit by the Catholic Church against the National Gallery of Victoria for its planned display of *Piss Christ*, the judge first noted the aesthetic beauty of the piece ("It shows the crucified Christ as if enveloped in a mist which is infused with the colours of a red and gold sunset. Of itself, it is not only inoffensive, but might be thought to be a reverent treatment of a sacred symbol of the Christian Church") before explaining why such a beautiful piece might be controversial:

> This is entirely understandable. The title "Piss Christ" provides one reason why. The account of its creation provides another. The crucifix was, according to the artist, immersed in urine when the photograph was taken. In other words, the person who for Christians is the son of God and the founder of their church, is shown immersed in excrement.[24]

Excrement often also plays a role in the most common contemporary obscenity case: the decision of whether or not a pornographic movie—typically one sold or distributed via the internet—is hard-core enough to amount to the level of obscene. As you might predict, the types of films at issue involve the same types of disgust-inducing depictions of excretion or nontraditional sexual practices (or

Figure 10.1. *Piss Christ*, Andres Serrano, 1987.
Courtesy of the artist and Nathalie Obadia gallery.

both) that we observed with taboo language. Recently prosecuted pornographic movies include, for example, *Ass Munchers, Filthy Things 6, Mako's First Time Scat, Scat Fist Fucking 2, Doggie3Some, Extreme Tit Torture 18, Breaking of Crista, Anal Doggie and Horse, Ragtime Red*, and *Gang Bang Horse Pony Sex Game*.[25]

But these examples—like the examples of taboo language—provide only *implicit* evidence for our contention, and while it would be difficult to reconcile this pattern with any other explanation, it would nonetheless strengthen our case if we could find explicit evidence, too. That is, since the world of prohibited speech is largely judge-made law, we should be able to find overt instances of courts discussing the relationship between disgust, morality, and the speech we choose to proscribe.

FROM THE HORSE'S MOUTH

In 2011, the Supreme Court decided *Brown v. Entertainment Merchants Association*, which established that videogames, like other, older, more established media of communication, were entitled to First Amendment protection as speech.

In striking down a California law prohibiting the sale or rental of "violent video games" to minors, the Court, in an opinion authored by Justice Antonin Scalia, explicitly decreed that "disgust is not a valid basis for restricting expression."[26] But this ostensibly unequivocal assertion isn't as definitive as it sounds. For one thing, Scalia was addressing disgust in reaction to *violence* in the videogames, not with respect to sex or excretion, the traditional categories of obscenity (violence has never received the same level of scrutiny by either Courts or the general populace of the United States that other forms of offensive conduct have).[27] For another, the extensive body of prior case law dealing with prohibited speech tells a slightly different story.

Whether they should or not, courts routinely conflate the ideas of disgust, morality, and obscenity in their opinions. In fact, in their evaluations of whether or not speech constituted obscenity, several Supreme Court decisions have cited the dictionary definition of obscene, which includes a component of disgust. The Court in the 1962 case *Manual Enterprises, Inc. v. Day* notes that the first definition of obscenity in Webster's dictionary was (at that time) "[o]ffensive to taste; foul; loathsome; disgusting."[28] And the Court in *Miller*, attempting to distinguish pornography from obscenity, goes into a lengthy footnote discussion of the etymology of the word *obscene*, noting that it is derived "from the Latin *obscaenus, ob*, to, plus *caenum*, filth" and citing multiple dictionary definitions that include the phrases "disgusting to the senses" and "[o]ffensive to the senses, or to taste or refinement, disgusting, repulsive, filthy, foul, abominable, loathsome."[29]

The US Court of Appeals for the Fourth Circuit, in a case concerning the interstate transportation of obscene films, explicitly addresses the relationship between the standard for obscenity and disgust in noting that "[t]he effect upon less susceptible persons must be put in the balance. As the offensiveness requirement in the *Miller* test is more than minimally met, however, the greater the number of people who would react to the material with revulsion and disgust."[30] Likewise, the US District Court for the Eastern District of Pennsylvania, in evaluating whether or not a mailing called "The Housewife's Handbook on Selective Promiscuity" rose to the level of obscenity, also explicitly addresses disgust:

> The Handbook, standing bare of any socially redeeming value, is a patent offense to the most liberal morality. The descriptions leave nothing to the imagination, and in detail, in a clearly prurient manner offend, degrade and sicken anyone however healthy his mind was before exposure to this material. It is a gross shock to the mind and chore to read. Pruriency and disgust coalesce here creating a perfect example of hardcore pornography.[31]

And here is the Supreme Court itself, in the *Miller* decision, lamenting the difficulty of disentangling these concepts:

> The impossibility of defining the precise line between permissible uncertainty in statutes caused by describing crimes by words well understood through long use in the criminal law—obscene, lewd, lascivious, filthy,

indecent or disgusting—and the unconstitutional vagueness that leaves a person uncertain as to the kind of prohibited conduct—massing stories to incite crime—has resulted in three arguments of this case in this Court. The legislative bodies in draftsmanship obviously have the same difficulty as do the judicial in interpretation.[32]

The sheer frequency with which courts refer to obscene material as "filth" or some similar euphemism demonstrates just how deep-seated the conflation of disgust, morality, and obscenity can be. Here, for example, is an excerpt from a 1977 opinion by the Supreme Court of Utah, reviewing a conviction for exhibiting an obscene motion picture at an adult theater:

The motion picture exhibited revealed an entirely naked man and woman in various acts of sodomy (fellatio, cunnilingus, buggery) and adultery all shown with close-up camera photography.

A more sickening, disgusting, depraved showing cannot be imagined. However, certain justices of the Supreme Court of the United States have said that before a matter can be held to be obscene, it must be ". . . when taken as a whole, lacks serious literary, artistic, political, or scientific value."

Some state judges, acting the part of sycophants, echo that doctrine. It would appear that such an argument ought only to be advanced by depraved, mentally deficient, mind-warped queers. Judges who seek to find technical excuses to permit such pictures to be shown under the pretense of finding some intrinsic value to it are reminiscent of a dog that returns to his vomit in search of some morsel in the filth which may have some redeeming value to his own taste. If those judges have not the good sense and decency to resign from their positions as judges, they should be removed either by impeachment or by the vote of the decent people of their constituency.[33]

Note the use of disgust as moral signal as well as moral spotlight. And even more flamboyantly, here is a dissent from *Commonwealth v. Robin*, a 1966 case from the Pennsylvania Supreme Court ruling that the state could not stop a bookseller and publisher from selling the book *Tropic of Cancer* by Henry Miller:

The decision of the Majority of the Court in this case has dealt a staggering blow to the forces of morality, decency and human dignity in the Commonwealth of Pennsylvania. If, by this decision, a thousand rattlesnakes had been let loose, they could not do as much damage to the well-being of the people of this state as the unleashing of all the scorpions and vermin of immorality swarming out of that volume of degeneracy called "The Tropic of Cancer." Policemen, hunters, constables and foresters could easily and quickly kill a thousand rattlesnakes but the lice, lizards, maggots and gangrenous roaches scurrying out from beneath the covers of "The Tropic of Cancer" will enter into the playground, the study desks, the cloistered confines of children and immature minds to eat away moral resistance and wreak damage and harm which may blight countless lives for years and decades to come. . . .

Then the defendants say that "Cancer" is entitled to immunity under the First Amendment because court decisions have declared that only worthless trash may be proscribed as obscene. To say that "Cancer" is worthless trash is to pay it a compliment. "Cancer" is the sweepings of the Augean stables, the stagnant bilge of the slimiest mudscow, the putrescent corruption of the most noisome dump pile, the dreggiest filth in the deepest morass of putrefaction. . . .

"Cancer" is not a book. It is a cesspool, an open sewer, a pit of putrefaction, a slimy gathering of all that is rotten in the debris of human depravity. And in the center of all this waste and stench, besmearing himself with its foulest defilement, splashes, leaps, cavorts and wallows a bifurcated specimen that responds to the name of Henry Miller. One wonders how the human species could have produced so lecherous, blasphemous, disgusting and amoral a human being as Henry Miller. One wonders why he is received in polite society.[34]

Of course, these last two excerpts are extreme examples. Of these opinions, one (Salt Lake City) has been overruled, and the other is a dissent, so neither are binding precedent. But they nonetheless illustrate just how entangled, especially at the margins, the concepts of disgust, morality, and law can become.

I KNOW IT WHEN I SEE IT

Obscenity law provides a tidy microcosm for our theory, an illustration for how disgust becomes institutionalized. In crafting laws proscribing (or allowing the proscription of) obscenity, indecency, and profanity, judges have relied heavily on intuition, both in how they've specified the general categories of content that should be considered obscene, and in crafting standards that require future decision-makers to consult their own instincts in considering whether individual cases of such content rise to the level of obscene. Again, this reliance on intuition is frequently blind. That is, the different actors don't know where those intuitions come from, and sometimes aren't even aware that they are relying on them. Nevertheless, insight into the speech we find offensive can be found in our systems for aversion: the words or images that wind up being prohibited often track the words or images we find disgusting.

We want to make a point here that even though we've selected colorful passages to illustrate our arguments, the examples we've chosen are not cherry-picked outliers with regard to the principles they convey. We don't think, for example, that it is a particularly novel or controversial claim that decisions of the offensiveness of speech are guided by hidden intuitive processes. In one of the most famous phrases in the history of the Supreme Court, for example, Justice Potter Stewart explicitly articulates this contention. In his concurrence attempting to delimit the bounds of "hard-core pornography," Justice Stewart opined that "I shall not today attempt to further define the kinds of material I understand to be embraced within that shorthand description; and perhaps I could never succeed in intelligibly doing so. But I know it when I see it, and the motion picture involved in this case is not that."[35]

To the extent that we *are* advancing a novel claim, it is about the particular unconscious psychological mechanisms that generate such intuitions, and the role that disgust plays in those processes. More specifically, that individual estimates of the value of engaging in particular acts dictate levels of intuitive aversion, which, when elevated, serve as a beacon to our moral trawlers that are searching for candidate norms. In truth, it's difficult to reconcile the body of obscenity law with *any other* broader theory of speech proscription. By limiting the definitions of prohibited speech to excretion and prurient sexual content, courts have essentially foreclosed the option of relying on any rationale that does not include a disgust component. That being said, to some, this still might seem an unobjectionable method of deciding rules. After all, if we've decided that we are going to ban *some* speech based on the unpleasantness it causes the listener, why not draw that line at the things that conjure disgust? In later chapters, we'll make a thorough case for why disgust is an inadequate rubric, but for now consider the following.

In each case in which the Supreme Court upholds a law restricting speech, it means carving out an exception that contradicts the explicit language ("Congress shall make no law . . . abridging the freedom of speech") of the foremost amendment of the Constitution. The Supreme Court is exceedingly cautious about granting such exceptions, and the limited exceptions they do grant—obscenity, fraud, defamation, incitement, speech integral to criminal conduct—generally include both a component of harm and of a history and tradition of proscription.

The harm component of obscenity, though, is much more ambiguous than the other categories of prohibited speech. Unlike fraud, defamation, incitement, or speech integral to criminal conduct, all of which involve a reputational, monetary, or physical manifestation of harm, the "harm" caused by obscenity is a type of psychological harm—a subjective state of unpleasantness. This raises the question: If we are truly worried about psychological harm, why single out excretion and prurient sexual material? Though words like "motherfucker" and "cocksucker" undoubtedly cause displeasure to many who hear them, surely they do not inflict the type of harm on the listener—or for that matter, on society—that the words "nigger" or "faggot" have the potential to do. Why provide constitutional protection for the latter, but not the former? If we single out the psychological harm of obscenity because of a historical tradition of prohibiting obscene speech (and not other types, such as derogatory insults), then perhaps it is time to take a closer look at that tradition, and ask whether the psychological mechanisms promoting that tradition are the type of ideals that we truly wish to codify. By taking a critical look at *why* certain speech has traditionally been proscribed, or *why* we find certain words or images unpleasant—essentially, why "we know it when we see it"—we can approach the task of deciding what speech to ban (or not) with a clearer framework for evaluation.

Disgust as Moral Weapon

In *A Moveable Feast*, Ernest Hemingway describes meeting the painter Wyndham Lewis for the first time, on a spring afternoon in Paris:

> Wyndham Lewis wore a wide black hat, like a character in the quarter, and was dressed like someone out of *La Bohème*. He had a face that reminded me of a frog, not a bullfrog but just any frog, and Paris was too big a puddle for him . . . I watched Lewis carefully without seeming to look at him, as you do when you are boxing, and I do not think I had ever seen a nastier-looking man. Some people show evil as a great racehorse shows breeding. They have the dignity of a hard *chancre*. Lewis did not show evil; he just looked nasty.
>
> Walking home I tried to think what he reminded me of and there were various things. They were all medical except toe-jam and that was a slang word. I tried to break his face down and describe it but I could only get the eyes. Under the black hat, when I had first seen them, the eyes had been those of an unsuccessful rapist.[1]

By our count, Hemingway compares Lewis, either directly or indirectly, to at least five different objects intended to elicit our disgust, summoning impressions of bad hygiene, a slimy amphibian, bodily discharge/excrement, toe-jam, and sexual assault (and a failed sexual assault, at that). This isn't even counting Hemingway's allusion to a "hard chancre" (an infectious lesion typically associated with syphilis) or his assertion that he had never seen a "nastier-looking" man. It's obvious that Hemingway doesn't care for Lewis, but why is he so heavy-handed with the disgust imagery? What is he trying to do here? Without being able to ask him, our best guess is that he is unwittingly operationalizing our theory, putting the quirks of our psychological machinery for disgust to use to make us dislike Lewis as much as he does.

So far we've taken a look at which things we find disgusting, and why. We've also seen how the convergence of our psychological systems for disgust and morality can unconsciously engineer a leap from the descriptive to the normative, from "gross" to "wrong." In this chapter, we'll look at how, even if humans haven't *explicitly* understood the mechanics of these systems, we've nonetheless exploited this descriptive-to-proscriptive link for quite some time by using disgust to trigger moral condemnation.

The archetypal use of this technique is by authors—like Hemingway—and other artists looking to engineer an audience's disapproval of a character. It is a tried-and-true device for storytellers: to make villains seem bad, simply make them disgusting. Give them festering sores, contemptible manners, layers of fat or gaunt bones, odious smells and other emetic qualities that allude to disease, decay, poor health, bodily or facial asymmetries, or bad hygiene. Vladimir Nabokov, relishing the author's power to do such a thing, wrote: "The twinkle in the author's eye as he notes the imbecile drooping of a murderer's underlip, or watches the stumpy forefinger of a professional tyrant exploring a profitable nostril in the solitude of his sumptuous bedroom, this twinkle is what punishes your man more surely than the pistol of a tiptoeing conspirator."[2] From Shakespeare's Richard III (a "diffused infection of a man," a "poisonous bunch-back'd toad" and a "lump of foul deformity")[3] to J. K. Rowling's Lord Voldemort ("with wide, livid scarlet eyes and a nose that was flat as a snake's with slits for nostrils")[4] and nearly every monster in every horror story in between—as long as writers have been writing stories, they have been prejudicing the social value attached to their villains by loading them with disgust.

Consider the propensity of Charles Dickens to paint each of his antagonists with a collection of repulsive traits. Daniel Quilp in The Old Curiosity Shop is "so low in stature as to be quite a dwarf, though his head and face were large enough for the body of a giant" with "a grotesque expression," "discoloured fangs that were yet scattered in his mouth," and fingernails that "were crooked, long, and yellow."[5] Fagin in Oliver Twist is described as "a very old shriveled Jew, whose villainous-looking and repulsive face was obscured by a quantity of matted red hair . . . dressed in a greasy flannel gown."[6] Uriah Heep, in David Copperfield, is sullied with "a cadaverous face . . . whose hair was cropped as close as the closest stubble; who had hardly any eyebrows, and no eyelashes, and eyes of a red-brown, so unsheltered and unshaded, that I remember wondering how he went to sleep."[7] And when Pip meets Miss Havisham in Great Expectations, he observes that

> Once, I had been taken to see some ghastly waxwork at the Fair, representing I know not what impossible personage lying in state. Once, I had been taken to one of our old marsh churches to see a skeleton in the ashes of a rich dress that had been dug out of a vault under the church pavement. Now waxwork and skeleton seemed to have dark eyes that moved and looked at me. I should have cried out, if I could.[8]

Long before we actually observe the behavior of any of these characters, their wickedness is foreshadowed in Dickens' descriptions. We're against them before they've ever done anything wrong. Heep's cloying, his reptilian writhing, his "umble" servility, all serve to index his social value and predispose us to his coming treachery. Fagin's darker side is likewise portended in everything from his appearance to the way he moves: "As he glided stealthily along, creeping beneath the shelter of the walls and doorways, the hideous old man seemed like some loathsome reptile, engendered in the slime and darkness through which he moved: crawling forth, by night, in search of some rich offal for a meal."[9]

Dickens happened to favor gruesome physical features for his villains, but plenty of other authors rely on sexual disgust to do the trick, too. In *Lolita*, Nabokov, in what is perhaps the most disgusting sentence ever written in literature, combines both pathogen and sexual disgust to thoroughly vilify his antagonist Humbert Humbert. In the story, Humbert, after repeatedly attempting to coerce his underage stepdaughter—who also happens to be feverishly ill and barely lucid—into having sex with him that night, gives up only after observing that "Her brown rose tasted of blood."[10] Therefore, without actually using any words that would be offensive in isolation, Nabokov manages to taint his character with allusions to incest, pedophilia, rape, sodomy, sickness, blood, and feces—all in the span of a mere six words.

The next time you read a novel or watch a movie, pay attention to the villain and look for one of the many disgust-activating characteristics that we often subconsciously attach a value judgment to: a physical deformity (Richard III, Quilp, the Cyclops, Long John Silver, Captain Hook); scarring or other skin conditions (Harvey Dent, Tony Montana, Number 1, Freddy Krueger); slimy, green, or serpentine features (Heep, Fagin, the Wicked Witch of the West, the Grinch, Medusa); obesity (Jabba the Hutt, Kasper Gutman); gauntness (Miss Havisham, Mrs. Sliderskew, Gollum, Cruella de Vil); cannibalism (Dracula, Hannibal Lecter); or incestuous or other atypical sexual tendencies (Humbert Humbert, Jezebel, Cersei and Jamie Lannister). It's a quick and easy psychological heuristic that artists can use to exploit the disgust system and stack the deck against their antagonists. As exceptions that prove the rule, stories like *Beauty and the Beast, The Phantom of the Opera*, and *The Hunchback of Notre Dame* succeed by flipping this psychological trap on its head and having off-putting characters do good things. Because we're predisposed to use "gross" as shorthand for "bad," we are surprised when our expectations are upended and the Beast, the Phantom, and Quasimodo end up being virtuous characters.

DISGUST FOR A CAUSE

Now, why does this little technique matter, in the grand scheme of things? Why do the evocative tools used by storytellers matter from a larger, societal perspective? The reason is that this tactic—using the imagery of disgust to prejudice value judgments—is not just a favorite of raconteurs; it has also been an effective tool for social, political, and legal activists as well. Unlike the case of obscenity, in which certain words or images are banned at least in part by their tendency to elicit disgust, here we'll discuss an inverse case: how words or images are instead proactively used *specifically to* rouse disgust and engender moral disapproval toward a behavior, person, or group. As we'll see, advocates looking to advance a cause—like President Trump and his evocative campaign tactics discussed in

Chapter 1—have long capitalized on the persuasive power of disgust to make their case.

Some of the most prominent examples come, again, from literature, where authors like Émile Zola and Upton Sinclair used graphic imagery to engender moral condemnation of disgusting social conditions. In *Germinal*, Zola centered his story on a coalminers' strike in northern France in the 1860s and used harsh descriptions of the poor health and severe working conditions of miners to condemn the effects of a capitalist mining system on a provincial French town. Sinclair used the same approach to great effect in *The Jungle* to attack the working conditions of immigrants in industrialized American cities. The revolting descriptions of the Chicago meatpacking industry were so influential that they are at least partially responsible (and some would argue primarily responsible) for a series of reforms, including President Roosevelt's commissioning the Neil-Reynolds report investigating the meatpacking industry, the Federal Meat Inspection Act of 1906, and the Pure Food and Drug Act of 1906. Would a dispassionate, clinical list of the problems of the meatpacking industry have had the same effect? Perhaps. But it seems hard to believe that such a list would have had the resonance of descriptions like this:

> Cut up by the two-thousand-revolutions-a-minute flyers, and mixed with half a ton of other meat, no odor that ever was in a ham could make any difference. There was never the least attention paid to what was cut up for sausage; there would come all the way back from Europe old sausage that had been rejected, and that was moldy and white—it would be dosed with borax and glycerin, and dumped into the hoppers, and made over again for home consumption. There would be meat that had tumbled out on the floor, in the dirt and sawdust, where the workers had tramped and spit uncounted billions of consumption germs. There would be meat stored in great piles in rooms; and the water from leaky roofs would drip over it, and thousands of rats would race about on it. It was too dark in these storage places to see well, but a man could run his hand over these piles of meat and sweep off handfuls of the dried dung of rats. These rats were nuisances, and the packers would put poisoned bread out for them; they would die, and then rats, bread, and meat would go into the hoppers together.[11]

Visual artists are no stranger to this technique, either. Several have used gruesome depictions to invoke antiwar sentiment. Rather than rely on cold, rational arguments in favor of peace, works such as Picasso's *Guernica*, Dix's *The War*, and Goya's *The Disasters of War* employ grisly imagery—portrayals of mangled bodies, maggot-infested corpses, dead children, severed limbs—to tap straight into the rapid, unconscious moral intuitions generated by disgust (Fig. 11.1). The same is true for anti-abortion protestors who use disturbing images of aborted fetuses, or animal-rights activists who use images of injured and abused livestock. In his recent law-review article "Gruesome Speech," the First Amendment scholar Eugene Volokh highlights a host of examples where gruesome images were used

Grande hazaña. con muertos.

Figure 11.1. Francisco Goya, *Grande hazana! Con muertos!* (Great deeds! Against the dead!), 1810s.

for political effect, including the use of photographs showing slaves' whipping scars or hanged African Americans, Emmett Till's mother displaying his body in a glass-topped casket at his funeral, and a recent *Time* magazine cover displaying a woman who had her nose cut off by the Taliban for escaping her abusive in-laws.[12]

Volokh's article is concerned with the constitutionality of gruesome images, and whether government officials can prohibit pictures of aborted fetuses or injured animals, or whether such images are protected by the First Amendment. In his discussion he points out that some courts are upholding restrictions of gruesome images (and in doing so are carving out heretofore unrecognized exemptions to the First Amendment) based solely on the images' deep-seated psychological effect. Though his discussion focuses primarily on First Amendment doctrine, he also recognizes the disgust-to-morality pathway we've been outlining here. "Photographs," he says, "are not syllogisms. Photographs of awful things aim at awakening viewers' consciences with an appeal to deeply seated emotional reactions and moral intuitions." Volokh also recognizes a difference between the intuition and the ultimate procedure of deciding rules, noting that "images are not rationalistic debate" and would not "be at home in a university economics or philosophy department" before acknowledging that "[m]uch of what we believe comes not just from logic but from experience—from what we have seen, and from the visceral moral reactions that this seeing has aroused."[13] What Volokh recognizes is the same phenomenon that storytellers recognize, and the same phenomenon that the anti-abortion and animal-rights groups recognize: the imagery of disgust is an effective tool for prejudicing moral judgment.

DEFAMATION PER SE

Other areas of the law also seem to recognize the powerful influence of disgust on moral judgments, even where the precise psychological mechanics are not understood. Consider, for example, the case of defamation per se. Usually, in civil cases, one of the essential elements that plaintiffs must prove is damages. That is, they must show that a defendant's wrongdoing or negligence caused some kind of actual, quantifiable harm. There are, however, certain limited exceptions to this requirement, including cases of defamation per se. In these cases, courts have traditionally recognized that there are some false statements that are so readily harmful that damages are presumed. In other words, if you can prove that the defendant made a false statement about you that falls into one of the four traditional categories of defamation per se, it's simply acknowledged that these things are so injurious to reputation that the plaintiff need not prove damages in order to recover. Two of the categories have minimal or no disgust components (they are actually more related to anger): damages are presumed if you make a false statement that someone committed a crime, or a false statement that injures another in trade, business, or occupation. The other two categories, however, do: it is considered defamation per se to falsely accuse someone either of having a "loathsome disease" or of "serious sexual misconduct."[14]

Although the definitions of "loathsome disease" and "serious sexual misconduct" differ from jurisdiction to jurisdiction, there are some general guidelines. The Restatement of Torts leaves an open end to the definition of "loathsome disease" but gives as examples sexually transmitted diseases, leprosy, and the plague.[15] The fact that "leprosy" and "the plague" are specified gives some idea as to the deep-seated roots of the doctrine. It was adopted by the United States from English common law, where early cases found defamation per se in statements such as "Thou wert laid of the French pox,"[16] "Thou art a pocky knave, get thee home to thy pocky wife, her nose is eaten with the pox,"[17] "You are a damned bitch, whore, and a pocky whore, and if you have not the itch you have the pox,"[18] and "He has got that damned pox from going to that woman on the Derby Road."[19] Aside from just providing us with amusing phrases, these early cases are useful because their opinions explain the rationale for the rule—namely, that accusations of disease can brand their targets as objects to be avoided by society. The opinion of the court in the 1863 Massachusetts case *Joannes v. Burt* is prototypical in the assertion that "imputation of such loathsome and infection maladies . . . would make [someone] an object of disgust and aversion, and banish him from human society."[20]

The same rationale is applied in the case of falsely accusing someone of "serious sexual misconduct." Like loathsome diseases, there is no one-size-fits-all definition—acts considered "serious sexual conduct" can run the gamut. For example, in some jurisdictions it was (and arguably still might be) considered defamation per se to accuse someone of being homosexual or bisexual. The quintessential case of serious sexual misconduct, though, involves falsely accusing a woman of being "unchaste." Again, the rationale for singling out this category is based on the type of reputational damage and societal repulsion that such an insult can cause. Here's the Supreme Court of Nebraska, in a case from 1906, establishing false accusations of promiscuity as per se defamation:

> [A] female against whom the want of chastity is established is driven beyond the reach of every courtesy and charity of life, and sometimes even beyond the portals of humanity. By common consent such an imputation is now everywhere treated as the deepest insult and the vilest charge that could be given or inflicted upon the victim or her friends. She is denied the society in which she has been wont to move.[21]

Interestingly, retaining these categories as defamation per se in the contemporary political climate places courts in a difficult position. By retaining unchaste or homosexual behavior as per se categories of defamation, courts are forced to balance the fact that such behavior is repulsive to many people with the political decorousness of such an acknowledgment. In other words, by recognizing that such allegations can taint the reputation of the person toward whom they are directed to such a reliable degree as to be deemed defamation per se, it could be argued that courts are lending credence to such value judgments themselves. In any event, the point stands: in deciding what kinds of statements are likely to produce societal exile, courts have placed a special emphasis on those that rouse disgust.

GRUESOME PHOTOS

Another example of how disgusting imagery can prejudice value judgments in the legal process comes from the area of evidence law, and the judge's decision whether or not to allow gruesome photographs to be introduced as evidence at trial. Under Rule 403 of the Federal Rules of Civil Procedure, a judge, when deciding whether or not to admit evidence into a trial, must decide if the probative value of the evidence is substantially outweighed by the danger of unfairly prejudicing the jury. Unfair prejudice, in turn, is defined as "an undue tendency to suggest decision on an improper basis, commonly, though not necessarily, an emotional one."[22]

One of most frequently litigated issues in this domain revolves around photographs of autopsies and crime scenes. The concern is whether such photos would prejudice the jury's ability to accurately determine guilt and, in some cases, whether or not a murder was committed in an especially "heinous, cruel, or depraved" manner and is thus punishable with death. In such cases, the judge is tasked with weighting the probative value of a gruesome photo—for instance, the trajectory of a stab wound or the position of a body—against the danger of un-fairly skewing the jury's ability to objectively evaluate other questions, such as whether or not the defendant committed the crime in question. The legal scholar Susan Bandes and the psychologist Jessica Salerno, in an article discussing the cognitive science of viewing gruesome photos, note that gruesome photos might "elicit moral outrage that influences the jury's decision on the question of guilt or innocence, a question on which they should have no bearing." Or the photos might "engender strong anger toward the defendant that interferes with the jury's ability to evaluate other relevant evidence in the case—and makes them overcon-fident as well," an effect they contend is unfairly prejudicial because it "deflects the jury from its deliberative task."[23] Consider also that several states include whether a murder is "vile," "horrible," "heinous," "atrocious," or "depraved" as an aggra-vating factor in determining whether or not the defendant should be sentenced to death. Though such factors are often meant to indicate that there had been torture or serious physical abuse of the victim, the use of words like "vile" and "heinous" invites jurors to integrate gruesome, albeit non-salient, aspects of the crime into their evaluations.

Generally, courts are hesitant to exclude otherwise relevant evidence and thus err on the side of admitting gruesome photographs, but not always. Here is the Supreme Court of Colorado ruling that photographs of a murdered woman were inadmissible:

> The two pictures of the naked body of Mary Macri Archina, taken at the morgue 17 days after the shooting showing the results of extensive surgery performed after the shooting, are clearly inadmissible. The pictures do not prove or tend to prove any issue in the case. It may be suggested they prove the nature and extent of her injuries—they do not, but rather prove the hand-iwork of surgeons who, in their efforts to save her life, had largely covered up evidence of the handiwork of the defendant.[24]

Further in the opinion, the court continues:

> None of these pictures is admissible, they are without probative value, they serve only to incite the jurors to passion, prejudice, vengeance, hatred, dis-gust, nausea, revolt and all of the human emotions that are supposed to be omitted from the jury's deliberations. Their admission was highly prejudiced and calls for a reversal.[25]

A significant body of empirical research substantiates the Colorado Supreme Court's fears. Several mock jury studies have found that gruesome photographs (i) increase the likelihood of finding liability in civil trials and issuing guilty ver-dicts in criminal trials, (ii) lower the amount of evidence that jurors need to make such findings, and (iii) raise the level of jurors' assuredness that their decisions are correct.[26] In one of the studies, the researchers even looked specifically at the relationship between disturbing photographs and emotions. They found that compared to anger, disgust was a more consistent predictor of moral outrage, and that as jurors' moral outrage increased, so too did their confidence in a guilty verdict.[27]

Again, this disgust-to-morality pathway that courts are intuitively recognizing—and that psychological research is confirming in the lab—occurs, in large part, outside of conscious awareness. In a different study, for example, the jurors who viewed gruesome photographs and issued more guilty verdicts thought they acted with the same degree of fairness as the jurors who were not shown the photographs, despite issuing greater numbers of guilty verdicts.[28] Because the mechanics are hidden from view (much like the case of split brain patients and subjects in studies examining functional fixedness and the by-stander effect discussed in Chapter 2), jurors are unaware of how their decisions are being cast. All that is deposited into consciousness is the final output: the increased moral outrage, the decision of the guilty verdict, the assuredness of a correct decision.

Research also shows that when it comes to gruesome evidence, photographs are stronger than verbal descriptions,[29] and color photographs more effective than black-and-white ones.[30] This should come as no surprise given the environment in which these cognitive systems were built. In the milieu of our ancestors, hearing about something disgusting (or wrong) would have been indicative information but certainly not as reliable as witnessing the thing with your own two eyes. Moreover, since photographs didn't exist until relatively recently, they are effective only to the extent that they can mimic real life and the actual visual cues that that particular system was built to detect and process. Since video is closer to real life than color photographs, and color photographs are closer than black-and-white photographs, we should expect that their potency and ability to "trip" our disgust sensors would be ordered in kind.

CRIMINAL SCUM

Defamation per se and the exclusion of gruesome photographic evidence are two cases where the law has identified the potentially prejudicial effects of disgust and has sought, in one way or another, to account for the prejudice. In the case of defamation per se, the law has attempted to account for the effect by lowering the threshold required to recover damages. The implication is that in the cases of false accusations of serious sexual misconduct, or of having a loathsome disease, the likelihood and severity of resulting reputational damage are so great that plaintiffs are excused from the onerous burden of proving quantifiable harm. In the case of gruesome photographs, courts are again carving out an exception, excluding otherwise relevant evidence because its gruesomeness presumably hinders jurors' ability to accurately assess guilt.

It's important to reiterate that disgust is not being targeted simply because it disgusts. Rather, inherent in both of these examples is the assumption that disgust is a mediator of some other unwanted consequence. The fear of jurors viewing a gruesome photograph is not that they will be disgusted, but rather that disgust will disrupt their ability to accurately weigh evidence and evaluate the likelihood that someone engaged in a particular act. Similarly, being unchaste or carrying a sexually transmitted disease causes reputational harm not just because it disgusts, but because disgust acts as a Trojan horse for value judgments of the person's general character or aptitude.

These two particular cases are examples where the law has identified the prejudicial effects of disgust, and where lawmakers have taken overt steps to account for it. But there are plenty of other avenues where the phenomenon occurs less obviously, and may go unnoticed or unregulated. One example of this—an example that has been given some attention by researchers—is when lawyers take a page out of Dickens' playbook and embellish their descriptions of defendants with disgust-eliciting details.

From courtrooms to novels to the media to everyday conversation, criminals are frequently described in disgust-inducing terms: vile, slime, scum, dirt bags, pieces of garbage, pieces of shit. They are associated with dirt, refuse, reptiles, insects, and excrement. In her article "In Slime and Darkness: The Metaphor of Filth in Criminal Justice," the legal scholar Martha Duncan illustrates this phenomenon using the example of the Botany Bay venture, Britain's 18th century formation of a penal colony in Australia, and its practice of shipping its convicts off to live there (a practice that the preeminent British jurist Jeremy Bentham described as projecting an "excrementitious mass"[31]). Duncan's research reveals a historical record "replete with descriptions of convicts as 'sewage' and of their island-prison as a 'dunghill,' a 'cesspool,' and a 'sink of wickedness.'"[32] (In *Euclid v. Ambler Realty Co.*, a zoning case that reached the US Supreme Court, Euclid city officials made an unsuccessful run at institutionalizing similar sentiments by attempting to group correctional institutions and mental health facilities in the same zone as sewage and gas plants, garbage and refuse incinerators, scrap metal storage, cemeteries, crematories, oil and gas storage, and manufacturing and industrial operations.[33])

While writing her article, Duncan also found 34 American cases "in which the prosecutor's characterization of the defendant as filth was an issue on appeal." She notes: "these cases show prosecutors calling defendants by such terms as 'little scums,' 'slimy creature,' 'type of worm,' and 'skunk.'"[34] Some of these decisions were overturned by the appeals courts; others were not. But even where lawyers are prevented from *overtly* using this technique—by calling a defendant "scum," for example—research suggests that they may be able to nonetheless exploit the same prejudicial mechanisms by simply using disgust-eliciting descriptions. For example, in one recent study, a team of United Kingdom researchers led by Eduardo Vasquez asked mock jurors for sentencing recommendations based on a description of a violent crime. There were two different versions of the description. In one version, the crime was described using phrases such as "the perpetrator *slunk*" and "[t]he attack was *savage*" and "the victim's blood *splattered*." In the second version, the crime was described in a more sterile manner: "the perpetrator *stole*" and "[t]he attack was *sustained*" and "the victim's blood *painted*" (all emphases ours).[35] Unsurprisingly, the first version resulted in significantly harsher punishment for the perpetrator. So even where prosecutors are prevented from calling a defendant a snake or slime, they may still be able to describe snake-like or slime-like behavior to achieve similar results.

CASTES AND CONTAMINATION

There's one more example that Duncan raises in her article that hints at just how perniciously this tactic can be put to use. She points to laws against vagrants that often use allusions to dirt or filth to malign them, citing a Supreme Court case that describes vagrants as "crowding together, in the open country and in camps, under living conditions shocking both as to sanitation and social environment,"[36] and a New York county court that characterizes vagrants as "sordid individuals who infest our stations such as the dirty, disheveled, besotted character whose state is but a step short of intoxication."[37] Though the case of vagrants might seem like a fringe example, Duncan here is scratching the surface of a much more pervasive phenomenon—namely, the use of disgusting imagery to spark or foment discriminatory sentiment toward an outside group.

So far in this chapter we've looked at how the imagery of disgust has been used to exploit the disgust-to-morality—or more specifically, gross-to-wrong—pathway that reliably develops in human brains. We've also approached our various examples in a relatively hierarchical order, starting with the most innocuous uses and then graduating to higher-stakes examples. We might, for example, think it interesting or even enjoyable when authors and artists use this psychological shortcut to vilify their fictional characters. And we might recognize the effectiveness of the technique when it is used to advance a political cause (we might even find it admirable or worthwhile, but this of course probably turns on whether we support the underlying cause). But the true danger of employing this technique becomes apparent when we see how it can be used to prejudice guilt and liability determinations, or to stereotype and taint entire classes of people, such as ex-convicts and vagrants.

It's this last example that has the potential for especially destructive use, a danger that has been extensively detailed by the law professor Martha Nussbaum, who notes: "throughout history, certain disgust properties—sliminess, bad smell, stickiness, decay, foulness—have repeatedly and monotonously been associated with, indeed projected onto . . . Jews, women, homosexuals, untouchables, lower-class people."[38] We needn't look far for evidence: the historical records of wartime propaganda, genocidal movements, slavery, class- and race-based segregation, and other forms of discrimination are replete with examples of one group harnessing the moral sway of disgust to rouse negative sentiment (read: lower their perceived social value) toward another group.

To do this, subjugating groups often look for an existing trait of the group they wish to subjugate, and amplify that trait to foment discriminatory sentiment. For women, this often means focusing on menstruation (the third-century Carthaginian theologian Tertullian, for example, called women "a temple built over a sewer"[39]), while for lower socioeconomic classes, the target is often sanitation and hygiene. Groups like the European Cagot, the Japanese Burakumin, and the Indian Dalit, for instance, were labeled "untouchable" (read: low estimated value of contact) based at least partly on their occupations dealing with butchering, tanning, death, and the removal of refuse and excreta.

But even where there is not an obvious disgust-eliciting element of the subjugated group to exploit, the discriminating group often simply turns to metaphor. In the period preceding the 1994 Rwandan genocide, for example, Hutus would commonly refer to Tutsis as "*inyenzi*" (Kinyarwanda for "cockroach"), and "*inzoka*" (Kinyarwanda for "snake") during "animation sessions" used to drum up anti-Tutsi fervor.[40] Anti-Semitic Nazi propaganda similarly likened Jews to worms, snakes, vermin, and diseases. A particularly heavy-handed example is the German Nazi propaganda film *The Eternal Jew*, where Jews were compared to parasitic rats through both visual images (in one scene, a montage juxtaposes a crowd of Jews with rats emerging from a sewer) and voiceover narration.[41] At different points during the film, the narrator insinuates that Jews, like rats, spread disease, travel in large packs, and "represent the rudiment of an insidious, underground destruction"—an extension of the imagery that Hitler used in *Mein Kampf*: "Was there any form of filth or profligacy, particularly in cultural life, without at least one Jew involved in it? If you cut even cautiously into such an abscess, you found, like a maggot in a rotting body, often dazzled by the sudden light—a kike!"[42]

This imagery is often extended to genocidal movements where the killings are framed as "exterminations" or as "cleansings" and is likewise used as a way to condemn friendship or association between groups with allusions to "taint" or "contamination." This is especially true of sexual or romantic intermingling, where one might be accused of impurity or bodily corruption for sleeping with a person of another race or lower class. The legal record is again illustrative here, going all the way back to colonial-era decisions. In 1630, for example, Hugh Davis was ordered "to be soundly whipped, before an assembly of negroes and others for abusing himself to the dishonor of God and shame of Christians, by defiling his body in lying with a negro."[43] Another example of this type of framing is illustrated in an 1869 Georgia Supreme Court case upholding an anti-miscegenation statute, where the Court pronounced that:

> The amalgamation of the races is not only unnatural, but is always productive of deplorable results. Our daily observation shows us, that the offspring of these unnatural connections are generally sickly and effeminate, and that they are inferior in physical development and strength, to the full-blood of either race. It is sometimes urged that such marriages should be encouraged, for the purpose of elevating the inferior race. The reply is, that such connections never elevate the inferior race to the position of the superior, but they bring down the superior to that of the inferior. They are productive of evil, and evil only, without any corresponding good.[44]

There is a hard question lurking here about the extent to which disgust is a *cause* of discrimination—a catalyst for coalitional exploitation—and the extent to which it is simply a tool used to perpetuate it. Though there is not a clear-cut answer, we can still probably formulate a few useful rules of thumb. First, when the aversion is triggered by a trait *actually occurring* in the subjugated population, disgust is probably at least a partial cause of the discrimination. This would likely include groups such as vagrants, the handicapped, the ill, or the obese, where the individuals might exhibit some trait that signaled pathogen presence or deleterious reproductive characteristics in the ancestral environment. But where the aversion is triggered by metaphor or allusion to a disgust-eliciting object (e.g., comparing a group to cockroaches, rats, slime, or scum), disgust is probably not the underlying catalyst of the discrimination and is instead being recruited to deepen a coalitional rift. This would likely include groups defined by race, national origin, and political or religious affiliation (in short, out-groups), none of which, as a class, necessarily presented the same type of static ancestral fitness risks as the first group of individuals.

A useful heuristic to differentiate between the two (disgust as impetus or spotlight, as we've called it, and disgust by analogy or as a signal or shield) is simply to look at the rhetorical device being used. If a statement focuses on an actual trait of the subjugated group to induce disgust, then disgust is probably a psychological impetus of the discrimination. But if the statement instead uses a metaphor or comparison to another object that induces disgust, then disgust is probably just a tool being used to enflame a different coalitional division. Is there a meaningful difference between the two? Perhaps not in how they are deployed, but at least psychologically the difference is noteworthy. The latter example is easier to detect and see through; the former, not as much. Interestingly, it is also the latter group of classifications—race, national origin, religion, and alienage—that have traditionally been offered the highest level of protection in the US legal system (under the Fourteenth Amendment, laws attempting to classify individuals along these lines are subjected to "strict scrutiny" and rarely survive), whereas courts have been hesitant to extend such protections to the former groups (e.g., vagrants, the handicapped, the ill, or the obese).

Finally, it is worth noting that immigrants, as a group, are often caught in a perfect storm of these various mechanisms—sitting right at the nexus of our adaptations for coalitional exploitation, moral judgment, and disgust. Not only are they often targeted specifically because of some trait that might trigger disgust (under the Immigration and Nationality Act, for example, the list of potential immigrants considered ineligible for visas or admission include, among others, prostitutes, practicing polygamists, drug abusers, carriers of certain infectious diseases, and individuals with certain physical or mental disorders[45]). But even when those traits are absent or rare, disgust is often still recruited as a means to derogate immigrants as a class (Rush Limbaugh has both compared undocumented immigrants to an "invasive species" and asked whether "the CDC ever published a story about the dangers of catching diseases when you sleep with illegal aliens?").[46]

Empirical research corroborates these anecdotes. One 2004 study, for instance, found that arousing feelings of vulnerability to disease increased negativity toward foreign immigrant groups.[47] Another study in 2006 produced similar results, finding that the more one perceived oneself to be vulnerable to disease, the more ethnocentric one's attitudes toward out-groups.[48] Moreover, interpersonal-disgust sensitivity (for example, not wanting to "wear clean used clothes" or to "sit on a warm seat vacated by a stranger") has been found to predict negative attitudes toward immigrants and foreigners—an effect that was mediated by, among other things, "dehumanizing perceptions of the out-group."[49] And in a 2014 study of Dutch citizens, disgust sensitivity—the tendency to feel disgust across a range of dimensions, such as seeing maggots on a piece of meat or seeing a man with his intestines exposed after an accident—predicted views on immigrants and immigration policy. In other words, the greater one's tendency to experience disgust—especially with respect to contamination—the stronger one's anti-immigrant sentiment and anti-immigration policy views.[50] These studies are the perfect illustration of why—at a time when the president of the United States is pushing to build a wall on the Mexican border and to outright ban immigrants from several predominantly Muslim countries, and when Europe is experiencing one of the most significant influxes of migrants in history—sitting at this nexus is so perilous for immigrant populations.

Relationships

As long as humans have been entering into sexual relationships—which is to say, always—other humans have made it their business to try and regulate those relationships. And as long as humans have been regulating the sexual and marital practices of others, those regulations have been driven and influenced by the various moral systems that draw on disgust. With relationships, as with obscenity, defamation, discrimination, and many of the other examples we've covered thus far, subconscious programs designed to steer us away from sources of disease and sexual partners that jeopardize our reproductive success become conscripted by mechanisms for generating and coordinating explicit moral norms, spawning a host of proscriptions with the general logic of *what is gross to me is wrong for you.*

The Code of Hammurabi punished incest between a father and daughter with exile,[1] and sex between mother and son with being burned to death.[2] The Hittite laws punished all cases of incest with death but had a tiered structure for punishing sex with animals:[3] sex with a horse or mule resulted in being banned from the company of the king, while sex with a cow, sheep, pig, or dog was punished with death—*unless* the "ox leaps on a man" in sexual excitement, in which case the man's life was spared and a sheep was sacrificed in his stead.[4] The Code of the Assyrians prescribed death for both incest and bestiality, and likewise contained the earliest known prohibition of sodomy, decreeing that "if a man have intercourse with his brother-in-arms, they shall turn him into a eunuch."[5] Ancient Greece was famously tolerant of homosexual behavior (that is, at least, unless you were the "passive" participant in the act), and ancient Rome may have been as well (this point is more contested), at least for a period of time. But by the sixth century, when the Eastern Roman Emperor Justinian compiled the Corpus Juris Civilis, the state's position was clear: men "who dare to commit acts of vile lust with [other] men" were to be punished with death.[6]

The political dominance of Christianity in the Middle Ages produced perhaps the peak of sexual regulation in the West, a rather unsurprising occurrence for an ideology that derives its lodestar from the Book of Leviticus—a text that prescribed death for, among other things, "uncovering the nakedness" of blood relatives, having sexual relations with animals, and lying with a male as one lies with a female. Medieval Christian penitentials—guidebooks for church priests on how to conduct confession that assign specific penances for individual sins—frequently targeted incest, bestiality, homosexuality, and sodomy.[7] The seventh-century *Penitential of Theodore*, for example, prescribed 10 years for fornication with a man or with a beast, 15 years for fornication with a sister or a mother, and 7 years of penance for "qui semen in os miserit" (whoever sends seed into the mouth).[8] In 1524, while the Holy Roman Emperor Charles V was signing a law punishing "impurity" with a beast or someone of the same sex with death by burning, Pope Clement VII was handing jurisdiction of sodomy cases over to the Inquisition, and in the process precipitating hundreds of executions for both homosexuality and bestiality.[9] Not long after, in 1533, England's Parliament passed the Buggery Act—England's first civil sodomy law, which punished both homosexual and zoophilic sex with "pains of death and losses and penalties of their good chattels debts lands tenements and hereditaments."[10]

One of the earliest existing examples of traditional Chinese law, the seventh-century T'ang Code, in addition to prohibiting sex with slaves or persons of lower social classes, cast incest as such a heinous offense that it was included in "The Ten Abominations," a list of crimes understood to be especially reprehensible.[11] Roughly two thousand years before that, the Laws of Manu, in addition to warning that "one should not sit in a lonely place with one's mother, sister, or daughter; for the senses are powerful, and master even a learned man,"[12] also forbade "bestial crimes," "unnatural offences with a male," and even "smelling at things which ought not to be smelt at" (the penalties for which ranged from bathing while clothed to being paraded through the town with a shaved head and dismembered limbs).[13] In the American colonies, the fervor for prosecuting bestiality took on near-witchcraft proportions. In one incident, the incredibly named Thomas Hogg was (perhaps non-randomly) accused of buggery when a sow gave birth to a deformed piglet with eyes that reminded the townspeople of the hang of Hogg's scrotum (the composition of which was common knowledge due to the steel truss Hogg wore for his hernia, which frequently cut his pants, revealing his genitals, an event, we note, that likely incited disgust in on-lookers). As part of his trial, Hogg was first made to fondle the sow in question (which resulted in an immediate "working of lust in the sow") and then a different sow (which did not result in any similar arousal). Hogg was remarkably spared execution, presumably because he refused to confess, but he was nonetheless whipped and imprisoned.[14] The hapless colonial farmhand George Spencer was not as lucky; Spencer was executed for "buggery" when a deformed piglet was born with a single, cloudy, cyclops-like eye that reminded the townspeople of Spencer's own.[15]

Laws against having sex with women during menstruation—though absent from modern Western legal codes (a state of affairs that is probably helped by the proliferation of amplified hygienic practices/technology)—can be found everywhere from the early laws of the ancient Near East, to religious texts of the Abrahamic religions, ancient Hindu texts, and Christian penitentials. Indeed, while it might not be illegal, strong taboos both at the individual and cultural levels prevail, often via reference to the "unclean" or "impure" nature of the blood, and often accompanied by a tangential taboo of contamination. Among the !Kung of the Kalahari, menstruating women were forbidden from touching the arrows men use for hunting.[16] In *Sex and Punishment*, Erik Berkowitz notes that in Babylon "everything a woman touched during her period, from furniture to people, was considered contaminated" and that the "Torah, which decrees that women and everything they touch are unclean during their periods, also pronounces that this contamination extends to things touched by people who are themselves touched by menstruating women."[17]

Many other of these historic sexual proscriptions have endured until fairly recently, and many others still are alive and well in parts of the world today. Sodomy, for example, persisted as a capital offense in France until the 18th century, and in the United Kingdom until the mid-1800s.[18] Here in the United States, the ink is only starting to dry on *Obergefell v. Hodges*, the Supreme Court opinion protecting gay marriage. And up until 2003 (*2003!*) sodomy remained a punishable offense in several states. According to the International Lesbian, Gay, Bisexual, Trans and Intersex Association, while same-sex marriage or civil unions are now at least partially allowed in 37 countries, more than 70 countries still have criminal laws against sexual activity by lesbian, gay, bisexual, transgender, or intersex people. And in nine of those countries (Afghanistan, Iran, Mauritania, Nigeria, Qatar, Saudi Arabia, Somalia, Sudan, and Yemen), homosexuality is still punishable by death.[19] Bestiality likewise remains a crime in 46 US states (the exceptions: Hawaii, Kentucky, New Mexico, and Wyoming, plus the District of Columbia) and in most of the world's countries.

Several countries that have recently repealed their sodomy laws (which often included both homosexual sex and bestiality in the definition of sodomy) in an effort to deregulate same-sex intimacy have also passed corresponding bestiality statutes to ensure that the behavior did not go unpunished, and this includes a litany of countries that might otherwise be considered socially liberal, such as Brazil (2015), Denmark (2015), Sweden (2014), the Netherlands (2010), Norway (2008), Belgium (2007), France (2004), and Poland (1997). In many US states, necrophilia is either a crime unto itself or falls under abuse-of-corpse statutes, while in some states necrophilia is not a crime at all (though we suppose it is safe to assume that the taboo remains strong enough, both in the United States and elsewhere, to render a known necrophile a pariah).[20] And incest—through either marriage or sexual contact—remains as close to a "universal" taboo as there is: it is prohibited in some capacity in every US state (punishable in some cases by up to life imprisonment) as well as almost every other country and culture in the world.

The psychological pathways by which these judgments can be formed are myriad (low expected sexual value and low expected value of contact being two), but the end results are fairly consistent and stable: mechanisms designed to deter relationships with biologically deleterious partners—relatives, individuals of the same sex, individuals both too young and too old to reproduce, the dead and dying, individuals with diseases or illnesses, and even other species—become recruited by moral mechanisms designed to promote self-interest (which norms could benefit me or my kin's or my friends' best interests?) or to coordinate and solidify coalitions (which behaviors—usually those not practiced by the individual, or the majority—could serve as focal points for organizing and rallying a group for the purpose of exploiting another group?) to produce norms, taboos, and laws regulating, for example, incest, sodomy, homosexuality, bestiality, sex with minors, and necrophilia. Such laws are, and have always been, persistent features of human societies. They aren't dispersed with perfect uniformity across all cultures and across all times within a culture, which we shouldn't expect given individual differences and the contingencies of the moralization process discussed earlier. But many of these laws and norms have been reliably recurrent over long time-scales and across cultures, and many also persist today.

By now, this pattern should be familiar. And we should make explicit that all laws, including those regulating sexual and marital behaviors, result from the confluence of many forces, including cultural, religious, institutional, historical, and procedural ones. For centuries, for example (and today in many places still), state and religious institutions had a vested interest in the fruitful propagation of their wards; more people meant more vassals to work, more citizens to tax, more soldiers to fight, and more congregants to tithe. The state or church's interest in deterring non-procreative sex undoubtedly contributed (and contributes) to the ubiquity of laws restricting it—many of which overlap with those sexual practices we have evolved to reject as part of a naturally selected impulse to efficiently reproduce. We aren't suggesting that disgust and disgust only is the driving force of these laws, merely that it is often a catalyst or contributing factor, and, perhaps most importantly, it helps to solve the riddle of why people should care so much about the activities of others that do not appear to affect the well-being of anyone other than those engaged in the activities.

This confluence of factors is especially enlightening when it comes to mismatches, instances in which these reliably developing tendencies are contravened by actual societal practices or customs. We've already considered the case of the Taiwanese minor marriages in which unrelated children were raised together effectively as siblings (and presumably developed the strong sexual aversions that go along with prolonged childhood co-residence) and then forced to marry at the earliest signs of adulthood. Despite their marriages, these pairs often had sex with more desirable partners (reminding scholars that we should keep the matter of marriage and sex distinct). Consider also cases of incestuous marriages among royal families, such as the intermarriages among the ruling families of ancient Egypt, or of the European Hapsburgs, whose inbreeding was recurrent enough to reliably produce a prominent underbite (the "Hapsburg jaw"). That members of the same royal family would get married probably has little to do with how their psychological systems for mate choice, disgust, and morality operated, and more to do with maintaining succession, consolidating power, and reducing exterior claims to the throne. That is, the marrying relatives very likely were married *in spite of* their aversion, because other factors outweighed those feelings, not because those feelings were absent. Of course, if the relatives were not in fact raised together, then perhaps aversions were lessened. Regardless, there have been various reasons across cultures and across time why two people who find each other sexually aversive might be wed.

Laws restricting sex with minors are another example. If we were to predict—based solely on our psychological mechanisms for disgust and mate choice—the age at which it might be considered acceptable for adolescents to engage in sex, we would probably predict the age of puberty. Puberty is the time in which humans become reproductively viable and, not coincidentally, the time in which members of the opposite sex become less disgusted and more enticed by the thought of sex with the maturing individual. So, all other things being equal, if we had to guess at an age where society gave a green light for sexual behavior, we could do worse than puberty. And for much of history, and still in many parts of the world, this prediction would be accurate. The age of first marriage (for a female) in traditional hunter-gatherer or foraging societies, for example, ranges anywhere from 18 all the way down to 12, depending on the society.[21] In more than 60 countries around the world today, the age of consent is 15 or younger, including Burkina Faso, Japan, and Niger at 13, Angola and the Philippines at 12, and Nigeria at 11.[22] And until the late 19th and early 20th century in the United States, the age of consent in most states was 10 to 12 years old.[23]

Yet in the United States today this is not the case. Instead, statutory rape laws (and their variants) set the age of consent usually between ages 16 and 18, with "Romeo-and-Juliet" allowances made for parties who are close to one another in age. In other words, what ended up carrying the day was not the age at which our disgust mechanisms are turned "off" (puberty), but rather the age at which lawmakers (with daughters?) thought people were mentally mature enough to voluntarily consent to the sexual activity (usually 16 to 18).[24] The result represents a disconnect between our natural inclinations and the line that the law has chosen to draw—a conflict borne out by the fact that roughly 60 percent of female statutory-rape victims in the United States are 14 or 15 years of age and 96 percent are between 12 and 17 years of age.[25] That is, almost all cases of statutory rape fall between what we might call the natural age of sexual maturity (puberty) and the legal age of sexual maturity (adulthood) for the victim.

Now, to make sure we are being clear, we are not suggesting that statutory-rape laws based on the idea of voluntary consent are inferior or unworkable by way of this disconnect. Putting aside important questions about *whether* an adolescent possesses the requisite mental maturity to voluntarily consent, or how that line can be drawn with any real precision, the idea of requiring voluntary consent strikes us as a promising criterion. Our contention, rather, is that the social taboo underlying statutory-rape laws generally is initially *propelled* not by a natural inclination for consent, but ultimately by psychological mechanisms meant to deter and condemn sex with pre-reproductive adolescents. Indeed, many of the ostensible justifications put forward for laws used to regulate relationships—not just with respect to minors, but relationships generally—appear quite rational, devoid of the emotional impulse we are attempting to document here. But when we take a closer look, either by carrying these rationales to their logical conclusions or examining the language used in conjunction with these laws, we find an instinctual revulsion not far from the surface.

LOOKING FOR CLUES

To illustrate how these laws stem from a gut objection, let's stay, for a moment, with the consent rationale behind statutory rape laws—this time in light of the Romeo-and-Juliet exceptions. Romeo-and-Juliet provisions are generally structured such that if one participant in a sexual relationship is below the legal age of consent and the other above, the sexual activity is either considered legal or the penalties are reduced or eliminated if certain conditions are met. Typically, those conditions include both that (a) the older participant is not more than a certain number of years older than the younger participant, and (b) the younger participant not be below a certain minimum age. A majority of US states have such exceptions. The law in Texas is representative: the age of consent is 17 years old unless the older participant was not more than 3 years older than the younger participant *and* the younger participant is at least 14 years of age.[26] So, if the younger participant is 14, the older participant can be no older than 17. If the younger participant is 15, the older participant can be no older than 18, and so on.

If consent was truly the end being pursued here, then why allow for these exceptions? If we think that the mental maturity required to consent does not develop until 17 or 18, then why carve out these provisions? And why do we consider a 14-year-old unable to consent to sex with a 30-year-old, but able to consent to sex with someone their own age? Could this be explained at least partly by the fact that, even though we have decided to make mental maturity the fulcrum of the law, we implicitly recognize that puberty is the age at which people begin to become both sexually attracted and sexually attractive? If not, then (a) why set a hard floor in the first place, and (b) why does that floor just happen to approach the age at which puberty completes (of the 27 states that set hard floors to their Romeo-and-Juliet provisions [i.e., below which Romeo-and-Juliet exceptions are not applicable, no matter how close in age] the average minimum age required of the younger participant is 14).

Further, what if tomorrow all of the world's psychologists declared that a consensus had been reached, and it had been determined without a doubt that children eight years and older had the mental maturity to give the type of consent required of the law; would society leap to extend the age of consent to pre-pubescence? Or, by the same token, imagine a rare disease in which a person's body ceases to age past age 8 even while their mind ages at the normal rate—would we be untroubled by the thought of an adult having sex with a 22-year-old person if he or she still had the body of an 8-year-old (a body lacking cues to an elevated mate value and, hence, elevated sexual value)?

This same line of thinking can be extended to laws prohibiting sex with animals. Bestiality proscriptions have principally been justified based on (1) the impermissibility of using animals as "means," and (2) the idea that non-human animals, like children, are unable to give the kind of consent that we typically require for sexual activity.[27] And again such rationales look suspect when the lens is zoomed out even just a little bit. We certainly have no problem using animals as means when it comes to food, farming, agriculture, transportation, and entertainment, and animals no more consent to any of these activities than they do to sexual relationships with humans. Assuming that there is no (other) harm being done to the animal, the real issue seems to be using animals for *sexual* means, or that the animals are not consenting to *sexual* activity. (We'd guess they'd prefer sex to death!) Not only is this distinction logically incoherent, but it is also undermined even further by the fact that many bestiality laws contain animal husbandry exceptions for sexual activity between a person and an animal. If we are indeed worrying about the animal participant in this act, then we will leave it to the reader to explain why the animal's consent is simply disregarded if it is being sexually stimulated for animal husbandry purposes but not for the sexual gratification of the person doing the stimulating . . .

Defenders of incest laws, on the other hand, tend to abandon the consent rationale and instead focus on the increased risk of genetic defects in offspring (we should note here that we are talking about *consensual* incest between adults—*not* rape or statutory rape). That is, they proffer that it is in society's best interests to ban incest because close relatives have a heightened risk of passing on deleterious recessive alleles to their offspring. But as a society we permit plenty of other relationships that pose similar genetic hazards. We do not, for instance, prohibit aging adults—who pose high risks of birth defects or pregnancy complications—from attempting to have children, nor do we prevent individuals who have already had children with birth defects from further reproduction.[28] Likewise, we don't prohibit marriages or sexual relationships between individuals who have Huntington's disease or other conditions with a high likelihood of inheritance. The chances of producing offspring with defects and disease are probabilistic in *all* cases of reproduction. For incest, this probability is, on average, higher, but children of related parents can also be of perfect health. This is no different than, for instance, having the dominant gene that gives rise to Huntington's disease, and rolling the reproductive die, giving your child a 50/50 chance of inheriting the same syndrome. And if we were able to *guarantee* that there was no risk of genetic defect, for instance by showing that one of the individuals was infertile; do you think this would stem societal objections to a brother and sister having sex or getting married?[29]

We know that in many cases it would not. Recall our hypotheticals from Chapter 1; we know from Haidt's study that people will remain steadfast to their instinctual objections even once the rationally defensible justifications are preempted. In the case of incest, for example, we know that even when the incest is consensual, is between adults, does not result in regret, and poses no risk of pregnancy, people will still insist that the practice is wrong. Remember also our hypothetical for the woman who sells her corpse to be defiled after her death. Although necrophilia and desecration-of-corpse statutes are often buttressed with a nexus of justifications involving consent, ownership of property, and public health, did it matter when reading the hypothetical that those concerns weren't present?

As the porous rationales of these prohibitions suggest, the objections that are driving these laws run deeper than the surface-level justifications of consent or genetic integrity. When we examine the various justifications put forward for these laws, often we are not looking at fundamental guiding principles, but rather post-hoc rationalizations for intuitive reactions (in these cases, to disgust). Indeed, for all of the sophisticated reasoning that proponents of these laws put forth, the rhetoric used by such proponents often betrays an instinctual objection. When a Tennessee judge calls necrophilia "the most loathsome, degrading and vile sexual activity imaginable ... so horrible as to be repugnant to all but the most depraved,"[30] it is hard to envision him forming this judgment based on the legal and philosophical subtleties involved with postmortem consent.[31] And when the Colorado Supreme Court characterizes the objection to incest as a "natural repugnance," it would seem a stretch to assume that this is shorthand for a deliberate, policy-driven choice meant to promote the optimal health of potential children.[32]

Indeed, we often need not look any further than the name of the statute for evidence that these are instinct-driven proscriptions, where crimes pertaining to "indecent" or "unnatural" sexual behavior carry labels such as *sodomy* (derived from the biblical story of Sodom and Gomorrah), *crimes against morality, crimes against nature*, or sometimes the longer *detestable and abominable crime against nature, committed with mankind or beast*. To underline the point, for many years in several states it was sufficient to merely charge the accused with a "crime against nature" without identifying the particular details of the act: "the crime being too well-known and too disgusting to require other definition or further details or description."[33]

Now, it is of course perfectly reasonable to argue that these pretextual arguments should carry the day, but first let us call a spade a spade. The reason that laws against incest, bestiality, sodomy, necrophilia, and the like can be traced back through almost every system of laws on the planet is not a result of all of these cultures across all of these time periods each deliberately weighing the various policy issues at play and independently arriving (in an odds-defying manner) at the same conclusions. No. The reason these laws have been so pervasive for so long is that they emanate from a shared psychological architecture that has been deployed under similar environmental circumstances. Often, people disapprove of these sexual behaviors now for the same reasons that people in the time of Hammurabi, Justinian, and Charles V disapproved of them: because the behaviors are *icky*, they *gross them out*, and they just plain *feel wrong*.

THE EXAMPLE OF HOMOSEXUALITY

Perhaps the most instructive example of this phenomenon is the case of homosexuality. Laws against incest, bestiality, necrophilia, and sex with minors are similar in that they all have rational arguments to be made in their favor. That is to say, even if the justifications put forth for these laws are pretextual or are logically incoherent when viewed in context, there might still be objective, utilitarian arguments to be made in their defense. It is possible to at least have an argument about whether such laws should exist that extends beyond "it's just wrong" or "it just grosses me out." So, for instance, one can admit that their objection to sex with animals emanates from an instinctual revulsion designed for the propagation of genes and yet simultaneously believe that, regardless of the usefulness of this instinct, there are genuine concerns over whether or not an animal is consenting to such activity and that those concerns ought to factor into the question of whether sex with an animal should be legal (after all, we can't just ask sheep to "baaa" once for yes and twice for no). Laws prohibiting sex or marriage between homosexuals, however, are unique in that they have largely been sustained absent an even plausible justification beyond "it's just wrong."

To illustrate, let's consider the quartet of cases in the US Supreme Court that have dealt explicitly with the rights of homosexuals to have sex or get married: *Bowers v. Hardwick, Lawrence v. Texas, United States v. Windsor*, and *Obergefell v. Hodges*. In the earliest case, *Bowers*, which was decided in 1986, the Court, in a 5–4 decision, upheld a Georgia statute that made sodomy a crime where a person "performs or submits to any sexual act involving the sex organs of one person and mouth or anus of another." The crux of the issue, as framed by the majority opinion in the case, was whether the Constitution confers a fundamental right upon homosexuals to engage in sodomy. In ruling that it did not, the Court stressed that this case—unlike prior cases where the Court had found fundamental rights for heterosexuals to marry and procreate—involved conduct whose proscriptions had "ancient roots." Citing a need for a fundamental right to be "deeply rooted in this Nation's history and tradition," the Court refused to grant consensual homosexual conduct the heightened protection of a fundamental right.[34]

The majority concluded their opinion by addressing the claim that there was no basis for the law "other than the presumed belief of a majority of the electorate in Georgia that homosexual sodomy is immoral and unacceptable." The Court dismissed this objection too, declaring that the law "is constantly based on notions of morality, and if all laws representing essentially moral choices are to be invalidated under the Due Process Clause, the courts will be very busy indeed."[35] In a concurring opinion, Justice Warren Burger traced proscriptions against sodomy back through various legal systems, noting that they were "firmly rooted in Judeo-Christian moral and ethical standards" before concluding that protecting homosexual sodomy as a fundamental right "would be to cast aside millennia of moral teaching."[36]

Seventeen years later, in 2003, the Supreme Court changed its mind. In *Lawrence v. Texas*, the Court overruled *Bowers* ("*Bowers* was not correct when it was decided, and it is not correct today. It ought not to remain binding precedent"), citing an "emerging awareness that liberty gives substantial protection to adult persons in deciding how to conduct their private lives in matters pertaining to sex."[37] But the three dissenting justices, in an opinion authored by Justice Antonin Scalia, reiterated the arguments of the *Bowers* majority, asserting that rights should only be considered "fundamental" (and hence deserving of heightened protection) when they are "deeply rooted in this Nation's history and tradition" and arguing that the idea that a majoritarian sexual morality is *not* a legitimate reason for upholding a law is "so out of accord with our jurisprudence—indeed, with the jurisprudence of *any* society we know—that it requires little discussion."[38]

In 2013, the Court then began extending this protection from homosexual sex to marriage, ruling in *U.S. v. Windsor* that the Defense of Marriage Act (DOMA)—which limited the definition of marriage for federal purposes to opposite-sex partners—was unconstitutional.[39] And in 2016, the Court dropped the other shoe, ruling in *Obergefell v. Hodges* that states no longer had that option either: "same-sex couples may exercise the fundamental right to marry." In both of these cases, as in *Lawrence*, the dissenters carried the flag of the *Bowers* majority, emphasizing both the role of the voting majority in making such determinations, as well as the longstanding tradition of opposite-sex marriages in this country. In his *Obergefell* dissent, for example, Justice John Roberts opined that "the Court today not only overlooks our country's entire history and tradition but actively repudiates it." In doing so, Roberts noted, the Court "invalidates the marriage laws of more than half the States and orders the transformation of a social institution that has formed the basis of human society for millennia, for the Kalahari Bushmen and the Han Chinese, the Carthaginians and the Aztecs. Just who do we think we are?" In his own incendiary dissenting opinion in *Obergefell*, Justice Scalia argued that the Court was usurping the task of defining marriage from (and, assumedly, supplanting the moral judgment of) "the People" to such an extent that it was a "threat to American democracy."[40]

Casting aside the complex questions of Constitutional interpretation, of *stare decisis* (the obligation of judges to adhere to principles established in earlier cases), and of the roles of the various branches of government that loom large over these decisions, the point we are making with these four cases is this: the best that the various Justices of the Supreme Court could do to provide a justification for laws prohibiting same-sex intimacy and marriage were (a) the existence of a majoritarian moral disapproval of the act, and (b) a "history and tradition" of prohibiting the practice. (This view was also echoed and succinctly stated in the 1996 House Judiciary Committee report on DOMA, which stated, "Civil laws that permit only heterosexual marriage reflect and honor a collective moral judgment about human sexuality. This judgment entails both moral disapproval of homosexuality and a moral conviction that heterosexuality better comports with traditional [especially Judeo-Christian] morality.") Thus, unlike the proffered justifications for laws against incest, necrophilia, or bestiality, for example, which at least have the pretextual appearance of an objective good, the justifications for laws against homosexual sex or marriage frequently boil down to little more than "a lot of people just don't like it" and "people have felt this way for a very long time."[41]

Of course, the Supreme Court is arguably the most visible judicial entity in the world, and when we are hearing the Supreme Court's argument in favor of a principle, we are often hearing the most palatable version of that argument, which also becomes armored by very sharp, very seasoned, and very cunning legal minds. Which is why—if you take seriously our contention that these judgments are often propelled by disgust—you would expect to find the more revealing rhetoric at the periphery, where pundits proclaim that our instinct is to "recoil" from homosexuals in "some kind of disgust"[42]; activists label homosexuals "vile beastly creatures" and compare exposing children to homosexuals to "feed[ing] them garbage"[43]; religious figures argue that Christians "shouldn't be mourning the death of 50 sodomites" in the Orlando club shooting[44]; and lower-court judges refer to sodomy as "moral filthiness and iniquity."[45] Even Justice Burger, in his concurrence in *Bowers*, couldn't help citing William Blackstone's description of sodomy as "an offense of 'deeper malignity' than rape, a heinous act 'the very mention of which is a disgrace to human nature', and 'a crime not fit to be named.' "[46]

All this is to say that when the Supreme Court and other lawmakers couch these rationales in the nobility of a moral consensus, or of history and tradition, what they are actually doing is aggregating these sentiments of revulsion, along with the sentiments found under blog posts, on Westboro Baptist Church picket signs, and in YouTube comments sections, and repackaging them in the shiny patina of a collective ideal, all the while without any scrutiny of the underlying sentiment.

This is inadequate. Moral intuitions are outputs of human psychological mechanisms—they are not sacred and they shouldn't be immune from the type of rigorous analysis that judges and legal scholars might apply to, say, administrative or contract laws. By simply rubber-stamping a storied or collective sentiment, we are replacing normative analysis with mere tallying. And where the instinct is flawed, having many of these instincts does nothing to alleviate any underlying problems with the instinct itself.

Decades of research in the behavioral sciences—most visibly in behavioral economics—has demonstrated that while human instincts might be extremely proficient from an evolutionary perspective (in other words, at optimizing genetic propagation), they are deeply flawed instruments in other contexts, frequently producing irrational results in the modern milieu. We overestimate our abilities and chances of success, we misjudge the probabilities of events occurring based on how recently we've encountered them, we ignore base rates, we evaluate spending decisions based on relative instead of absolute cost, and we disproportionately discount the future, to name just a few examples. Across a range of domains, it is not just suggested, but generally accepted, that blindly following our gut can lead to *suboptimal* results.

It is time for the law, too, to consider strongly what we know of our evolved human psychology—from our disease-avoidance and sexual-choice systems to the systems that motivate coalitional actions for the purpose of exploiting vulnerable minorities—to make sure that it does not fall into the same trap.

Closing Arguments

Over the course of this book, we've attempted to do two things. First, we've tried to give you a sense of just *how* pervasive and instrumental a role disgust plays in legal and political affairs. We've seen how it shapes doctrine, permeates judicial opinions, and influences juror determinations. We've shown how disgust is present in everything from free-speech discourse to debates about privacy rights; from decisions about what words can be said on broadcast television to decisions about whom we are free to sleep with, and to marry. Disgust is there, working behind the scenes when a lawyer describes a defendant as scum, and when a juror is applying "contemporary community standards." And we've also seen just how transcendent these features are—shaping legal institutions in very similar ways, across different cultures, and over historical time.

Second, we've tried to show *why* disgust has played (and continues to play) such a significant role by giving a comprehensive account of the psychology of disgust—including an explanation of what it is built to do, and a computational schematic for how it goes about achieving these goals. We've shown the evolutionary forces that shaped disgust into a multipurpose tool for guiding food selection, avoiding contact with surfaces and individuals bearing cues to disease, and steering clear of sexual partners who increase the chances of jeopardizing reproduction. We have also shown how group-level psychological adaptations for generating and maintaining moral norms use outputs of our disgust system. For all of these processes, we've attempted to sketch the cognitive procedures by which these tasks are accomplished. We hope that in doing so, we've given an illustrative account of how the various functional properties of disgust have shaped many of our societal norms and ethical taboos, taboos that often become institutionalized proscriptions.

In this chapter, we'll make our own turn from the descriptive to the normative and argue that disgust should play a very limited role in legal affairs, if any at all. We think it should not be used to create sympathy for victims, nor to condemn defendants; it should not be incorporated into guilt or liability or capital punishment determinations of a jury, or into courtroom arguments made by lawyers. We don't think it should be given any weight in choosing what words, images, or behaviors warrant protection from the First Amendment. And it should not be incorporated into moral decisions about what kinds of behaviors and personal relationships are acceptable for society.

Contrary to what some others have argued, we see no profundity in the intuition of disgust. Because of its evolutionary history and resultant psychological structure, we see it as an elegant, yet imperfect and unreliable, feat of natural engineering. Disgust is quite effective at its original functions: as a device for avoiding the consumption of harmful items, touching surfaces causing disease, and procreating with biologically costly mates. But the further we get away from these evolved functions, and the further we deviate from the ancestral setting in which they were designed to operate, the less effective and the less reliable disgust becomes. Each new use inherits features of its prior functions—features that may have been salient for a prior purpose, but are unfitting for a subsequent one. And as the modern environment increasingly becomes more novel and more dissimilar from the environment in which disgust evolved (e.g., we now inhabit worlds in which sugary treats come in feces shapes and cockroaches can be plastic), disgust loses accuracy, reliability, and, in the case of morality-driven proscriptions, relevance.

But even if it didn't, even if disgust operated in a perfectly accurate and reliable fashion, we would nonetheless remain opposed. Humans have science, the capacity for logic and abstract reasoning, and a vast sea of knowledge from which to draw. We need not rely on biologically driven intuitions, like disgust, to shape society, particularly when they are so often used to exploit, marginalize, and eliminate. If we are going to claim a moral high ground, it will not be built atop disgust.

FRAMING THE DEBATE

That disgust plays such a prominent role in legal affairs seems beyond dispute—we aren't aware of any real controversy over its presence. The critical disagreement for scholars, rather, has revolved around whether, and to what extent, disgust *should* play a role. The modern version of this debate was instigated in 1997, when two important, but unrelated, works were published. The first was an article by the bioethicist Leon Kass in *The New Republic* titled "The Wisdom of Repugnance." Kass—who would later serve as chairman of George W. Bush's President's Council on Bioethics—argued that disgust should play a vital role in the decision not to clone human beings, noting that "repugnance is the emotional expression of deep wisdom, beyond reason's power to fully articulate it." Kass urged his readers to embrace the mysterious intuitiveness of disgust and to use disgust as a moral compass, asserting that "we intuit and feel, immediately and without argument, the violation of things that we rightfully hold dear"; that "[r]epugnance, here as elsewhere, revolts against the excesses of human willfulness, warning us not to transgress what is unspeakably profound"; and that "repugnance may be the only voice left that speaks up to defend the central core of our humanity."[1]

The second work (published that same year) was law professor William Ian Miller's book *The Anatomy of Disgust*. In essence, Miller gave a qualified endorsement of disgust, casting it as an indiscriminate but powerful moral force to be harnessed for good:

> What we need are ways of knowing when to trust our disgusts and contempts. But despite their considerable warts contempt and disgust do proper moral work. More strongly, even their warts are moral; it is just that other criteria make us nervous about constituting official Morality that way. . . . The view that moral emotions like disgust and contempt are necessary evils does not do them justice; they do much salutary work if we inhibit their excesses . . . limiting the scope of their legitimacy by recourse to other norms we accept.[2]

Shortly following the publication of *Anatomy*, the law professors Dan Kahan and Martha Nussbaum each wrote a review of the book in which they took opposite positions. Kahan's review, *The Anatomy of Disgust in Criminal Law*, championed Miller's account and transposed it to make a normative legal argument, acknowledging the "indispensability" of disgust in criminal law and endorsing its role in shaming punishments and in capital punishment decisions of "horribly vile" murders.[3] Nussbaum, on the other hand, cast a leery eye at Miller's claims, noting in her review "Foul Play" that "Miller might have been expected to expand on the theme of disgust's political and legal irrationality . . . There is certainly a lot to be said about the role played by appeals to disgust in the oppression of homosexuality, and about the links between anti-Semitism, misogyny, and homophobia."[4]

Not long after those reviews were published, Kahan and Nussbaum sharpened their arguments and returned for a second round of debate with a pair of essays published in the anthology *The Passions of Law*. In his essay "The Progressive Appropriation of Disgust," Kahan reinforced his qualified support for disgust. His central arguments were that (1) it would be a mistake to accept the guidance of disgust uncritically, but it would also be a mistake to dismiss it completely, (2) disgust is an inevitable feature of our psychology, and will be directed at something, so we should take steps to properly direct it at objects warranting disgust, and (3) disgust is "indispensable to a morally accurate perception of what's at stake in the law" and "attempting to banish it risks making the law morally blind."[5]

Nussbaum's essay, "Secret Sewers of Vice," was in essence a counterpunch to the claims of Miller and Kahan. It was clear that, between the time of her review of Miller's book and her writing "Sewers," Nussbaum had thought a great deal about disgust, and had decided that the law would "do well to cast disgust onto the garbage heap where it would like to cast so many of us." She argued that disgust should never be used as a criterion for legal decision-making, and though she has no qualms with relying on an emotional or moral intuition, she would much prefer outrage and indignation instead of disgust. Basing her psychological view of disgust largely on the findings of Paul Rozin, Nussbaum argued that because disgust:

embodies a shrinking from contamination that is associated with the human desire to be non-animal, it is more than likely to be hooked up with various forms of shady social practice, in which the discomfort people feel over the fact of having an animal body is projected outwards onto vulnerable people and groups.

In light of this psychological model, Nussbaum argued that disgust was an irrational, untrustworthy device for use in the law—a view that she echoed and expounded in several subsequent books.[6]

Recently, scholars from outside the legal sphere have also been weighing in on the disgust-in-law debate. In her book *Don't Look, Don't Touch*, the epidemiologist Valerie Curtis argues that "to entirely dismiss moral disgust as a basis for social justice, as Nussbaum suggests we do, is to throw the baby out with the bathwater." She takes the approach of Miller and Kahan, arguing that "we need to listen to some kinds of disgust and not to others" and that "without moral disgust of cheating, violence, and exploitation, we would be unable to function as a social species."[7] On the flipside, the philosophers Daniel Kelly and Nicolae Morar take a hard stance against disgust, asserting that "disgust is not fit to do any moral or social work whatsoever."[8] Kelly and Morar, like Nussbaum, view disgust, especially in its moral domain, as a dehumanizing, untrustworthy tool. Like us, they believe that disgust's peculiar evolutionary history has furnished it with a series of "bugs" that render it unreliable.

We can classify the various extant views of the role disgust should play in law into three basic positions: *deep support, qualified support,* and *qualified opposition.* The deep support position finds normative value in the ancient, universal, subconscious origins of disgust. It is precisely *because* disgust has these properties that it should be used as a guidepost. This is Kass's view—that of a disgust with "deep wisdom." The position of qualified support is the position of Miller, Kahan, and Curtis. They lack Kass's reverence for the origins of disgust, and instead hedge their position by endorsing some features and uses of disgust, but not others. They focus more on using disgust as a harnessable tool rather than a guidepost to be blindly followed. Finally, Nussbaum, Kelly, and Morar are the qualified oppositionists, who have no particular qualms with disgust's origins and status as an intuition, but rather object to it based on its design features, and the potential it has to mislead and to be abused.

Our view is a fourth position: *deep opposition.* Like the qualified oppositionists, we reject the idea that disgust should (and perhaps even *could*) be tamed and directed as a tool for social good—we think the design features of disgust are so unreliable as to render it an unusable tool. (To the extent that we differ from Nussbaum, Kahan, and Curtis, that difference is rooted in the underlying psychological model of disgust being used, and the rationale for exactly why disgust is unfit for social use.) But we also object to the deference Kass grants to disgust as an intuition and, for reasons we'll detail shortly, would also oppose finding any "deep wisdom" in any other similar intuition, such as the outrage or indignation that Nussbaum favors—at least with respect to moral decisions. In our view, any such intuition should be met with similar skepticism.

HUME'S LAW AND THE APPEAL TO NATURE

Throughout this book, we've attempted to highlight the many ways in which disgust "sneaks" into the law. We've shown how the rapid, deeply rooted, subconscious structure of disgust often shepherds it into normative judgments, and often also spares it from the type of rigorous criticism that nonintuitive moral judgments might receive. We've also seen, though, how disgust and its attendant moral intuitions are often not only recognized but *embraced* as evaluative criteria. That a certain word, image, murder, or relationship disgusts us more than another has often been explicitly offered as reason enough to proscribe it, or to punish it more severely. Kass's view is characteristic of this approach, where he openly and unapologetically endorses the wisdom of disgust that extends "beyond reason" and that occurs "immediately and without argument."

Kass and the others who endorse this position are guilty of committing two closely related logical fallacies: the violation of Hume's Law and the Appeal to Nature. Hume's Law is the mistake of confusing "is" with "ought" and inferring a normative conclusion from a descriptive state of affairs. Here is Hume's famous passage from *A Treatise of Human Nature* that describes this tendency:

> In every system of morality, which I have hitherto met with, I have always remarked, that the author proceeds for some time in the ordinary ways of reasoning, and establishes the being of a God, or makes observations concerning human affairs; when all of a sudden I am surprised to find, that instead of the usual copulations of propositions, *is*, and *is not*, I meet with no proposition that is not connected with an *ought*, or an *ought not*. This change is imperceptible; but is however, of the last consequence. For as this *ought*, or *ought not*, expresses some new relation or affirmation, 'tis necessary that it should be observed and explained; and at the same time that a reason should be given, for what seems altogether inconceivable, how this new relation can be a deduction from others, which are entirely different from it.[9]

A pithy way of capturing Hume's idea is that an argument that something is true is not an argument that it is good, and an argument that something is (or would be) good is not an argument that it is true. The error in this line of thinking is echoed in the closely related Appeal to Nature, or the assumption that what is natural is per se good, and "unnatural" per se bad. When we blindly defer to our gut-level revulsions, we commit both of these fallacies, assuming that simply because evolution has endowed us with an instinctual aversion to a particular object or behavior, this aversion is therefore sacrosanct, and is automatically worth canonizing in our system of laws. This conflates the descriptive question of "what disgusts us?" with the normative question of "what should disgust us?" or, perhaps more specifically, "what should we prohibit?"

In *Lawrence v. Texas*, the Supreme Court decision invalidating anti-sodomy laws, Justice Anthony Kennedy alluded to this conflation in his majority opinion, noting that:

> [F]or centuries there have been powerful voices to condemn homosexual conduct as immoral. . . . For many persons these are not trivial concerns but profound and deep convictions accepted as ethical and moral principles to which they aspire and which thus determine the course of their lives. These considerations do not answer the question before us, however. The issue is whether the majority may use the power of the State to enforce these views on the whole society through operation of the criminal law.[10]

In our view, the reason these questions become so frequently conflated, and the reason disgust is so frequently given deference, is because of its more enigmatic properties: its rapidness, its automaticity, its subconscious origins, its universality, and its visceral nature—qualities that Kass mistakes for profundity and deep wisdom, but in truth are nothing more than effective design features that have been engineered by the evolutionary process. As we've argued, disgust isn't a mandate from the heavens, or a rulebook handed down from on high—it's a physical set of procedures, built by natural selection and realized in neural circuitries. Humans come "factory equipped" with a set of reliably developing programs for navigating the world, instincts that were good enough to promote survival and reproduction, but were not designed to produce rational, objective legal standards. Our intuitions were retained in our species because they had the tendency to enable ancestors to live to see another day and to reproduce (those intuitions). But the applicability of these intuitions is limited. If we were to disregard rational inquiry in favor of intuition in the realms of geography, physics, and biology, for example, we would still endorse a flat, motionless Earth that sits at the center of a revolving cosmos and a view of life that emanates from vitalism, essentialism, or creationism. Over time many of our folk-scientific intuitions—intuitions that perhaps worked for hunter-gatherers navigating ancestral social environments—have been exposed as flawed approximations of reality. Why should we give our moral intuitions—especially intuitions that were in part selected to coordinate exploitation—the benefit of the doubt?

There is a noteworthy objection to this view that is reasoned along the following lines: humans tend, by virtue of a common, species-wide psychology, to share many intuitions, values, and moral beliefs. To the extent that the law deviates from these shared intuitions, it runs the risk of being perceived as unfair or out of touch, and of losing the support, deference, and obedience of the general populace. The law professor Paul Robinson, who is the most prominent proponent of this kind of position, notes for example that "whatever the source of people's shared intuitions of justice, those intuitions are something to which system designers and social reformers would be wise to give special attention.

Reformers ought not to assume they can simply educate people out of a core in-tuition of justice the way they would persuade people to change their views on a purely reasoned matter."[11]

To us, this is an administrative problem—a challenge of *how* to implement a more reasoned approach, but not a challenge to *whether* we should. Like "is" and "ought," these are two separate questions. The analogy to the natural sciences is again useful: imagine how absurd it would feel to suggest to a biologist or a phys-icist that they should demur to people's commonsense observations of the world because it might threaten the credibility of their enterprise. This isn't to say the challenge is not a difficult one, as both evolutionary theorists and climate scien-tists will attest. (And just think what it must have been like in the 16th century to try and convince someone that the Earth, which all methods of sensory ob-servation indicated was motionless, was in truth simultaneously spinning on an axis, revolving around the sun, and hurtling outward into the vast expanse of space.) But this difficulty doesn't mean that we should therefore simply abandon our attempts to reason and persuade. After all, despite the strength of our "mo-tionless Earth" observations, every mainstream elementary-school science book says otherwise, and most of us have come to accept that—our observations not-withstanding—the scientists have it right.

If there is a "deep wisdom" to be found in repugnance, as Kass proposes, it is a wisdom that benefits our genes, not us as individuals. Natural selection is an incredible engineer, capable of producing wondrous mechanisms of survival and replication, but the process of natural selection is also amoral and apolitical. Disgust is designed to help propagate the genes that code for it—it cares not one lick for individual or societal welfare to the extent that individual and societal welfare do not aid in accomplishing this goal. This is worth saying again to make the point plain: your genes have an "interest" in your happiness and well-being, and the happiness and well-being of your neighbors, friends, and the rest of so-ciety, *only to the extent that that happiness and well-being aided in the survival and reproduction of those genes*. When we defer to disgust on decisions of right or wrong, good or bad, we are ceding the privilege of dictating our affairs to a cosmic accident, a process that happened to arise and happened to outperform available alternatives in helping the units that code for it to survive and reproduce in the particular conditions of a particular time period on this planet—that's all.

THE ERRORS OF DISGUST

Of course, it isn't enough to simply point out the fallacious Appeal to Nature or the violation of Hume's Law, because behind them lurks a second challenge: even if "is" doesn't *automatically* equal "ought," one can still make the argument that it can, or should. In other words, one can argue, based on outside criteria, that the natural state of affairs is also the desirable state of affairs. In a general sense, this is the position of Robinson, who feels that enforcing the natural state of affairs is worthwhile because of the stabilizing and legitimizing effect that this has for the legal system. With respect to disgust, this is also the general position of Miller and Kahan, who acknowledge the need to critically examine disgust but nonetheless feel it can be "properly directed" in some situations and used as a social tool.

Kelly and Morar have a first-line rebuttal to this thinking, which is that you will still always need another principle or standard to determine how to "properly direct" disgust, and that it's this second principle, not disgust, that is the useful moral compass. They argue:

> Some independent criterion is required to tell the difference, above and be-yond the brute presence of feelings of disgust. Indeed, Kahan even acknow-ledges this not just with his emphasis on "properly directed" disgust, but also by suggesting that it would be a mistake "to accept the guidance of disgust uncritically." The appeal to critical faculties or this kind of *proper* orienta-tion is an appeal to exactly the kind of independent criterion that we agree is required. But this appeal and Kahan's apparent acceptance of the need for it defeats his argument. . . . When push comes to shove, it is always an inde-pendent criterion, like the reference point provided by the "proper orienta-tion," that is calling the shots, and doing the real justification work, rather than the feelings of disgust themselves.[12]

We agree, but we have a secondary response, which is that disgust is simply too prone to error to be "properly directed" in any reliable fashion. The sources of these errors are multiple, but all originate from the evolutionary history and resultant mechanical properties of disgust. In this section, we'll discuss three, which we'll call *inherent error, mismatch error*, and *error from repurposing*. To do this, we'll revisit several of the properties of disgust that we outlined in pre-vious chapters. But whereas before we approached these features with an eye toward descriptive explanation of how disgust works, here we approach them with a normative lens, considering their reliability for use in the institutional-ization of norms.

Inherent Error

Inherent errors are "inherent" in that they were necessary to the effective oper-ation of disgust in the ancestral environment, but "errors" in that they deviate from optimal accuracy. They aren't design flaws, as they produce the best results on average over time, but some amount of inaccuracy is nonetheless intrinsic in their operation.

The various recurrent situations faced by our hunter-gatherer ancestors, in-cluding the situations that disgust is designed to navigate, often had to be solved with incomplete information. Decisions such as whether a piece of food was safe to eat or whether a potential mate posed any potential fitness costs had to be made in a finite time period, under novel conditions with never-before-encountered substances and people, and without perfect knowledge of the consequences for choosing one way or another. This means that, in effect, each time disgust is initiated, your mind is making a "bet" on a particular outcome based on what has worked *in the past*.

To help minimize the amount of uncertainty in these bets, natural selection has equipped us with a number of information-gathering mechanisms and behaviors. Take, for example, the cat-and-mouse game played during the courtship of a sexual partner. On the one hand, the person represents a prospective mate and all the attendant benefits that go along with it: a chance at producing offspring, a potential cooperative partner for gathering and cooking food, for creating shelter and other basic survival needs, for raising children, and for emotional support. On the other hand, the person also represents a potential carrier of disease—both sexually transmitted and otherwise—as well as a possible waste of time and reproductive resources. To counterbalance these two concerns, our systems regulating mating and disease-avoidance behavior seem to have produced a resultant courtship ritual consisting of a gradual ramping up of pathogen exposure. First, there is skin-to-skin contact, such as hugging or holding hands, next mouth-to-mouth, where closed-mouth kisses usually precede open-mouth kisses of gradually escalating durations of time. Hand-to-genital touching or mouth-to-genital contact is usually next, followed eventually by genital-to-genital contact and sexual intercourse.[13]

Driving one side of this equation is the "need" to have sex to pass on our genes. Driving the other is the "need" to avoid contracting a disease. This gradual escalation of pathogen probing is a kind of compromise between the two goals, allowing us to gather information at a safe rate before an irreversible error is made. If a person appears to have a skin disease, disgust might activate immediately, ending the ritual before it starts. If the person shows no visible signs of disease, then you might proceed to kissing. Here, clues like a foul taste or bad breath or evidence of poor health or disease might trip disgust, ending the ritual. If not, then proceed to the next step, and so on.[14] This same type of information-gathering game of cat-and-mouse can also be seen in other contexts, such as the decision whether or not to eat potentially spoiled food: visually inspect it, smell it, ask other people to smell it, taste a small amount, then eat; but if there is sufficient information to indicate spoliation at any step, stop there.

Systems such as these are designed to minimize the chances of, and the costs of, making an error when making a decision under uncertainty. Nonetheless, even with such safeguards in place, it is still impossible to gather all the information necessary to make consequence-certain decisions. Any system operating under such conditions (with imperfect information) is going to be wrong sometimes. The system that is going to do the best, on average, under these circumstances is going to be the one that produces the best overall net gains over many rounds of these decisions by maximizing the number and benefits of correct choices and minimizing the overall costs of errors. In making these calculations, a good system is one that takes into account the potential costs of being wrong in either direction: not all errors are created equal. In many of the cases involving disgust, the costs of a miss (failing to detect a harmful toxin or pathogen, for instance) are going to greatly outweigh the costs of a false positive (detecting a harmful pathogen where there is none, for instance). As a result, disgust tends to be extra-cautious, playing a better-safe-than-sorry approach, which leads to us getting disgusted more often than would occur if the system were acting with perfect information.

How does this overly sensitive system bias manifest itself in practice? Consider the experience of eating a food that gives you food poisoning, or drinking too much of a certain type of liquor and becoming sick. Even though that particular food or drink might be perfectly acceptable at a later time—when the food isn't spoiled and the drink is consumed in more reasonable quantities—your disgust systems nevertheless catalog the offending substance to ward off future consumption. In a similar way, people will not drink apple juice from a brand-new bedpan or consume drinks that have briefly contacted a sterilized, dead cockroach, even when they know the beverages are perfectly safe for consumption—our disgust systems find it safer to assume potential contamination risk than to play more precise odds. Likewise, noncommunicable diseases such as psoriasis, alopecia, eczema, and acne—diseases that *look* like communicable diseases even though (at least as far as we know) they can't be "caught"—can trigger the disgust response despite the fact that they pose no risk of infection.

All of these examples are a result of our disgust system playing a better-safe-than-sorry strategy: better to miss a single meal and live to fight another day rather than risk an extremely costly case of food poisoning. Better to avoid bodily contact even if it only "looks" like a contagious disease than to risk infection. Even though the risks are small, the costs are so large that your psychological immune system literally *errs* on the side of caution. On average over historical time, these are functionally adaptive errors, but in any given single case, they might drive an inaccurate and deleterious result.

Mismatch Error

In addition to inherent errors, disgust is also plagued by errors resulting from the mismatch between the ancestral environment in which it evolved and the modern environment in which it is deployed. As we've discussed, the various algorithms of disgust are designed to rely on inputs and cues that were reliable indicators of things like pathogen presence and potentially fitness-reducing sexual partners in the ancestral environment. To the extent that these cues are different in the modern environment—that there is a mismatch between the environment of our ancestors and the one in which we live—we can expect some amount of resultant error. For example, food and drink containing high concentrations of pesticides, fluoride, high-fructose corn syrup, red-dye #5, and other potentially harmful substances tend not to trigger disgust because these substances were not present or readily available in such high concentrations in the ancestral environment. Similarly, the need for disgust to be triggered by sexual partners posing genetic risks to offspring (e.g., siblings) has been neutralized by the advent of birth control and prophylactics, but such inventions are so evolutionarily novel that our disgust system hasn't had enough time to account for them, even if there were an adaptive reason to do so.

This isn't to say that things that weren't present in the ancestral environment can't disgust us. As noted above, certain mechanisms of the disgust system may rely on inputs such as "foods that have made me sick before," and so things like gummy bears or whiskey might become elicitors of disgust if consuming too much of them once made you sick—even though they weren't present in the time of our ancestors. Moreover, to the extent that modern objects and situations mimic the inputs and cues that the various algorithms of disgust are designed to detect, they can still trigger disgust; a rancid Hot Pocket will still set off the alarms of our spoliation detectors. As an even more extreme example, things like fake cockroaches, plastic feces, and fart-scented aerosol sprays (none of which were present in the ancestral environment) trigger disgust precisely by mimicking the visual and olfactory cues that disgust is designed to detect, even though they pose no risk of toxins or pathogens. In his account of living with the indigenous Yanomamö of Venezuela, the anthropologist Napoleon Chagnon recounts an instance that nicely illustrates the point:

> I found peanut butter and crackers a very nourishing "trail" meal, and a simple one to prepare. . . . More importantly, it was one of the few foods the Yanomamö would let me eat in relative peace. It looked suspiciously like animal feces to them, an impression I encouraged. I referred to the peanut butter as the feces of babies or "cattle." . . . On another occasion I was eating a can of frankfurters and growing very weary of the demands from one of the onlookers for a share in my meal. When he finally asked what I was eating, I replied: "Beef." He then asked: "Shaki! What part of the animal are you eating?" To which I replied, "Guess." He muttered a contemptuous epithet, but stopped asking for a share.[15]

Chagnon's story also illustrates a related point: in some cases, we may be able to "update" the disgust system so that it is no longer activated in the face of cues that once would set it off. In other words, the system can "learn" not to be disgusted. Just as an aversion to gummy bears or whiskey might be altered after repeated exposures to safe samples, Chagnon (like most people of the industrialized world) has been able to retrain his system to accept the peanut butter and frankfurters that disgust the Yanomamö.[16]

But this malleability should be taken with a grain of salt. We may be able to "learn" and "unlearn" certain elicitors of disgust, but, again, as we've previously outlined, the ability to do so depends on the underlying mechanisms that are coding such elicitors, and those mechanisms were influenced at least partly by the amount of variance in risk that the object at hand posed in the ancestral environment. On one end of the spectrum, food has a very high variance—there are many different *kinds* of foods, and encountering a novel food was probably quite common for our ancestors. Potential food carries with it potential nutritional benefits, but also the risk of spoliation or of defense mechanisms of the plant producing it (e.g., poisonous berries). Because of this wide variance in potential foods, disgust in the food domain tends to show higher rates of variation between people and cultures. On the other end of the spectrum, having children with your brother or sister was almost always a genetically deleterious endeavor, and so with such little variance in outcome, and such detrimental consequences, sexual disgust at the thought of incest—unlike toxin/pathogen disgust in the face of food—is not very malleable at all.

The point is this: we are not claiming that disgust is a fixed set of intuitive prohibitions, and that *only* those items and no others are going to trigger disgust in every situation. Disgust has certain limited ways of updating its various algorithms and acquiring and shedding elicitors—that is, by virtue of its architecture, disgust *is* a flexible system. But there is a glut of research demonstrating that, by and large, there are universal features of disgust that we can expect to reliably develop in humans—including the cues in our environment that will trigger disgust, as well as the mechanisms by which those cues can be acquired and updated—and, most importantly, *these features have been dictated largely by the conditions of the ancestral environment*. As a result, to the extent that our modern world differs from those conditions, the ability for disgust to adapt will be limited, and errors will occur.

One more example to illustrate the point. Consider the intuitive repulsion that some people feel toward homosexuality—toward the thought of kissing or making love with a person of the same sex. That repulsion, as we've outlined, is a tool (at least for females) to discourage nonprocreative sex (for males, pathogen avoidance might explain more) and reflects your genes saying *Don't waste your time here, there's no future in this for me!* Yet, today, homosexuals have plenty of options for having kids. Techniques such as donor insemination and surrogacy allow homosexuals to pass on their genes at the same rates as traditional heterosexual reproduction, but because such techniques were not recurrent features of the environment in which our psychological mechanisms were selected, their potential isn't ingrained in the system.

Error from Repurposing

The final category of errors includes those resulting from the continuous repurposing of disgust for different roles. As we've shown, our systems for generating moral decisions are often recruiting the output of systems for avoiding toxins and disease, and for avoiding potentially costly (in evolutionary terms) sexual partners. The available evidence also indicates that the development and repurposing of disgust were sequential: disgust began first as a consumption/contact-avoidance system, then was recruited to engineer the avoidance of certain sexual partners, and then, finally, once in place was available for the use of moral mechanisms designed to promote self-interest and facilitate coalitional action.

From an evolutionary point of view, this repurposing is efficient engineering: why build entirely new systems when such an effective one already exists?

In fact, natural selection frequently repurposes existing equipment to perform subsequent functions. We breathe and ingest food through a common tube, for example, and our spine—designed as a bridge for walking on all fours—is now used as a column to support walking and standing on two feet.[17] But efficiency in these cases doesn't come without its trade-offs; the "good enough" solution achieved by repurposing a thing for an ancillary task is often far from optimal—precision is sacrificed, complications arise, and secondary functions carry residual features of an antecedent use. To wit, because we have a common passageway for food and air, we also run the risk of choking on food or saliva. Similarly, because our spine is a repurposed bridge instead of a column designed for vertical support, we suffer from an array of back problems later in life.

Repurposed psychological functions, like disgust, are no different. They are prone to the same type of trade-offs as our physical features when repurposed for another use. When disgust was appropriated to function in the sexual domain and then subsequently co-opted by moral programs, it retained relics of its role as a system for avoiding toxins, pathogens, and other infectious agents. Nausea and retching, for example—while great ways to prevent (or reverse) the ingestion of toxins—are carried over into the sexual domain (at the thought, say, of having sex with a family member or a baby) even though there is little risk of toxin ingestion, or little benefit of nausea. Likewise, the same facial muscles that are activated to curl your lip and wrinkle your nose in the presence of toxins and pathogens are also often activated when you feel morally slighted, or while imagining dishonest behavior.[18]

In fact, it is in this context, when disgust is used in the condemnation of behavior, that the carryover of vestigial features is most problematic. Several different lines of research have demonstrated that because the various functions of disgust share infrastructure, they often "cross wires." Eliciting pathogen disgust by seating people at a dirty desk, introducing a smelly wastebasket or noxious odor in the room, or watching a disgusting video can increase the severity of a range of moral judgments on everything from committing minor social infractions to homosexual behavior.[19] Likewise, the propensity to experience pathogen disgust (or having a high "disgust sensitivity" in the "pathogen domain") correlates with the propensity to disapprove of homosexual behavior and gay marriage, and also with having more negative attitudes toward out-groups. Moreover, the cues of kinship that predict personal incest aversion also predict moral opposition to third-party incest,[20] and individuals who live in areas with greater pathogen threats place a greater emphasis on disgust intuitions in moral decision-making.[21] The fact that moral decisions may be swayed by factors as immaterial as how bad the room smells or how sensitive one is to touching germs reveals the danger of not (where possible) identifying and excising disgust.

In sum, our disgust system is prone to error. If moral systems survey the disgust system to render decisions on which behaviors to condemn, then moral systems will also be prone to these errors. To yoke a legal rule or other evaluative standard to disgust means that the rule will inevitably be saddled with, and ultimately tainted by, various design quirks. All this on top of the fact that, even if these systems operated free from any operational errors, there is no prima facie reason to privilege them in moral or legal decision-making.

PURGING DISGUST

We've spent several chapters here cataloging what happens when disgust is woven into the legal process, and how these various operational errors of our psychological disgust systems translate into real-world consequences in legal and political affairs. We've seen how disgust can prejudice juror decisions of guilt and degree of appropriate punishment, as when lawyers use disgust-inducing descriptions of defendants or when gruesome photographs are introduced as evidence. We've also seen how disgust contributes to us drawing seemingly arbitrary distinctions between which words we can say and which images we can display, and which we cannot. We've seen it used as a political wedge, forming and deepening fissures between groups, and as a primary fulcrum in seemingly illogical distinctions between which relationships are OK and which aren't. These are not low-stakes concerns. They involve issues relating to free speech, death penalty determinations, discrimination, homosexuality, privacy rights, and equal protection—a literal "greatest hits" of the most important and contentious legal issues of the past 50 years, both in the United States and around much of the world.

In our view, disgust, where present in the legal and political domain, should be identified and, to the extent possible, eliminated so as to avoid any prejudicial influence.[22] To be clear, our claims relate to the *process* for legal and political decision-making. For us, the critical issues are not which words are protected, or which couples are allowed to marry, but rather *how* we decide these questions. We aren't advocating for any ultimate positions, for instance that all speech should be allowed or none of it should; we are simply arguing for removing disgust as a criterion. Rather than concocting post-hoc arguments for our error-ridden and genetically focused intuitions of disgust—or as Francis Bacon phrased it, fitting arguments to practice, in reversed order—we should be deciding these questions using logic, reason, rational inference, and other tools that do not ultimately regress to gut-level intuitions.

Sometimes removing disgust might have no effect on the ensuing result. For example, in the cases of bestiality or pedophilia, it is almost certainly the case that issues of consent would necessitate the same outcome. Even when our natural intuitions about the "wrongness" of these issues are taken out, the fact that animals and children cannot offer the type of permission that we typically require for other lawful sexual activity—the same logic used in cases of rape and sexual assault of adults—points us toward the same result. But the important thing to keep in mind is that, in cases such as these, when disgust lines up with a more objective, more reasoned approach, it's a coincidence, not evidence of fit. Ultimately, as Kelly and Morar argued, it's the other, more objective criterion that is critical. That it also engenders disgust is incidental to the ultimate function of the law.

This logic is equally applicable to zoning or other public-health issues that involve threats to sanitation. Disgust will often serve as a very useful heuristic for identifying potential pathogen threats—and in this very limited role we have no complaint. More often than not, those instincts will be in sync with some other objective rubric (e.g., threats to health or safety). But once our intuitional alarm bells are set off, those instincts still need to be vetted via reference to that other rubric. As the *Euclid v. Ambler Realty Co.* case discussed earlier (the case in which city officials attempted to group correctional institutions and mental health facilities in the same zone as industrial waste facilities) demonstrates, relying simply on disgust—and in the process ceding rigorous assessment via the objective criterion to imperfect heuristic decision-making processes—is perilous.

On the other end of the spectrum are those instances in which, once we've removed the intuitional motivation of disgust, we're confronted with a case of Haidt's moral dumbfounding: *I can't really justify it, but I know it's wrong.* It is precisely these cases where we would urge voters and lawmakers to discard their gut reactions in favor of a more reasoned approach. As Judge Richard Posner (echoing John Stuart Mill) wrote in a recent opinion defending the rights of gays to marry, "there is a difference . . . between the distress that is caused by an assault, or a theft of property, or an invasion of privacy, or for that matter discrimination, and the behavior that disgusts some people but does no (other) harm to them."[23] In our view, if society cannot point to criteria beyond an instinctual disgust or aversion, criteria that aren't artifacts of genetic self-interest, and that aren't so prone to so much error, then perhaps we should reconsider the rule. Just as cases like pedophilia and bestiality are easy to justify without disgust, rules against sodomy, homosexual marriage, consensual incest, segregation of races and castes, and most forms of obscenity appear equally difficult to reconcile absent a reliance on gut aversions.

As we've seen, courts do frequently attempt to justify such rules, often by relying on concepts like contemporary community standards, traditional mores, or a historical practice of proscription. In other words, the logic is either *many people share these intuitions now* or *people have had these intuitions consistently for a long time.* But because disgust is a species-wide program built by an evolutionary process that takes thousands of generations to alter, many of our moral intuitions become both widespread within communities and consistent over long time courses. Hence, contemporary community standards and historical traditions aren't examples of more reasoned or deliberative frameworks, and they aren't part of a larger, more coherent political philosophy. Rather, they are simply aggregated and repackaged intuitions—statistical observations rather than value assessments. The collateralized debt organizations responsible for the subprime mortgage crisis provide an apt metaphor: if the original instruments are faulty, aggregating them is merely superficial—it doesn't remedy the underlying flaws.

Our contentions are truly put to the test, though, in cases like the two hypotheticals we opened this book with—necrophilia (or desecration of a corpse) and incest—cases where there may not be an obvious rational justification, and yet our disgust intuitions are the strongest and most universal. This tension was on full display in Europe recently, when both the German Ethics Council and a branch of the Swedish Liberal People's Party advocated for the legalization of consensual incest—proposals that were swiftly dismissed by the governing bodies in Germany and Sweden, respectively.

As we've seen, our aversion to incest is so strong that even when all rational objections are removed from the hypothetical, we still refuse to accept that it's OK. And in practice, many rational objections (such as, say, the genetic risk to offspring) are undermined by the widespread availability of birth control, as well as the scores of other genetic risk factors to potential children (e.g., Huntington's disease or a female's advanced age) that are not singled out for prohibition. Of course, there may be perfectly defensible reasons for prohibiting incest. There are undoubtedly sound arguments to be made on either side; our contention is merely that those are the conversations we should be having, and that such decisions should be made without regard to instinct-level revulsions. Even for laws governing the behaviors that we might have the strongest gut aversions to, the challenge is to view and evaluate the law with a reasoned, rational eye and decide whether or not it is worth keeping—or as Justice Oliver Wendell Holmes Jr. phrased it, to "get the dragon out of his cave on to the plain and in the daylight" where you can "count his teeth and claws, and see just what is his strength" and thus decide, when everything is laid bare, "either to kill him, or to tame him and make him a useful animal."[24]

CONCLUSION

It is one of the great accomplishments of the discipline of psychology, and indeed one of the great intellectual achievements of our species, that we have started to unravel the origins and mechanical workings of our deep-seated instincts. Unlike other animals, humans are endowed with an extraordinary gift: the capacity to ascertain and investigate our own biological and psychological makeup, and even more importantly, the capacity to evaluate it—to reinforce the parts of it that we deem worthy, and to try our best to moderate the parts of it that we deem undesirable. As far as we know, we're the only species on the planet that has this capacity, and we're also the only species with an institutional infrastructure that is powerful enough either to value the intuition and license it, or to move society away from these deep-seated intuitions. It is an extraordinary gift and, accordingly, should be exercised with great responsibility. The starting point of this responsibility is to separate biology from philosophy, to disentangle the reliably developing tendencies that evolution has equipped us with from the state of the world that we seek to effectuate.

Disgust was built by natural selection to solve, or help solve, a few of the many recurrent problems faced by our ancestors: finding a safe next meal, avoiding disease, and producing healthy children. Moreover, it was built to do so in ways that optimized genetic propagation when the typical human life was, to use Hobbes' phrase, poor, nasty, brutish, and short. In shaping the law, we face a different set of problems. The goal of the law is not to optimize or maximize the survival and re-production of individuals or their genes, but rather to move the populace toward a desired state of affairs, or to realize a particular moral or political ideology or principle—to prevent harm, to facilitate commerce, to enact the procedural ar-chitecture necessary to maintain a complex modern state. And while the goals of these enterprises might align in certain circumstances, there's certainly no reason to *presume* that they will, or that they should.

In a sense, there's nothing specific about this argument that limits it to dis-gust. Instead, it serves as a particularly illuminating example of why we should be taking a closer look at *all* of our intuitions, motivations, feelings, judgments, and moral inclinations and asking the same types of questions we've been asking here: Where do they come from? How do they work? What features are hidden from consciousness, and how does our blindness to them color our appraisal of the intuition itself? By answering those questions, we can start to evaluate whether, and how, they fit into the framework generated by a separate set of ques-tions: Which types of behaviors do we want to encourage, and which do we want to proscribe? What ends do we want to see our legal systems pursue? What values and ideas do we want to privilege in our policy?

Our general contention—that these are *independent* sets of questions—applies equally to other legally relevant psychological phenomena such as, say, retributive punishment urges or intuitions of property ownership. Disgust happens to be an especially illustrative test case because of its prevalence and impact, but it cer-tainly isn't unique in its standing.

From a historical perspective, we've never been in a better position to under-take these tasks. For one, the framework for investigating human behavior is as advanced—both technologically and theoretically—as it has ever been. We are in an unprecedented position to answer the *how* and *why* questions of psychology that seem so mysterious to our everyday, folk-intuitionist, experiencing selves. What is more, the size and sophistication of our governmental and legal institu-tions have also risen to a level such that we can implement policy with a remark-able level of both force and complexity. We have our Leviathan; the question now is: What are we going to do with it?

We opened this book by discussing the slow and incremental change that's nec-essary to an effective system of laws, and the balance that must take place between stability on the one hand and accounting for the advances of the behavioral sciences on the other. On the pages in between, we've tried to make our case that the scientific advances in the psychology of disgust have been significant, and that, because disgust is so pervasive in the law, these advances have substantial implications in the legal and political domains, and render many of the areas of law worth a fresh look—most importantly to ensure that they rely on something other than an instinctual revul-sion. And so we'll close with a passage taken from a letter from Thomas Jefferson to Samuel Kercheval, who captures the underlying thrust of our position nicely:

> I am certainly not an advocate for frequent and untried changes in laws and constitutions. I think moderate imperfections had better be borne with;

because, when once known, we accommodate ourselves to them, and find practical means of correcting their ill effects. But I know also, that laws and institutions must go hand in hand with the progress of the human mind. As that becomes more developed, more enlightened, as new discoveries are made, new truths disclosed, and manners and opinions change with the change of circumstances, institutions must advance also, and keep pace with the times. We might as well require a man to wear still the coat which fitted him when a boy, as civilized society to remain ever under the regiment of their barbarous ancestors.[25]

Chapter 1

1. Haidt, J., Bjorklund, F., & Murphy, S. (2000). *Moral Dumbfounding: When Intuition Finds No Reason*. Unpublished manuscript, University of Virginia; Haidt, J. (2001). The emotional dog and its rational tail. *Psychological Review, 108*, 814–834.

2. For more on human universal patterns of behavior, see Brown, D. E. (1991). *Human Universals*. Philadelphia: Temple University Press.

3. Curtis, V. (2013). *Don't Look, Don't Touch, Don't Eat: The Science Behind Revulsion*. Chicago: University of Chicago Press.

4. Book of Leviticus, New International Version, in the order in which they appear in the text: 15:1–33; 17; 12:2–6; 13:1–46; 21:18–20; 21:10; 11:20; 22:5; 11; 11:32–40; 5:1; 19:6; 19:10; 19:28; 21:18–20; 19:35; 18:7–18; 18:19; 18:23; 19:29; 20:13; 13:47–59; 21:11; 24:22.

5. *Lawrence v. Texas*, 539 U.S. 558 (2003), p. 590 (Scalia, J., dissenting).

6. The Criminal Justice and Immigration Act 2008 (section 63) (United Kingdom).

7. *Daubert v. Merrell Dow Pharmaceuticals, Inc.*, 509 U.S. 579 (1993), pp. 596–597.

8. Ibid., p. 597.

9. Cardozo, B. (1924). *The Growth of the Law*. New Haven: Yale University Press, p. 133.

10. Miller, W. I. (1998). *The Anatomy of Disgust*. Cambridge, MA: Harvard University Press, pp. ix–x.

11. Menninghaus, W. (2003). *Disgust: Theory and History of a Strong Sensation*. Albany: State University of New York Press, pp. 1, 43.

12. Kristeva, J. (1982). *The Powers of Horror: An Essay on Abjection*. New York: Columbia University Press, pp. 2–3.

13. Kant, I. (2006). *Anthropology from a Pragmatic Point of View*, translated by R. B. Loudon. Cambridge, UK: Cambridge University Press (original work published in 1798).

14. Pinker, S. (1997). *How the Mind Works*. New York: Norton, p. 383.

15. Darwin, C. (1872). *The Expression of the Emotions in Man and Animals*. London: John Murray, p. 257.

16. Menninghaus, W. (2003). *Disgust: Theory and History of a Strong Sensation*. Albany: State University of New York Press, p. 1.

17. Rozin, P., Haidt, J., & McCauley, C. (1993). Disgust. In *Handbook of Emotions*, edited by M. Lewis & J. M. Haviland. New York: Guildford Press, p. 584.

18. Miller, W. I. (1998). *The Anatomy of Disgust*. Cambridge, MA: Harvard University Press, p. 40.
19. McGinn, C. (2011). *The Meaning of Disgust*. New York: Oxford University Press, pp. 89–90.
20. For further reading, see, for instance, Haidt, J. (2007). The new synthesis in moral psychology. *Science, 316*, 998–1002 (Haidt maintains that morality does indeed extend beyond concepts of harm and fairness to include concerns regarding purity); Schein, C., & Gray, K. (2016). Moralization and harmification: the dyadic loop explains how the innocuous becomes harmful and wrong. *Psychological Inquiry, 27*, 62–65 (in contrast to Haidt, Gray maintains that disgust's link to morality is mediated by concerns regarding harm).
21. Kass, L. R. (1997, June 2). The wisdom of repugnance. *The New Republic*, p. 20.
22. Nussbaum, M. C. (2004). *Hiding from Humanity: Disgust, Shame, and the Law*. Princeton: Princeton University Press, p. 116.

CHAPTER 2

1. Nisbett, R. E., & Wilson, T. D. (1977). Telling more than we can know: verbal reports on mental processes. *Psychological Review, 84*, 231–259.
2. It is possible to target the left brain hemisphere by presenting information to the *right* visual field and the right brain hemisphere by presenting information to the left visual field.
3. Gazzaniga, M. S. (1995). Principles of human brain organization derived from split-brain studies. *Neuron, 14*, 217–228. Also see the following website for a depiction of a study on split-brain patients: http://thebrain.mcgill.ca/flash/capsules/experience_bleu06.html.
4. Maier, N. R. F. (1931). Reasoning in humans: II. The solution of a problem and its appearance in consciousness. *Journal of Comparative Psychology, 12*, 181–194; see pp. 188–189.
5. Latané, B., & Darley, J. M. (1970). *The Unresponsive Bystander: Why Doesn't He Help?* New York: Appleton-Century Crofts.
6. Cosmides, L., & Tooby, J. (1994). Beyond intuition and instinct blindness: the case for an evolutionarily rigorous cognitive science. *Cognition, 50*, 41–77.
7. Tooby, J., & Cosmides, L. (1995). The language of the eyes as an evolved language of mind. Foreword to: *Mindblindness: An Essay on Autism and Theory of Mind* by Simon Baron-Cohen. Cambridge, MA: MIT Press, p. xii.
8. Marr, D. (1982). *Vision*. Cambridge, MA: MIT Press.
9. Scheib, J. E., Gangestad, S. W., & Thornhill, R. (1999). Facial attractiveness, symmetry and cues of good genes. *Proceedings of the Royal Society B: Biological Sciences, 266*, 1913–1917.
10. Møller, A. P. (1997). Developmental stability and fitness: a review. *American Naturalist, 149*, 916–932.
11. For instance: Little, A. C., Jones, B. C., & DeBruine, L. M. (2011). Facial attractiveness: evolutionary based research. *Philosophical Transactions of the Royal Society B: Biological Sciences, 366*, 1638–1659.
12. Little, A. C., DeBuine, L. M., & Jones, B. C. (2011). Exposure to visual cues of pathogen contagion changes preferences for masculinity and symmetry in opposite-sex faces. *Proceedings of the Royal Society B: Biological Sciences, 278*, 2032–2039.

13. Symons, D. (1995). Beauty is in the adaptations of the beholder: the evolutionary psychology of human female sexual attractiveness. In *Chicago Series on Sexuality, History, and Society. Sexual Nature, Sexual Culture*, edited by P. R. Abramson & S. D. Pinkerton. Chicago: University of Chicago Press, pp. 80–119.

14. Pinker, S. (1994). *The Language Instinct*. New York: HarperCollins.

15. Tooby, J., & Cosmides, L. (1992). The psychological foundations of culture. In J. H. Barkow, L. Cosmides, & J. Tooby (Eds.), *The Adapted Mind* (pp. 19–136). New York: Oxford University Press.

16. For more on the conditions present over the course of human evolution, see Lee, R. B., & DeVore, I. (1968). *Man the Hunter*. New Brunswick, NJ: Aldine Transaction; and Boyd, R., & Silk, J. B. (2014). *How Humans Evolved*, 7th ed. New York: Norton.

17. Marr, D. (1982). *Vision*. Cambridge, MA: MIT Press.

18. We are, of course, also interested in questions of what and where, but limit our discussion here to questions of why and how.

19. Holmes, W. G., & Sherman, P. W. (1983). Kin recognition in animals. *American Scientist, 71*, 46–55; Hepper, P. G. (1991). *Kin Recognition*. New York: Cambridge University Press.

20. Ibid.

21. Westermarck, E. A. (1891/1921). *The history of human marriage*. Fifth Edition. London: Macmillan.

22. Talmon, Y. (1972). *Family and Community in the Kibbutz*. Cambridge, MA: Harvard University Press.

23. Shepher, J. (1983). *Incest: A Biosocial View*. New York: Academic Press.

24. Lieberman, D., & Lobel, T. (2012). Kinship on the Kibbutz: Co-residence duration predicts altruism, personal sexual aversions, and moral attitudes among communally reared peers. *Evolution and Human Behavior, 33*, 26–34.

25. For those looking for a more in-depth explanation of an evolutionary approach to psychology and also for a discussion of common misconceptions of the field, we recommend the classics *The Adapted Mind* by Jerome Barkow, Leda Cosmides, and John Tooby, *How the Mind Works* and *The Blank Slate*, by Steven Pinker, and the more recent *The Shape of Thought*, by H. Clark Barrett.

CHAPTER 3

1. Birkeland, C., Cheng, L., & Lewis, R. A. (1981). Mobility of dideminid ascidian colonies. *Bulletin of Marine Science, 31*, 170–173; Melillo, R., & Leisman, G. (2009). *Neurobehavioral Disorders of Childhood*. New York: Springer; see Chapter 2, Evolution of the Human Brain.

2. There is some evidence that, in humans, moms "eat their brains" too in a trade-off favoring greater energy expenditure on a growing child over costly neural functions like memory. See Hoekzema, E., et al. (2017). Pregnancy leads to long-lasting changes in human brain structure. *Nature Neuroscience, 20*, 287–296.

3. Spatial navigation can occur via multiple mechanisms. Organisms can navigate along concentration gradients, for instance gradients of salinity, acidity, electromagnetic radiation, etc. Here we are not speaking of uni-gradient movement but rather movement requiring the integration of multiple sources of information, whether it be multiple gradients or more complex mental representations.

4. For discussions of the counterintuitive nature of physics, see Styer, F. S. (2000). *The Strange World of Quantum Mechanics*. New York: Cambridge University Press; and Feynman, R. P. (1970). *The Feynman Lectures on Physics*. Boston: Addison Wesley Longman.

5. See Pinker, S. (2002). *The Blank Slate: The Modern Denial of Human Nature*. New York: Penguin Books.

6. There has been much written on consciousness. Here are two suggestions: Dennett, D. C. (1991). *Consciousness Explained*. Boston, MA: Back Bay Books; Chalmers, D. J. (2010). *The Character of Consciousness*. New York, NY: Oxford University Press.

7. There are a number of articles and books that address these issues. Here are a few: Schachter, S., & Singer, J. E. (1962) Cognitive, social and physiological determinants of emotional states. *Psychological Review, 69*, 379–399; Myers, D. G. (2004). Theories of emotion. *Psychology*, 7th ed. New York: Worth Publishers; Dennett, D. (1991). *Consciousness Explained*. Boston, MA: Back Bay Books; Chalmers, D. (1996). *The Conscious Mind*. New York: Oxford University Press; Kaszniak, A. (various). *Emotions, Qualia, and Consciousness*. River Edge, NJ: World Scientific Publishing Co.

8. See, for instance, Myers, D. G. (2004). Theories of emotion. *Psychology*, 7th ed. New York: Worth Publishers.

9. Our discussion derives from ideas published by John Tooby and Leda Cosmides. See, for example, Tooby, J., & Cosmides, L. (1990). The past explains the present: Emotional adaptations and the structure of ancestral environments. *Ethology and Sociobiology, 11*, 375–424; Cosmides, L., & Tooby, J. (2000). Evolutionary psychology and the emotions. In M. Lewis & J. M. Haviland-Jones (Eds.), *Handbook of Emotions, 2nd Edition* (pp. 91–115). NY: Guilford.

10. This could be one reason (of many) why it is difficult to motivate people to act in response to claims of climate change.

11. 1. Fear, 2. Disgust, 3. Sexual jealousy, 4. Anger, 5. Gratitude, 6. Shame, 7. Hunger, 8. Lust, 9. Love.

12. Seligman, M. E. P. (1971). Phobias and preparedness. *Behavior Therapy, 2*, 307–320.

13. For more on an evolutionary account of emotions, see Cosmides, L., & Tooby, J. (2000). Evolutionary psychology and the emotions. In *Handbook of Emotions*, 2nd ed., edited by M. Lewis & J. M. Haviland-Jones. New York: Guilford, pp. 91–115.

CHAPTER 4

1. Darwin, C. (1872/1965). *The Expression of the Emotions in Man and Animals*. New York: D. Appleton & Company. Quote is on p. 250.

2. Angyal, A. (1941). Disgust and related aversions. *Journal of Abnormal and Social Psychology, 36*, 393–412. Quote is on p. 394.

3. One of the influential papers in modern disgust research is Haidt, J., McCauley, C., & Rozin, P. (1994). Individual differences in sensitivity to disgust: a scale sampling seven domains of disgust elicitors. *Personality and Individual Differences, 16*, 701–713.

4. There have been a number of articles and books written on disgust. Readers interested in learning more about consumption might be interested in Herz, R. (2017). *Why You Eat What You Eat: The Science Behind Our Relationship with Food*. New York: W. W. Norton & Company.

5. Ewald, P. (2002). *Plague Time: The New Germ Theory of Disease*. New York: Anchor Books.

6. One study that used such odorants to induce disgust is Wicker, B., Keysers, C., Plailly, J., Royet, J. P., Gallese, V., & Rizzolatti, G. (2003). Both of us disgusted in my insula: the common neural basis of seeing and feeling disgust. *Neuron, 40*, 655–664.

7. Oum, R. E., Lieberman, D., & Aylward, A. (2011). A feel for disgust: tactile cues to pathogen presence. *Cognition and Emotion, 25*, 717–725.

8. Sarabian, C., Ngoubangoye, B., & MacIntosh, A. J. J. (2017). Avoidance of biological contaminant through sight, smell, and touch in chimpanzees. *Royal Society Open Science*. doi:10.1098/rsos.170968.

9. Sauter, D. A., Eisener, F., Ekman, P., & Scott, S. K. (2010). Cross-cultural recognition of basic emotions through nonverbal emotional vocalizations. *Proceedings of the National Academy of Sciences USA, 107*, 2408–2412.

10. Ekman, P., & Friesen, W. V. (1971). Constants across cultures in the face and emotion. *Journal of Personality and Social Psychology, 17*, 124–129.

11. There is controversy over whether there exists a dedicated system for detecting amino acids; some authors suggest that a desire for salt covers the need for meat, as meat is salty. For more on this, see the following: Bartoshuk, L. M. (1991). Taste, smell and pleasure. In *The Hedonics of Taste*, edited by R. C. Bolles. Hillsdale, NJ: Erlbaum; Herz, R. (2017). *Why You Eat What You Eat*. New York: W. W. & Norton; Chaudhari, N., Pereira, E., & Roper, S. D. (2009). Taste receptors for umami: the case for multiple receptors. *American Journal of Clinical Nutrition, 90*, 738S–742S.

12. Here we are talking about red peppers, capsicums. We are not talking about black pepper; peppercorns and ground pepper are products of *Piper nigrum*, a flowering cine of the family Piperaceae.

13. Caterina, M. J., Schumacher, M. A., Tominaga, M., Rosen, T. A., Levine, J. D., & Julius, D. (1997). The capsaicin receptor: a heat-activated ion channel in the pain pathway. *Nature, 389*, 816–824.

14. Tewksbury and colleagues have conducted a number of studies on hot chilies: Haak, D. C., McGinnis, L. A., Levey, D. J., & Tewksbury, J. J. (2012). Why are not all chilies hot? A trade-off limits pungency. *Proceeding of Biological Sciences, 279*, 2012–2017; Tewksbury, J. J., Reagan, K. M., Machnicki, N. J., Carlo, T. A., Haak, D. C., Calderón- Peñaloza, A. L., & Levey, D. J. (2008). The evolutionary ecology of pungency in wild chilies *Proceedings of the National Academy of Sciences USA, 105*, 11808–11811; Tewksbury, J. J., Levey, D. J. Huizinga, M., Haak, D., & Travaset, A. (2008). Costs and benefits of capsaicin-mediated control of gut retention in dispersers of wild chilies. *Ecology, 89*, 107–117; Levey, D. J., Tewksbury, J. J., Cipollini, M., & Carlo, T. A. (2006). A field test of the directed deterrence hypothesis in two species of wild chili. *Oecologia, 150*, 51–68; Tewksbury, J. J., Manchego, C., Haak, D., & Levey, D. J. (2006). Where did the chili get its spice? Biogeography of capsaicinoid production in ancestral wild chili species. *Chemical Ecology, 32*, 547–554; Tewksbury, J. J. (2002). Fruits, frugivores, and the evolutionary arms race. *New Phytologist, 156*, 137–144; Tewksbury, J. J., & Nabhan, G. P. (2001). Directed deterrence by capsaicin in chilies. *Nature, 412*, 403–404.

15. Roulette, C. J., et al. (2014). Tobacco use vs. helminthes in Congo basin hunter-gatherers: self-medication in humans? *Evolution & Human Behavior, 35,* 397–407.

16. Billing, J., & Sherman, P. W. (1998). Antimicrobial functions of spices: why some like it hot. *Quarterly Review of Biology, 73,* 3–49.

17. Rozin, P., & Kalat, J. W. (1971). Specific hungers and poison avoidance as adaptive specializations of learning. *Psychological Review, 78,* 459–486; Rozin, P. (1976). The selection of food by rats, humans and other animals. In *Advances in the Study of Behavior, Vol. 6,* edited by J. S. Rosenblatt, R. A. Hinde, E. Shaw, & C. Beer. New York: Academic Press, pp. 21–76.

18. Meier, L., et al. (2015). Rivalry of homeostatic and sensory-evoked emotions: dehydration attenuates olfactory disgust and its neural correlates. *Neuroimage, 114,* 120–127.

19. Hoefling, A., et al. (2009). When hunger finds no fault with moldy corn: food deprivation reduces food-related disgust. *Emotion, 9,* 50–58.

20. Paul Rozin has published a number of articles on specific types of hunger and diets sought to address particular deficiencies. See, for example, Rozin, P. (1968). Are carbohydrate and protein intakes separately regulated? *Journal of Comparative and Physiological Psychology, 65,* 23–29; Rozin, P., & Kalat, J. W. (1971). Specific hungers and poison avoidance as adaptive specializations of learning. *Psychological Review, 78,* 459–486.

21. Garcia, J., & Koelling, R. A. (1966). Relation of cue to consequence in avoidance learning. *Psychonomic Science, 4,* 123–124.

22. Seligman, M. E. P., & Hager, J. L. (1972, August). Biological boundaries of learning: the sauce-béarnaise syndrome. *Psychology Today,* pp. 59–61, 84–87; Seligman, M. E. P. (1970). On the generality of the laws of learning. *Psychological Review, 77,* 406–418; Seligman, M. E. P., & Hager, J. L. (1972). *Biological Boundaries of Learning.* New York: Appleton-Century-Crofts.

23. Profet, M. (1995). *Pregnancy Sickness: Using Your Body's Natural Defenses to Protect Your Baby-to-Be.* Da Capo Press. Quote is by Margie Profet in a November 28, 1995, *Washington Post* article by Rick Weiss, "Is nausea in pregnancy nature's way of protecting the fetus from toxins?"

24. Fessler, D. M. T., Eng, S. J., & Navarrete, C. D. (2005). Elevated disgust sensitivity in the first trimester of pregnancy: evidence supporting the compensatory prophylaxis hypothesis. *Evolution and Human Behavior, 26,* 344–351.

25. Rozin, P., et al. (1986). The child's conception of food: differentiation of categories of rejected substances in the 16 months to 5 year age range. *Appetite, 7,* 141–151.

26. Dencker, S. J., Johansson, G., & Milsom, I. (1992). Quantification of naturally occurring benzodiazepine-like substances in human breast milk. *Psychopharmacology, 107,* 69–72.

27. Cashdan, E. (1998). Adaptiveness of food learning and food aversions in children. *Social Science Information, 37,* 613–632; Cashdan, E. (1994). A sensitive period for learning about food. *Human Nature, 5,* 279–291.

28. Pliner, P., & Salvy, S. (2006). Food neophobia in humans. *Frontiers in Nutritional Science, 3,* 75.

29. Evidence of this type of social learning comes from studies on infants. Zoe Liberman, a developmental psychologist at UCSB, found that infants infer that if one person exhibits disgust toward a food item, others will as well, regardless of

their social affiliation. Liberman, Z., Woodward, A., Sullivan, K. R., & Kinzler, K. D. (2016). Early emerging system for reasoning about the social nature of food. *Proceedings of the National Academy of Sciences USA, 113*, 9480–9485.

30. As conceived, expected values of consumption can range along a continuum. In reaction to this idea, an anonymous colleague stated that we do not feel disgust at the thought of eating rocks or dirt. We disagree. Try and feed someone rocks and dirt. Put it to their mouth, close to their lips and we suspect you will observe strong disgust. Now the thought of dirt and rocks (pencils, paper, carpet fiber, etc.) might not evince a strong disgust reaction when imagining them, unlike, say, imagining maggots, puke, and diarrhea. But this is for good reason. These items vary in their cues to pathogen presence and contamination threat. But expected values of consumption track not just pathogen cues, but other cues correlating with palatability. Too much bitter (e.g., tea) can become disgusting. Too much sugar or salt can also render a substance disgusting by virtue of a lowered expected value of consumption.

31. See, for instance, Hart, B. (2005). The evolution of herbal medicine: behavioural perspectives. *Animal Behaviour, 70*, 975–989.

32. Krief, S., et al. (2006). Bioactive properties of plant species ingested by chimpanzees (*Pan troglodytes schweinfurthii*) in the Kibale National Park, Uganda. *American Journal of Primatology, 68*, 51–71; Barelli, C., & Huffman, M. A. (2017). Leaf swallowing and parasite explusion in Khao-Yai white-handed gibbons (*Hylobates lar*), the first report in an Asian ape species. *American Journal of Primatology, 79*, e22610; Huffman, M. A., & Seifu, M. (1989). Observations on the illness and consumption of a possibly medicinal plant *Vernonia amygdalina* (Del.), by a wild chimpanzee in the Mahale Mountains National Park, Tanzania. *Primates, 30*, 51–63.

33. There was a recent *New York Times* article, "The self-medicating animal" by Moises Velasquez-Manoff, May 18, 2017, regarding the medicinal use of plants by various animals and a discussion of evolved mechanisms.

34. Schaller, M., & park, J. H. (2011). The behavioral immune system (and why it matters). *Current Directions in psychological Science, 20*, 99–103.

CHAPTER 5

1. See also Curtis, V. A. (2014). Infection-avoidance behavior in humans and other animals. *Trends in Immunology, 35*, 457–464; Hart, B. L. (2011). Behavioural defences in animals against pathogens and parasites: parallels with the pillars of medicine in humans. *Philosophical Transactions of the Royal Society B: Biological Sciences, 366*, 3406–3417.

2. Hutchings, M. R., Kyriazakis, I., Papachristou, T. G., Gordon, I. J., & Jackson, F. (2000). The herbivores' dilemma: trade-offs between nutrition and parasitism in foraging decisions. *Oecologia, 124*, 242–251; Karvonen, A., Seppälä, O., & Valtonen, E. T. (2004). Parasite resistance and avoidance behavior in preventing eye fluke infections in fish. *Parasitology, 129*, 159–164; Meisel, J. D., & Kim, D. H. (2014). Behavioral avoidance of pathogenic bacteria by *Caenorhabditis elegans*. *Trends in Immunology, 35*, 465–470; Schulenburg, H., & Muller, S. (2004). Natural variation in the response of *Caenorhabditis elegans* towards *Bacillus thuringiensis*. *Parasitology, 128*, 433–443.

3. Christe, P., Oppliger, A., Bancalà, F., Castella, G., & Chapuisat, M. (2003). Evidence for collective medication in ants. *Ecology Letters*, 6, 19–22; Hemmes, R. B., Alvarado, A., & Hart, B. L. (2002). Use of California bay foliage by wood rats for possible fumigation of nest-borne ectoparasites. *Behavioural Ecology*, 13, 381–385; Clark, L., & Mason, J. R. (1985). Use of nest material as insecticidal and anti-pathogenic agents by the European starling. *Oecologia*, 67, 169–176; Hart, B. L. (2005). The evolution of herbal medicine: behavioural perspectives. *Animal Behaviour*, 70, 975–989.

4. Hart, B. L., & Hart, L. A. (1994). Fly switching in Asian elephants: tool use to control parasites. *Animal Behaviour*, 48, 35–45; Hofstede, H., & Brock Fenton, M. (2005). Relationships between roost preferences, ectoparasite density, and grooming behaviour of neotropical bats. *Journal of Zoology*, 266, 333–340; Mooring, M. S., McKenzie, A. A., & Hart, B. L. (1996). Grooming in impala: role of oral grooming in removal of ticks and effects of ticks in increasing grooming rate. *Physiology & Behavior*, 59, 965–971; Ribeiro, J. M. C. (1989). Role of saliva in tick/host interactions. *Experimental and Applied Acarology*, 7, 15–20.

5. Diez, L., Lejeune, P., & Detrain, C. (2014). Keep the nest clean: survival advantages of corpse removal in ants. *Biology Letters*, 10, 20140306; Behringer, D. C., Butler, M. J., & Shields, J. D. (2006). Avoidance of disease by social lobsters. *Nature*, 441, 421; Krause, J., & Godin, J-G. J. (1994). Influence of parasitism on the shoaling behaviour of banded killifish. *Canadian Journal of Zoology*, 72, 1775–1779; Poirotte, C., Massol, F., Herbert, A., Willaume, E., Bomo, P. M., Kappeler, P. M., & Charpentier, M. J. E. (2017). Mandrills use olfaction to socially avoid parasitized conspecifics. *Science Advances*, 3, e1601721; Medina, L. M., Hart, A. G., & Ratnieks, F. L. W. (2009). Hygienic behavior in the stingless bees *Melipona beecheii* and *Scaptotrigona pectoralis* (Hymenoptera: Meliponini). *Genetics and Molecular Research*, 8, 571–576.

6. Case, T. I., Repacholi, B. M., & Stevenson, R. J. (2006). My baby doesn't smell as bad as yours. *Evolution and Human Behavior*, 27, 357–365.

7. Stevenson, R. J., & Repacholi, B. M. (2005). Does the source of an interpersonal odour affect disgust? A disease risk model and its alternatives. *European Journal of Social Psychology*, 35, 375–401.

8. Wlodarski, R., & Dunbar, R. I. M. (2014). What's in a kiss? The effect of romantic kissing on mate desirability. *Evolutionary Psychology*, 12, 178–199; Kort, R., Caspers, M., van de Graaf, A., van Egmond, W., & Roeselers, G. (2014). Shaping the oral microbiota through intimate kissing. *Microbiome*, 2, 41.

9. Borg, C., & de Jong, P. J. (2012). Feelings of disgust and disgust-induced avoidance weaken following induced sexual arousal in women. *PloS One*, 7(9), e44111.

10. There are some interesting implications for explaining cannibalism. We defer this particular topic for a later time.

CHAPTER 6

1. Ridley, M. (1993). The power of parasites. Chapter 3 in *The Red Queen*. New York: Penguin Books.

2. It is true that our gastrointestinal cells and gut bacteria are symbionts, living together in a mutually beneficial relationship. However, it would be a mistake to assume cooperation is the default relationship (indeed, this is a larger theme of this book). If new routes of transmission presented themselves, genetic mutations that

caused commensal gut bacteria to begin exploiting our insides for their own gain would take hold. It's like having a tiger as a pet: so long as they're well fed, they won't see you as food.

3.   Tooby J. (1982). Pathogens, polymorphism, and the evolution of sex. *Journal of Theoretical Biology, 97*, 557–576.

4.   Tooby, J. (1988). *The evolution of sex and its sequelae*. Doctoral dissertation, Harvard University. University Microfilms.

5.   http://www.guinnessworldrecords.com/world-records/most-prolific-mother-ever

6.   Oberzaucher, E., Grammer, K. & Szolnoki, A. (2014). The case of Moulay Ismael—fact or fancy? *PLoS ONE, 9*(2), e85292.

7.   Betzig, L. (1997). Introduction: people are animals. In *Human Nature: A Critical Reader*, pp. 1–17. New York: Oxford University Press.

8.   Bermant, G. (1976). Sexual behavior: hard times with the Coolidge effect. In *Psychological Research: The Inside Story*, edited by M. H. Siegel & H. P. Zeigler. New York: Harper & Row, pp. 76–103.

9.   Clark, R. D. III, & Hatfield, E. (1989). Gender differences in receptivity to sexual offers. *Journal of Psychology & Human Sexuality, 2*, 39–55.

10. Clark, R. D., & Hatfield, E. (2003). Love in the afternoon. *Psychological Inquiry, 14*, 227–231; Guéguen, N. (2011). Effects of solicitor sex and attractiveness on receptivity to sexual offers: a field study. *Archives of Sexual Behavior, 40*, 915–919; see also Baranowski, A., & Hecht, H. (2015). Gender differences and similarities in receptivity to sexual invitations: effects of location and risk perception. *Archives of Sexual Behavior, 44*, 2257–2265.

11. Jones, D. (1996). An evolutionary perspective on physical attractiveness. *Evolutionary Anthropology, 5*, 97–109; Schmitt, D., Shackelford, T. K., Duntley, J., Tooke, W., Buss, D. M., Fisher, M. L., Lavallée, M., & Vasey, P. (2002). Is there an early 30s peak in female sexual desire: cross-sectional evidence from the United States and Canada. *Canadian Journal of Human Sexuality, 11*, 1–18.

12. Alterovitz, S. S.-R., & Mendelsohn, G. A. (2009). Partner preferences across the life span: online dating by older adults. *Psychology and Aging, 24*, 513–517; Skopek, J., Schmitz, A., & Blossfeld, H-P. (2011). The gendered dynamics of age preferences—empirical evidence from online dating. *Zeitschrift für Familienforschung, 23*, 267–290.

13. Kenrick, D. T., & Keefe, R. C. (1992). Age preferences in mates reflect sex differences in human reproductive strategies, *Behavioral and Brain Sciences, 15*, 75–133; Buunk, B. P., Dijkstra, P., Kenrick, D. T., & Warntjes, A. (2001). Age preferences for mates as related to gender, own age, and involvement level. *Evolution and Human Behavior, 22*, 241–250.

14. England, P., & McClintock, E. A. (2009). The gendered double standard of aging in U.S. marriage markets. *Population and Development Review, 35*, 797–816.

15. Dakin, R., McCrossan, O., Hare, J. F., Montgomerie, R., & Kane, S. A. (2016). Biomechanics of the peacock's display: how feather structure and resonance influence multimodal signaling. *PLoS One, 11*, e0152759.

16. This is well-trod material of evolutionary psychology, perhaps the most empirically validated findings of the field. For book-length treatments of the research, we recommend David Buss' *The Evolution of Desire*, revised and updated edition, 2016, New York, NY: Basic Books; Helena Cronin's *The Ant and the Peacock*, 1991,

Cambridge: Cambridge University Press; and Geoffrey Miller's *The Mating Mind*, 1996, New York, NY: Anchor Books.

17. Borgerhoff Mulder, M. (1988). Kipsigis bridewealth payments. In *Human Reproductive Behavior: A Darwinian Perspective*, edited by L. Betzig et al. Cambridge: Cambridge University Press, pp. 65–82.

18. For example, see Bittles, A. H., & Neel, J. V. (1994). The costs of human inbreeding and their implications for variations at the DNA level. *Nature Genetics, 8*, 117–121; Charlesworth, D., & Willis, J. H. (2009). The genetics of inbreeding depression, *Nature Reviews Genetics, 10*, 783–796; Liberg, O., Andrén, H., Pedersen, H-C., Sand, H., Sejberg, D., Wabakken, P., Åkesson, M., & Bensch, S. (2005). Severe inbreeding depression in a wild wolf (*Canis lupus*) population. *Biology Letters, 1*, 17–20.

19. Bittles, A. H., Mason, W. M., Greene, J., & Rao, N. A. (1991). Reproductive behavior and health in consanguineous marriages. *Science, 252*, 789–794; Bittles, A. H. (2005). Genetic aspects of inbreeding and incest. In *Inbreeding, Incest, and the Incest Taboo*, edited by A. P. Wolf & W. H. Durham. Stanford, CA: Stanford University Press, pp. 38–60.

20. Hrdy, S. B. (1974). Male–male competition and infanticide among the langurs (*Presbytis Entellus*) of Abu, Rajasthan. *Folia Primatologica, 22*, 19–58.

21. For instance, Quinlan, R. J., & Quinlan, M. B. (2008). Human lactation, pair-bonds, and alloparents: a cross-cultural analysis. *Human Nature, 19*, 87–102.

22. Another possible cue that has been suggested in prior research is that a man might also compare how much a particular baby resembles him when assessing paternity. Previous studies have found evidence to support this, though recent data call this proposed cue into question (e.g., Billingsley, J., Antfolk, J., Santtila, P., & Lieberman, D. [2018]. Cues to paternity: Do partner fidelity and offspring resemblance predict daughter-directed sexual aversions? *Evolution and Human Behavior*). From a theoretical perspective, given that humans did not evolve alongside mirrors, it is also not clear that a man would know what he actually looked like in ancestral times.

23. Lieberman, D., Tooby, J., & Cosmides, L. (2007). The architecture of human kin detection. *Nature, 445*, 727–731. We note that in the particular model presented here, we do not include a separate detection system for siblings, mothers, fathers, and offspring. There certainly could be dedicated systems for each type of relative. We present the more parsimonious model that takes as input all cues and generates an estimate of relatedness based on inputs available. We are, of course, happy to entertain models of greater modularity.

24. Especially striking are those reports of genetic relatives meeting later in life who profess to be exceptionally or uniquely attracted to one another. This is sometimes referred to as genetic sexual attraction (GSA). GSA has a relatively straightforward explanation. Relatives, by virtue of having an increased chance of sharing the same genes, also tend to share many attributes. By luck of the draw, your sibling is going to share many of the same preferences, desires, and even mindsets as you. (Imagine creating your ideal mate or friend. Likely this person would share many of your preferences and habits.) To boot, relatives also share physical features in common. Given that we come to know what counts as a healthy member of our species by observing those around us, our mental template of a "normal" or "typical" face and other features will resemble those with whom we most frequently interact: family, and, because we have mirrors

now, ourselves. The overall similarities and better-than-average chance that a relative will share preferences from A to Z makes it more likely that they will be valued highly (see discussion of association value in Chapter 8). Take away any naturally developing sexual aversion because kinship cues were absent and— voilà!—genetic sexual attraction.

25. For instance, Thieben, M. J., Duggins, A. J., Good, C. D., Gomes, L., Mahant, N., Richards, F., McCusker, E., & Frackowiak, R. S. (2002). The distribution of structural neuropathology in pre-clinical Huntington's disease. *Brain, 125*, 1815–1828; Shapira, N. A., Liu, Y., He, A. G., Bradley, M. M., Lessig, M. C., James, G. A., Stein, D. J., Lang, P. J., & Goodman, W. K. (2003). Brain activation by disgust-inducing pictures in obsessive-compulsive disorder. *Biological Psychiatry, 54*, 751–756; Gray, J. M., Young, A. W., Barker, W. A., Curtis, A., & Gibson, D. (1997). Impaired recognition of disgust in Huntington's disease gene carriers. *Brain, 120*, 2029–2038.

26. A study by Alan Feingold found that attractiveness ratings of men and women in relationships correlated between .39 and .49; the more attractive the women, the more attractive the man: Feingold, A. (1988). Matching for attractiveness in romantic partners and same-sex friends: a meta-analysis and theoretical critique. *Psychological Bulletin, 104*, 226–235.

27. Morgan, L. K., & Kisley, M. A. (2014). The effects of facial attractiveness and perceiver's mate value on adaptive allocation of central processing resources. *Evolution and Human Behavior, 35*, 96–102; Bailey, D. H., Durante, K. M., & Geary, D. C. (2011). Men's perception of women's attractiveness is calibrated to relative mate value and dominance of the woman's partner. *Evolution and Human Behavior, 32*, 138–146.

28. Lee, L., Loewenstein, G., Ariely, D., Hong, J., & Young, J. (2008). If I'm not hot, are you hot or not? Physical-attractiveness evaluations and dating preferences as a function of one's own attractiveness. *Psychological Science, 19*, 669–677. Quote is on p. 672.

29. Buss, D. M., & Shackelford, T. K. (2008). Attractive women want it all: good genes, economic investment, parenting proclivities, and emotional commitment. *Evolutionary Psychology, 6*, 134–146; Yong, J. C., & Li, N. P. (2012). Cash in hand, want better-looking mate: significant resource cues raise men's mating standards. *Personality and Individual Differences, 53*, 55–58.

30. Wolf, A. P. (1995). *Sexual Attraction and Childhood Association: A Chinese Brief for Edward Westermarck.* Stanford, CA: Stanford University Press.

31. Lieberman, D., Tooby, J., & Cosmides, L. (2007). The architecture of human kin detection. *Nature, 445*, 727–731.

32. http://www.sciforums.com/threads/is-it-wrong-to-be-disgusted-by-homosexuals. 62719/

33. Marsiglio, W. (1993). Attitudes toward homosexual activity and gays as friends: a national survey of heterosexual 15- to 19-year-old males. *Journal of Sex Research, 30*, 12–17.

34. LaMar, L., & Kite, M. (1998). Sex differences in attitudes toward gay men and lesbians: a multidimensional perspective. *Journal of Sex Research, 35*, 189–196; Herek, G. M. (1988). Heterosexuals' attitudes toward lesbians and gay men: correlates and gender differences. *Journal of Sex Research, 25*, 451–477.

35.   LaMar, L., & Kite, M. (1998). Sex differences in attitudes toward gay men and les-
      bians: A multidimensional perspective. *Journal of Sex Research*, *35*, 189–196.

36.   Ariely, D., & Loewenstein, G. (2006). The heat of the moment: the effect of sexual
      arousal on sexual decision-making. *Journal of Behavioral Decision Making*,
      19, 87–98.

37.   For instance, researchers have proposed a separate variable, association value, that
      is a more global index of the extent to which a person confers benefits, not just via
      a heightened sexual value, but because the individual is a good cooperator (for in-
      stance, they are honest and have good products to trade), or because the individual
      happens to value you for the positive attributes you possess. Thus, there is much
      more to human interactions beyond sexual value. Here we are only focusing on the
      particular traits that inform decisions about the expected costs or benefits another
      person holds as a sexual partner—that is, a person with whom to procreate. For
      more on association value and cooperation, see Tooby, J., & Cosmides, L. (1996).
      Friendship and the banker's paradox: other pathways to the evolution of adapta-
      tions for altruism. In *Evolution of Social Behaviour Patterns in Primates and Man*,
      edited by W. G. Runciman, J. Maynard Smith, & R. I. M. Dunbar. *Proceedings of the
      British Academy*, *88*, 119–143.

38.   Intragenomic conflict refers to the fact that different elements of our genome are
      in competition with one another and have different "interests" in the gender of off-
      spring that are produced. Some genes prefer only males to be born—this includes
      the Y chromosome, which is only inherited by males. And some genes prefer only
      females to be born—this includes DNA in mitochondria, the organelles responsible
      for producing energy for the cell. (Yes, our cells contain lots of DNA, not just in the
      nucleus on our 23 pairs of chromosomes, but outside the nucleus in various struc-
      tures like mitochondria.) DNA only gets passed down generation after generation via
      eggs—through daughters. Sperm only contribute nuclear DNA—they do not con-
      tribute any mitochondria or mitochondrial DNA. From the mitochondrial DNA's
      point of view, then, the production of which sex would have enhanced survival?
      Daughters and only daughters! Mitochondria have "no interest" in producing males
      and are under less pressure to even operate effectively in males. As a result, there are
      some interesting effects that can be attributed to the nefarious consequences of mi-
      tochondrial DNA. For instance, there is a sex bias in spontaneous abortions—more
      males are spontaneously aborted than females,[39] which might be due to mitochon-
      drial DNA attempting to "start again" in the hopes of producing a female.

      But what does mitochondrial DNA have to do with homosexuality and sexual
      variation? One provocative possibility: feminization of the body plan could be an
      attempt by nuclear DNA to "fool" mitochondrial DNA into thinking the growing
      fetus was female. This could lead to an over-feminization of females or a slight
      to severe feminization of males. By causing the biochemistry to look more fe-
      male, nuclear genes might score a win and prevent female-centric mitochondrial
      DNA from trying to abort the fetus. In general, over-feminization or over-mas-
      culinization could be a reflection of the never-ending conflict between different
      cohorts of genes, in this case the female-promoting cytoplasmic genes and the
      sex-equality–promoting nuclear genes. Sexual variation is complicated. For more
      on intragenomic conflict, see Cosmides, L., & Tooby, J. (1981). Cytoplasmic in-
      heritance and intragenomic conflict. *Journal of Theoretical Biology*, *89*, 83–129.

39. For instance, see Hassold, T., Quillen, S. D., & Yamane, J. A. (1983). Sex ratio in spontaneous abortions. *Annals of Human Genetics, 47,* 39–47. These researchers found that in mothers aged 20 to 34, the average ratio of spontaneously aborted males to females was approximately 1.3. When examining the sex ratio of spontaneously aborted fetuses as a function of menstrual age (gestation age), they found that at 9 to 12 weeks, just after sexual differentiation and development begins in utero, the ratio was 1.40.

40. As stated by John Rechy, quoted in Don Symons' *The Evolution of Human Sexuality,* 1979, Oxford University Press. New York, NY p. 295.

41. Kenrick, D. T., Keefe, R. C., Bryan, A., Barr, A., & Brown, S. (1995). Age preferences and mate choice among homosexuals and heterosexuals: a case for modular psychological mechanisms. *Journal of Personality and Social Psychology, 69,* 1166–1172; Kenrick, D. T., & Keefe, R. C. (1992). Age preferences in mates reflect sex differences in human reproductive strategies. *Behavioral and Brain Sciences, 15,* 75–133.

42. For a discussion developmental endocrinology, politics, and science, see Alice Dreger's *Galileo's Middle Finger,* 2016, New York, NY: Penguin Books.

43. Failure to recognize how complex our mate choice systems are and how they organize and deploy (in addition to the affliction of instinct blindness that we discussed in Chapter 2) can lead to knee-jerk, yet incorrect, assumptions that particular expressions of sexuality are simply learned. *60 Minutes* aired a program hosted by Oprah Winfrey in which seven Trump voters and seven Clinton voters discussed a number of current hot-button issues. See: https://www.cbsnews.com/news/post-election-is-the-u-s-still-a-nation-divided-oprah-winfrey-reports/. One issue was President Trump's ban of transgender individuals from the military. In the ensuing discussion, a panel member stated that he had no problem with homosexuals serving in the military because homosexuality is not a choice, but that he did have a problem with transgendered individuals serving in the military. The implication from this panelist's comments is that he believed that transgendered individuals choose to switch their sex. But this is not necessarily correct in the same way that most homosexuals (and heterosexuals for that matter) did not choose their sexual preferences. We need to have a deeper appreciation of the systems underlying sexual development.

44. Vasey, P. L., & VanderLaan, D. P. (2010). An adaptive cognitive dissociation between willingness to help kin and nonkin in Samoan Fa'afafine. *Psychological Science, 21,* 292–297.

45. Bobrow, D., & Baiey, J. M. (2001). Is male homosexuality maintained by kin selection? *Evolution and Human Behavior, 22,* 361–368.

CHAPTER 7

1. Perhaps the most notable scholar who has dealt with the role of disgust in law is Martha Nussbaum. In her writings, she adheres to the model of disgust proposed by Paul Rozin, Jonathan Haidt, and colleagues. For instance, see Nussbaum, M. (2010). *From Disgust to Humanity: Sexual Orientation and Constitutional Law.* New York: Oxford University Press.

2. Rozin, P., Lowery, L., & Ebert, R. (1994). Varieties of disgust faces and the structure of disgust. *Journal of Personality and Social Psychology, 66,* 870–881. Quote is on p. 870.

3. Rozin, P., Millman, L., & Nemeroff, C. (1986). Operation of the laws of sympathetic magic in disgust and other domains. *Journal of Personality and Social Psychology*, *50*, 703–712.

4. Rozin, P., Haidt, J., & McCauley, C. R. (2008). Disgust. In *Handbook of emotions*, 3rd ed., edited by M. Lewis, J. M. Haviland-Jones, & L. F. Barrett. New York: Guildford Press, pp. 757–776. Quote is on p. 761.

5. Martha Nussbaum, a legal scholar who has largely relied on the R-H model in her own treatment of law and disgust, has conceded that "the animal reminder view is too crude to account for the cases: some properties of animals, such as strength and speed, do not inspire disgust. I conclude that it is not just animality, but something about the *vulnerability to decay and dissolution* that is the lot of animal bodies, which inspires disgust." (emphasis added; see http://emotionresearcher.com/on-anger-disgust-love/)

    Though we applaud this step toward a theoretically coherent explanation, it still falls short. *All* animals, regardless of whether they are currently exhibiting signs of disease, are vulnerable to disease and death; this explanation still can't account for why disgust is triggered to a greater extent by particular animals and why we do not exhibit disgust toward every single animal all of the time given their mere vulnerability to disease and death. Rather than attempting to embalm the notion of animal-reminder disgust, it is time to let it completely decompose.

6. Rozin, P., Millman, L., & Nemeroff, C. (1986). Operation of the laws of sympathetic magic in disgust and other domains. *Journal of Personality and Social Psychology*, *50*, 703–712. Laws of sympathetic magic are detailed by Tylor (1871/1974). *Primitive Culture: Researches into the Development of Mythology, Philosophy, Religion, Art and Custom*. New York: Gordon Press; Mauss, M. (1902/1972). *A General Theory of Magic*., trans. R. Brain. New York: W. W. Norton; Frazer, J. G. (1890/1959). *The New Golden Bough: A Study in Magic and Religion*, abridged ed., edited by T. H. Gaster. New York: Macmillan.

7. Haidt, J., McCauley, C., & Rozin, P. (1994). Individual differences in sensitivity to disgust: a scale sampling seven domains of disgust elicitors. *Personality and Individual Differences*, *16*, 701–713. Quote is on p. 702.

CHAPTER 8

1. There is a vast literature on this topic. Here are a few articles and books that have been influential in our thinking: Haidt, J. (2007). The new synthesis in moral psychology. *Science*, *316*, 998–1002; Haidt, J. (2001). The emotional dog and its rational tail: a social intuitionist approach to moral judgment. *Psychological Review*, *108*, 814–834; Hauser, M. (2006). *Moral Minds: How Nature Designed our Universal Sense of Right and Wrong*. New York: HarperCollins; de Waal, F. (1996). *Good Natured: The Origins of Right and Wrong in Humans and Other Animals*. Cambridge, MA: Harvard University Press; de Waal, F. (2006). *Primates and Philosophers: How Morality Evolved*. Princeton, NJ: Princeton University Press; Wilson, J. Q. (1993). *The Moral Sense*. New York: Free Press; Wright, R. (1995). *The Moral Animal: Why We Are the Way We Are*. New York: Vintage Books; Boehm, C. (2012). *Moral Origins: The Evolution of Virtue, Altruism, and Shame*. New York: Basic Books; Alexander, R. D. (1987). *The Biology of Moral Systems*. Berlin: Walter de Gruyter.

2. A new wave of research has shown that many social emotions rely on estimates of social value, also referred to as a *welfare trade-off regulatory variable*. Robertson,

T. E., Delton, A. W., Klein, S. B., Cosmides, L., & Tooby, J. (2014). Keeping the benefits of group cooperation: domain-specific responses to distinct causes of social exclusion. *Evolution and Human Behavior, 35,* 472–480; Sell, A., Tooby, J., & Cosmides, L. (2009). Formidability and the logic of human anger. *Proceedings of the National Academy of Sciences USA, 106,* 15073–15078; Tooby, J., Cosmides, L., Sell, A., Lieberman, D., & Sznycer, D. (2008). Internal regulatory variables and the design of human motivation: a computational and evolutionary approach. In *Handbook of Approach and Avoidance Motivation,* edited by A. J. Elliot. Mahwah, NJ: Lawrence Erlbaum Associates, pp. 251–271; Smith, A., Pedersen, E. J., Forster, D. E., McCullough, M. E., & Lieberman, D. (2017). Cooperation: the roles of interpersonal value and gratitude. *Evolution and Human Behavior, 38,* 695–703; Sznycer, D., et al. (2017). Cross-cultural regularities in the cognitive architecture of pride. *Proceedings of the National Academy of Sciences USA, 114,* 1874–1879; Sznycer, D., Tooby, J., Cosmides, L., Porat, R., Shalvi, S., & Halperin, E. (2016). Shame closely tracks the threat of devaluation by others, even across cultures. *Proceedings of the National Academy of Sciences USA, 113,* 2625–2630.

3. Sznycer, D., De Smet, D., Billingsley, J., & Lieberman, D. (2016). Co-residence duration and cues of maternal investment regulate sibling altruism across cultures. *Journal of Personality and Social Psychology, 111,* 159–177; Dugatkin, L. A. (2002). Cooperation in animals: an evolutionary overview. *Biology and Philosophy, 17,* 459–476; Rachlin, H., & Jones, B. A. (2008). Altruism among relatives and nonrelatives. *Behavioral Processes, 79,* 120–123.

4. Tooby, J., & Cosmides, L. (1996). Friendship and the banker's paradox: other pathways to the evolution of adaptations for altruism. In *Evolution of Social Behaviour Patterns in Primates and Man,* edited by W. G. Runciman, J. Maynard Smith, & R. I. M. Dunbar. *Proceedings of the British Academy, 88,* 119–143.

5. Sell, A., Tooby, J., & Cosmides, L. (2009). Formidability and the logic of human anger. *Proceedings of the National Academy of Sciences USA, 106,* 15073–15078.

6. Sell, A., Sznycer, D., Cosmides, L., Tooby, J., Krauss, A., Nisu, S., Ceapa, C., & Petersen, M. B. (2017). Physically strong men are more militant: a test across four countries. *Evolution and Human Behavior, 38*(3), 334–340.

7. Sznycer, D., Tooby, J., Cosmides, L., Porat, R., Shalvi, S., & Halperin, E. (2016). Shame closely tracks the threat of devaluation by others, even across cultures. *Proceedings of the National Academy of Sciences USA, 113,* 2625–2630; Smith, A., Pedersen, E. J., Forster, D. E., McCullough, M. E., & Lieberman, D. (2017). Cooperation: the roles of interpersonal value and gratitude. *Evolution and Human Behavior, 38,* 695–703; Sznycer, D., et al. (2017). Cross-cultural regularities in the cognitive architecture of pride. *Proceedings of the National Academy of Sciences USA, 114,* 1874–1879.

8. Krasnow, M. M., Delton, A. W., Cosmides, L., & Tooby, J. (2016). Looking under the hood of third-party punishment reveals design for personal benefit. *Psychological Science, 27,* 1–14; Pedersen, E. J., Kurzban, R., & McCullough, M. E. (2013). Do humans really punish altruistically? A closer look. *Proceedings of the Royal Society B: Biological Sciences, 280,* 20122723.

9. Tooby, J., & Cosmides, L. (2010). Groups in mind: the coalitional roots of war and morality. In *Human Morality & Sociality: Evolutionary & Comparative Perspectives,* edited by Henrik Høgh-Olesen. New York: Palgrave MacMillan, pp. 91–234.

10. *Schadenfreude* is a German term that refers to the pleasure one takes in the misfortunes of others. Though the Germans coined the term, it is a feeling most people

can relate to: if someone reveals they do not value you as highly as you believe they ought to, the resulting lower social value you hold for them might turn a slight harm (a trip or blunder) into a pleasurable experience.

11. As we write, Hollywood is in upheaval over Harvey Weinstein's alleged treatment of employees and actresses. We suspect that his self-assessed leverage modified his perception of how he felt others should value him (and thus what he was entitled to) in various interactions. Not so anymore—leverage comes, leverage goes.

12. Interest in third-party interactions applies in the sexual domain too. The same man who, perhaps by virtue of his perceived leverage and a sense of his own mate value, might make repeated unwanted sexual advances toward a woman will likely find such advances highly objectionable when another man directs them toward his daughter. Of course, context will matter: if the man is perceived to be a high-quality mate for his daughter, then the father might view the daughter's attempts to rebuff the suitor's interest in a negative light. All to say that one's expected social value for each person in a third-party interaction will color how one views the nature and the outcome of various sexual and social interactions. Though we don't go into detail here, research in our own lab shows that people tend to find objectionable the incest that occurs between third parties as a function of the degree of genetic relatedness between the third parties. So for instance, subjects tend to object more strongly to sex between one's biological brother and sister than between one's biological cousins. Antfolk, J., Marcinkowska, U., Lieberman, D., & Santtila, P. (under review). Disgust and egocentric empathy in evaluations of third-party incest.

13. Here are some examples: Fertl, D., & Würsig, B. (1995). Coordinated feeding by Atlantic spotted dolphins (*Stenella frontalis*) in the Gulf of Mexico. *Aquatic Mammals, 21*, 3–5; Manson, J. H., et al. (1991). Intergroup aggression in chimpanzees and humans. *Current Anthropology, 32*, 369–390.

14. Tooby, J., & Cosmides, L. (2010). Groups in mind: the coalitional roots of war and morality. In *Human Morality & Sociality: Evolutionary & Comparative Perspectives*, edited by Henrik Høgh-Olesen. New York: Palgrave MacMillan, pp. 91–234.

15. Kummer, H. (1971). *Primate Societies: Group Techniques of Ecological Adaptation*. Chicago, IL: Aldine; Aureli, F., et al. (2008). Fission-fusion dynamics. *Current Anthropology, 49*, 627–654.

16. Manson, J. H., et al. (1991). Intergroup aggression in chimpanzees and humans. *Current Anthropology, 32*, 369–390.

17. Wrangham, R. W., & Peterson, D. (1996). *Demonic Males: Apes and the Origins of Human Violence*. Boston, MA: Houghton Mifflin; Wrangham, R. W. (1999). Evolution of coalitional killing. *Yearbook of Physical Anthropology, 42*, 1–30.

18. Goodall, J. (1986). *The Chimpanzees of Gombe: Patterns of Behavior*. Cambridge, MA: Belknap Press.

19. Wilson, M. L., Hauser, M. D., & Wrangham, R. W. (2001). Does participation in intergroup conflict depend on numerical assessment, range location, or rank for wild chimpanzees? *Animal Behaviour, 61*, 1203–1216.

20. Wrangham, R. W. (1999). Evolution of coalitional killing. *Yearbook of Physical Anthropology, 42*, 1–30. See pp. 11–12.

21. This position is not new; philosopher Kim Sterelny, in a critique of Phillip Kitcher's *The Ethical Project*, stated that "normative thought and normative institutions have

been more prominent as tools of exploitation and oppression than as mechanisms of a social peace that balances individual desire with collective co-operation." Sterelny, K. (2012). Morality's dark past. *Analyse & Kritik, 01*, 95–115.

22. See article here: http://www.npr.org/sections/goatsandsoda/2015/07/08/419569772/indian-governor-to-schoolkids-no-eggs-for-you. Critically, however, not *all* minority groups are necessarily targets of exploitation. Take the Amish: Why don't we find overt or implicit national moral campaigns against them? One possibility is that they publicly subscribe to a way of life that emphasizes their *lack of competition* over valued resources. They champion a lifestyle that is off the grid. They don't consume (much) oil, they educate their own, and they marry their own. Plus, they are possibly a net positive for the local majority—they bring in tourists and grow food for trade (though perhaps not all Pennsylvania residents perceive their Amish neighbors in such a positive light—we live in Florida and so are unaware of issues that might exist in Pennsylvania). There is nothing objectively protective about being Amish, though. Perceptions of the majority can shift and view any currently "positive-externality" group as potentially foreboding resource removers. Should this occur, moral sentiments and legal proscriptions too could change (e.g., one could imagine proposed laws against multigenerational housing, the use of horse-drawn carriages on state roads, and requirements to be "on the grid"). If we're right, a sad downstream consequence is that, in a world of shifting social and economic dynamics, no group is safe in the long run, and current majorities would do well to realize this fact.

23. This is a "keep your friends close and get rid of resource competitors" mentality. Though most of us are familiar with the common saying "keep your friends close and your enemies closer," we suspect this saying captures the same mentality— keep your enemies close *until you have the leverage to remove them*!

24. DeScioli, P., & Kurzban, R. (2013). A solution to the mysteries of morality. *Psychological Bulletin, 139*, 477–496; Tybur, J. M., Lieberman, D., Kurzban, R., & DeScioli, P. (2013). Disgust: evolved function and structure. *Psychological Review, 120*, 65–84.

25. Turner, J. C., Brown, R. J., & Tajfel, H. (1979). Social comparison and group interest in ingroup favouritism. *European Journal of Social Psychology, 9*, 187–204; Diehl, M. (1990). The minimal group paradigm: theoretical explanations and empirical findings. *European Review of Social Psychology, 1*, 263–292; Brewer, M. B. (1999). The psychology of prejudice: ingroup love or outgroup hate? *Journal of Social Issues, 55*, 429–444; Gaertner, L., & Insko, C. A. (2000). Intergroup discrimination in the minimal group paradigm: categorization, reciprocation, or fear? *Journal of Personality and Social Psychology, 79*, 77–94.

26. On August 12, 2017, there was a violent demonstration at the University of Virginia in Charlottesville. Though many were shocked to see David Duke and white nationalists out in force, they've always been there—lurking beneath the surface until favorable political conditions provide cover for further growth. As elections and political movements worldwide are now revealing, those "favorable" conditions seem to be on the rise (again), suggesting an increased frequency of future outbreaks.

27. http://www.pewresearch.org/fact-tank/2016/03/31/10-demographic-trends-that-are-shaping-the-u-s-and-the-world/

28. http://www.pewresearch.org/fact-tank/2017/04/06/why-muslims-are-the-worlds-fastest-growing-religious-group/

29. Inbar, Y., Pizarro, D. A., & Bloom, P. (2012). Disgusting smells cause decreased liking of gay men. *Emotion, 12*, 23–27.

30. Schnall, S., Haidt, J., Clore, G. L., & Jordan, A. H. (2008). Disgust as embodied moral judgment. *Personality and Social Psychology Bulletin, 34*, 1096–1109.

31. Olatunji, B. O., Puncochar, B. D., & Cox, R. (2016). Effects of experienced disgust on morally-relevant judgments. *PLoS ONE, 11*, e0160357. But, we should note, psychologist Kurt Gray might be correct in stating that harm is an important variable because in a separate study, subjects who put their hands in ice water (a pain-inducing manipulation) reported greater wrongness for moral offenses than did subjects who had their hands in fake vomit; see Schein, C., Ritter, R. S., & Gray, K. (2016). Harm mediates the disgust–immorality link. *Emotion, 16*, 862–876.

32. To read the back-and-forth between the different researchers, see first Landy, J., & Goodwin, G. P. (2015). Does incidental disgust amplify moral judgment? A meta-analytic review of experimental evidence. *Perspectives on Psychological Sciences, 10*, 518–536. Then read Schnall, S., Haidt, J., Clore, G. L., & Jordan, A. H. (2015). Landy and Goodwin (2015) confirmed most of our findings then drew the wrong conclusions. *Perspectives on Psychological Science, 10*, 537–538. And then: Landy, J., & Goodwin, G. P. (2015). Our conclusions were tentative but appropriate: a reply to Schnall et al. (2015). *Perspectives on Psychological Science, 10*, 539–540.

33. Wheatley, T., & Haidt, J. (2005). Hypnotic disgust makes moral judgments more severe. *Psychological Science, 16*, 780–784. But see Olantunji, B. O., & Puncochar, B. D. (2015). Effects of disgust priming and disgust sensitivity on moral judgment. *International Journal of Psychology, 51*, 102–108.

34. Lieberman, D., Tooby, J., & Cosmides, L. (2003). Does morality have a biological basis? An empirical test of the factors governing moral sentiments relating to incest. *Proceedings of the Royal Society B: Biological Sciences, 270*, 819–826.

35. Ekman, P. (1977). Facial expression. In *Nonverbal Behavior and Communication*, edited by A. Siegman & S. Feldstein. Mahway, NJ: Lawrence Erlbaum Associates, pp. 97–116; Sauter, D. A., Eisner, F., Ekman, P., & Scott, S. K. (2010) Cross-cultural recognition of basic emotions through nonverbal emotional vocalizations *Proceedings of the National Academy of Sciences USA, 107*, 2408–2412.

36. Bloom, P. (2004). *Descartes' Baby: How the Science of Child Development Explains What Makes Us Human*. New York: Basic Books; Pizarro, D. A., Detweiler-Bedell, B., & Bloom, P. (2006). The creativity of everyday moral reasoning: empathy, disgust, and moral persuasion. In *Creativity and Reason in Cognitive Development*, edited by J. C. Kaufman & J. Baer. Cambridge, UK: Cambridge University Press, pp. 81–98.

37. Bloom, P. (2004). *Descartes' Baby: How the Science of Child Development Explains What Makes Us Human*. New York: Basic Books, page 173, emphasis in original.

38. See recent articles by Roger Giner-Sorolla and Tom Kupfer, including Kupfer, T., & Giner-Sorolla, R. (2016). Communicating moral motives: the social signaling function of disgust. *Social Psychological and Personality Science, 8*, 632–640.

39. Lieberman, D. L. (2003). Mapping the cognitive architecture of systems for kin detection and inbreeding avoidance: the Westermarck hypothesis and the development of sexual aversions between siblings. University of California, Santa Barbara,

ProQuest Dissertations Publishing. 3103441; see also Fridlund, A. J. (1994). *Human Facial Expression: An Evolutionary View.* San Diego, CA: Academic Press.

40. Danovitch, J., & Bloom, P. (2009). Children's extension of disgust to physical and moral events. *Emotion, 9*, 107–112.

41. Nemeroff, C., & Rozin, P. (1994). The contagion concept in adult thinking in the United States: transmission of germs and of interpersonal influence. *Ethos, 22*, 158–186; Rozin, P., Markwith, M., & McCauley, C. R. (1994). The nature of aversion to indirect contact with other persons: AIDS aversion as a composite of aversion to strangers, infection, moral taint, and misfortune. *Journal of Abnormal Psychology, 103*, 495–504; Rozin, P., Nemeroff, C., Wane, M., & Sherrod, A. (1989). Operation of the sympathetic magical law of contagion in interpersonal attitudes among Americans. *Bulletin of the Psychonomic Society, 27*, 367–370.

42. Kupfer, T., & Giner-Sorolla, R. (working paper). Reputation management explains the apparent contagiousness of immorality. https://psyarxiv.com/rmh5t/download?format=pdf

43. DeScioli, P., & Kurzban, R. (2013). A solution to the mysteries of morality. *Psychological Bulletin, 139*, 477–496.

44. Royzman, E., Kim, K., & Leeman, R. F. (2015). The curious tale of Julie and Mark: unraveling the moral dumbfounding effect. *Judgment and Decision Making, 10*, 296–313; Schein, C., & Gray, K. (2016). Moralization and harmification: the dyadic loop explains how the innocuous becomes harmful and wrong. *Psychological Inquiry, 27*, 62–65.

45. Lieberman, D., & Linke, L. (2007). The effect of social category on third-party punishment. *Evolutionary Psychology, 5*, 291–307.

46. Asch, S. (1956). Studies of independence and conformity: a minority of one against a unanimous majority. *Psychological Monographs, 70*(9, Whole No. 416).

47. Haidt, J., & Kesebir, S. (2010). Morality. In *Handbook of Social Psychology*, 5th ed., edited by S. Fiske, D. Glibert, & G. Lindzey. Hoboken, NJ: Wiley, pp. 797–832.

CHAPTER 9

1. Qin, A. (2015, June 23). Chinese city defends dog meat festival, despite scorn. *New York Times.* Retrieved from https://www.nytimes.com/2015/06/24/world/asia/dog-eaters-in-yulin-china-unbowed-by-global-derision.html?mcubz=3&_r=0; Huang, S. (2016, June 9). China's dog meat festival is again at hand, and opponents are lining up. *New York Times.* Retrieved from https://www.nytimes.com/2016/06/10/world/asia/china-yulin-dog-meat-festival.html?mcubz=3; Qin, A. (2017, May 18). China's dog meat festival may have to cancel the dog, activists say. *New York Times.* Retrieved from https://www.nytimes.com/2017/05/18/world/asia/china-dog-meat-yulin-festival.html?mcubz=3.

2. On the number of dogs eaten in China: Qin, A. (2015, June 23). Chinese city defends dog meat festival, despite scorn. *New York Times.* Retrieved from https://www.nytimes.com/2015/06/24/world/asia/dog-eaters-in-yulin-china-unbowed-by-global-derision.html?mcubz=3&_r=0. On the number of dogs eaten in Vietnam: Rosen, E. (2014, December 30). To eat dog, or not to eat dog. *The Atlantic.* Retrieved from https://www.theatlantic.com/international/archive/2014/12/to-eat-dog-or-not-to-eat-dog/384107/.

3. Kim, R. E. (2007). Dog meat in Korea: a socio-legal challenge. *Animal Law, 14*, 201.

4. Haidt, J., Koller, S. H., & Dias, M. G. (1993). Affect, culture, and morality, or is it wrong to eat your dog? *Journal of Personality and Social Psychology*, 65(4), 613.

5. Though if Chinese immigrants began to advertise and hold their traditional dog festivals here in the United States, we suspect you'd begin to see many moral campaigns—and ultimately laws—proscribing the consumption of dog meat.

6. For example, Danziger, S., Levav, J., & Avnaim-Pesso, L. (2011). Extraneous factors in judicial decisions. *Proceedings of the National Academy of Sciences USA*, 108(17), 6889–6892.

7. Hallock, B. (2014, June 26). California Legislature repeals glove law for food handlers. *Los Angeles Times*. Retrieved from http://www.latimes.com/local/politics/la-me-glove-law-20140627-story.html.

8. Though we suspect this facet plays less of a role in proscriptions against homosexuality. Our larger point is that there are many reasons why people might endorse a particular norm or rule.

9. Douglas, M. (1966). *Purity and Danger: An Analysis of Concepts of Pollution and Taboo*. London: Routledge & Paul; Simons, F. J. (1994). *Eat Not This Flesh: Food Avoidances from Prehistory to the Present*. Madison: University of Wisconsin Press.

10. Begossi, A., Hanazaki, N., & Ramos, R. M. (2004). Food chain and the reasons for fish food taboos among Amazonian and Atlantic Forest fishers (Brazil). *Ecological Applications*, 14(5), 1334–1343.

11. It ends up that many Schedule I narcotics are plant derivatives: heroin is from the poppy plant, LSD is an alkaloid derived from ergot fungus that grows on rye and other grains, marijuana is from the cannabis plant, mescaline is an alkaloid derived from the cactus plant family, and MDMA (Ecstasy) is a compound manufactured using safrole, a phenylpropene compound from the sassafras plant. The connection to make here is that a low value of consumption, triggered by the presence of bitter toxin compounds, is a shared property of these proscribed substances. Far from random, we claim.

12. See, for example, Smith, P. (2002). Drugs, morality and the law. *Journal of Applied Philosophy*, 19(3), 233–244; Rozin, P. (1999). The process of moralization. *Psychological Science*, 10(3), 218–221; Rozin, P., & Singh, L. (1999). The moralization of cigarette smoking in the United States. *Journal of Consumer Psychology*, 8(3), 321–337; Frank, L. E., & Nagel, S. K. (2017). Addiction and moralization: the role of the underlying model of addiction. *Neuroethics*, 10(1), 129–139.

13. Fessler, D. M., & Navarrete, C. D. (2003). Meat is good to taboo: dietary proscriptions as a product of the interaction of psychological mechanisms and social processes. *Journal of Cognition and Culture*, 3(1), 1–40, see p. 10. Also, it is worth noting that in times before refrigeration, milk and meat products would have spoiled faster.

14. On the Matsigenka chicken taboo see Johnson, A., & Baksh, M. (1987). Ecological and structural influences on the proportions of wild foods in the diets of two Machiguenga communities. In *Food and Evolution: Toward a Theory of Human Food Habits*, edited by M. Harris & E. B. Ross. Philadelphia: Temple University Press, pp. 387–405. On the Somali fish taboo see Simoons, F. J. (1994). *Eat Not This Flesh: Food Avoidances from Prehistory to the Present*. Madison: University of Wisconsin Press.

15. Martins, Y., & Pliner, P. (2006). "Ugh! That's disgusting!": Identification of the characteristics of foods underlying rejections based on disgust. *Appetite*, 46(1), 75–85;

Al-Shawaf, L., Lewis, D. M., Alley, T. R., & Buss, D. M. (2015). Mating strategy, disgust, and food neophobia. *Appetite*, *85*, 30–35.

16. Badkhen, A. (2015, July 7). Eat not this fish. *Politico Magazine*. Retrieved from http://www.politico.com/magazine/story/2015/07/food-aid-mali-taboos-119605. html#.Wc5J1GhSyM8.

17. Fessler, D. M., & Navarrete, C. D. (2003). Meat is good to taboo: dietary proscriptions as a product of the interaction of psychological mechanisms and social processes. *Journal of Cognition and Culture*, *3*(1), 1–40, see pp. 18–19.

18. Ibid.

19. Warren, S. D., & Brandeis, L. D. (1890). The right to privacy. *Harvard Law Review*, *4*, 193.

CHAPTER 10

1. See the version of the routine performed in the 1978 HBO documentary *On Location: George Carlin at Phoenix.*

2. Cosgrove-Mather, B. (2004, April 9). FCC: big fine for airing Howard. *CBS News*. Retrieved from https://www.cbsnews.com/news/fcc-big-fine-for-airing-howard/.

3. *Jacobellis v. Ohio*, 378 U.S. 184 (1964), p. 197 (Stewart, J., concurring).

4. *Mishkin v. New York*, 383 U.S. 502 (1966), pp. 516–517 (Black, J., dissenting).

5. *Miller v. California*, 413 U.S. 15 (1973), p. 24.

6. *Roth v. United States*, 354 U.S. 476 (1957). See p. 487, footnote 20, citing the unabridged 1949 second edition of *Webster's New International Dictionary*.

7. Campbell, L. (2015). *The Book of Luke: My Fight for Truth, Justice, and Liberty City*. New York: HarperCollins, p. 156.

8. *Brockett v. Spokane Arcades, Inc.*, 472 U.S. 491, 504–505 (1985).

9. *Miller v. California*, 413 U.S. 15 (1973), p. 24.

10. See for example the Pennsylvania obscenity statute at 18 Pa. Code § 5903 or the Florida obscenity statute at Fla. Stat. § 847.011.

11. You can see the FCC's various definitions on its website: https://www.fcc.gov/consumers/guides/obscene-indecent-and-profane-broadcasts.

12. *Cohen v. California*, 403 U.S. 15 (1971), p. 25.

13. For an example, see Thibodeau, P., Bromberg, C., Hernandez, R., & Wilson, Z. (2014). An exploratory investigation of word aversion. In *Proceedings of the 36th Annual Conference of the Cognitive Science Society*, edited by P. Bello, M. Guarini, M. McShane, & B. Scassellati. Austin, TX: Cognitive Science Society.

14. *Federal Communications Commission v. Pacifica Foundation*, 438 U.S. 726 (1978). See also Carlin, G. (1972). Seven words you can never say on television. On *Class Clown*, Atlantic Records (recorded May 27, 1972).

15. See the version of the routine performed in the 1978 HBO documentary *On Location: George Carlin at Phoenix.*

16. And yet, we venture that "tits" will likely never gain the status as other terms like "breasts," at least not as long as half of the population finds it off-putting. To wit, we probably aren't going to be hearing the exchange, "Kids, we're having chicken tits tonight for dinner!" "Aw, mom, not chicken tits again!"

17. Pinker, S. (2007). *The Stuff of Thought: Language as a Window into Human Nature*. New York: Penguin, p. 344.

18. Ibid. See Chapter 7, "The Seven Words You Can't Say on Television," generally, and see pp. 344–345 for a discussion of the cited research.

19. Remnick, D. (2014, May 5). Putin's four dirty words. *The New Yorker*. Retrieved from https://www.newyorker.com/news/news-desk/putins-four-dirty-words.

20. For a purported list of all the words, see http://www.caravanmagazine.in/vantage/words-censor-board-does-not-want-you-hear.

21. Harbeck, J. (2015, March 6). *Mind Your Language! Swearing Around the World*. Retrieved from http://www.bbc.com/culture/story/20150306-how-to-swear-around-the-world.

22. Fakuade, G., Kemdirim, N., Nnaji, I., & Nwosu, F. (2013). Linguistic taboos in the Igbo society: a sociolinguistic investigation. *Language Discourse & Society*, *2*(2), 117–133.

23. Consider that in many parts of America, saying out in public "praise God" is likely met with a different reaction than saying "Allahu Akbar."

24. *Pell v. The Council of Trustees of National Gallery of Victoria*, 2 VR 391, 391 (1998); Young, A. (2000). Aesthetic vertigo and the jurisprudence of disgust. *Law and Critique*, *11*(3), 241–265.

25. Kinsley, J. M. (2015). The myth of obsolete obscenity. *Cardozo Arts & Entertainment Law Journal*, *33*, 607.

26. *Brown, et al. v. Entertainment Merchants Assn. et al.*, 564 U.S. 786 (2011), p. 798.

27. Here's one thought, though. Perhaps one reason why violence has not received as much attention as disgust harkens back to the differences between disgust and anger mentioned in the previous chapter. Anger, because it is an emotion that serves to benefit the individual displaying the anger, might not be able to operate under cover in the same way disgust can. To the extent that anger is both (a) involved in our reactions to violence, and (b) obvious, then it's more easily identified as a root for censorship and dismissed as an inappropriate basis. Disgust, on the other hand, is often working behind the scenes, popping up into consciousness only as a sensation of offense or moral wrong. To the extent the root of that moral intuition is harder to spot, perhaps it's being given more deference by lawmakers and others in charge of policy.

28. *Manual Enterprises, Inc. v. Day*, 370 U.S. 478 (1962). See p. 484, footnote 4, citing the 1956 unabridged second edition of *Webster's New International Dictionary*.

29. *Miller v. California*, 413 U.S. 15 (1973). See p. 20, footnote 2, citing the 1969 unabridged *Webster's Third New International Dictionary* and the 1933 edition of the *Oxford English Dictionary*.

30. *United States v. Guglielmi*, 819 F.2d 451 (4th Cir. 1987), p. 455.

31. *United States v. Ginzburg*, 224 F. Supp. 129 (E.D. Pa. 1963), p. 136.

32. *Miller v. California*, 413 U.S. 15 (1973), p. 18.

33. *Salt Lake City v. Piepenburg*, 571 P.2d 1299 (Utah 1977), pp. 1299–1300. Note the condemnation.

34. *Commonwealth v. Robin*, 421 Pa. 70 (1966), pp. 73–74, 83 (Musmanno, J., dissenting).

35. *Jacobellis v. Ohio*, 378 US 184 (1964), p. 197 (Stewart, J., concurring).

CHAPTER 11

1. Hemingway, E. (2010). *A Moveable Feast*. New York: Scribner (original work published in 1964), pp. 88–89.

2. Nabokov, V. (2002). *Lectures on Literature*. New York: Mariner Books, p. 376.

3. Shakespeare, W. (1999). *King Richard III*, edited by J. Hull. Cambridge, UK: Cambridge University Press (original work published in 1597), pp. 64, 82, and 63, respectively.

4. Rowling, J. K. (2000). *Harry Potter and the Goblet of Fire*. New York: Scholastic, p. 697.

5. Dickens, C. (1841). *The Old Curiosity Shop and Other Tales*. Philadelphia: Lea and Blanchard, p. 65.

6. Dickens, C. (2003). *Oliver Twist*. New York: Barnes & Noble Classics (original work published in 1838), p. 93.

7. Dickens, C. (2004). *David Copperfield*. Mineola, NY: Dover (original work published in 1850), p. 181.

8. Dickens, C. (2010). *Great Expectations*. Mineola, NY: Dover (original work published in 1861), p. 44.

9. Dickens, C. (2003). *Oliver Twist*. New York: Barnes & Noble Classics (original work published in 1838), p. 184.

10. Nabokov, V. (1997). *Lolita* (2nd international vintage ed.). New York: Random House, p. 240.

11. Sinclair, U. (1906). *The Jungle*. New York: Doubleday, Page & Company, p. 161.

12. Volokh, E. (2015). Gruesome speech. *Cornell Law Review*, *100*, 901–952.

13. Ibid. All quotes from p. 908.

14. Indeed, unpublished data from when Deb was in grad school and a member of the Tooby and Cosmides lab were used in an antidefamation case in which a man had been accused of child molestation. There, the data showed that child molestation and rape were ranked as most morally wrong out of a list of 19 acts that included consensual incest, assault, murdering a spouse, selling drugs, embezzlement, doing drugs, and speeding on the highway.

15. Restatement (Second) of Torts §572 commentaries (American Law Institute, 1975).

16. *Austin v. White*, Cro. Ellz. 214 (1591), p. 470.

17. *Brook v. Wise*, Cro. Ellz. 878 (1601), p. 1103.

18. *Grimes v. Lovel*, 12 Mod. 242 (1699), p. 1291.

19. *Bloodworth v. Gray*, 7 Man. G. 334 (1844), p. 334.

20. *Joannes v. Burt*, 88 Mass. (6 Allen) 236 (1863), p. 239.

21. *Battles v. Tyson*, 110 N.W. 299 (Neb. 1906), p. 300.

22. Am. Jur. 2d Evidence §331 (1999).

23. Bandes, S. A., & Salerno, J. M. (2014). Emotion, proof and prejudice: the cognitive science of gruesome photos and victim impact statements. *Arizona State Law Journal*, *16*, 1003–1057; see p. 1014.

24. *Archina v. People*, 135 Colo. 8 (1957), p. 32.

25. Ibid., p. 33.

26. Bright, D. A., & Goodman-Delahunty, J. (2006). Gruesome evidence and emotion: anger, blame, and jury decision-making. *Law and Human Behavior*, *30*(2), 183; Douglas, K. S., Lyon, D. R., & Ogloff, J. R. (1997). The impact of graphic photographic evidence on mock jurors' decisions in a murder trial: probative or prejudicial? *Law and Human Behavior*, *21*(5), 485.

27. Salerno, J. M., & Peter-Hagene, L. C. (2013). The interactive effect of anger and disgust on moral outrage and judgments. *Psychological Science*, *24*(1), 2069–2078; see p. 2074.

28. Douglas, K. S., Lyon, D. R., & Ogloff, J. R. (1997). The impact of graphic photo-graphic evidence on mock jurors' decisions in a murder trial: probative or prejudi-cial? *Law and Human Behavior*, *21*(5), 485.

29. See for example Bright, D. A., & Goodman-Delahunty, J. (2004). The influence of gruesome verbal evidence on mock juror verdicts. *Psychiatry, Psychology, and Law*, *11*(1), 154–166.

30. See for example Whalen, D. H., & Blanchard, F. A. (1982). Effects of photo-graphic evidence on mock juror judgement. *Journal of Applied Social Psychology*, *12*(1), 30–41.

31. Duncan, M. G. (1993). In slime and darkness: the metaphor of filth in criminal justice. *Tulane Law Review*, *68*, 725–802; see p. 763, citing Bentham, J. (1962). Panopticon Versus New South Wales. In *The Works of Jeremy Bentham*, edited by J. Bowring. New York: Russell & Russell, p. 176.

32. Ibid., p. 730 (Duncan's citations omitted).

33. *Village of Euclid v. Ambler Realty Co.*, 272 U.S. 365 (1926).

34. Duncan, M. G. (1993). In slime and darkness: the metaphor of filth in criminal justice. *Tulane Law Review*, *68*, 725–802; see p. 792 (Duncan's citations omitted).

35. Vasquez, E. A., Loughnan, S., Gootjes-Dreesbach, E., & Weger, U. (2014). The an-imal in you: animalistic descriptions of a violent crime increase punishment of perpetrator. *Aggressive Behavior*, *40*(4), 337–344; see p. 343.

36. *Edwards v. California*, 314 U.S. 160 (1941), p. 167.

37. *People v. Bell*, 125 N.Y.S.2d 117 (1953), p. 119.

38. Nussbaum, M. C. (2003). *Upheavals of Thought: The Intelligence of Emotions*. New York: Cambridge University Press, p. 347.

39. Myers, P. Z. (2013). *The Happy Atheist*. New York: Pantheon, p. 84.

40. Tirrell, L. (2012). Genocidal language games. In *Speech and Harm: Controversies over Free Speech*, edited by I. Maitra & M. K. McGowan New York: Oxford University Press, pp. 174–221 (see p. 176).

41. Goebbels, J. (producer), & Hippler, F. (director). (1940). *Der Ewige Jude* [motion picture]. Germany: Deutsche Film Gesellschaft.

42. Hitler, A. (1969). *Mein Kampf*. London: Hutchinson (original work published in 1925), p. 53.

43. Phillips, C. E. (1966). Miscegenation: the courts and the Constitution. *William & Mary Law Review*, *8*(1), 133–142; see p. 133 (citing 1 Laws of Virginia 146 [Hening 1823]).

44. *Scott v. State*, 39 Ga. 321 (1869), p. 323.

45. 8 U.S.C. § 1182.

46. The "invasive species" quote can be found at Limbaugh, R. (host). (2005, April 1). *The Rush Limbaugh Show* [radio program]. Sherman Oaks, CA: Premiere Networks. The "catching diseases" language can be found at Limbaugh, R. (host). (2011, January 31). *The Rush Limbaugh Show* [radio program]. Sherman Oaks, CA: Premiere Networks.

47. Faulkner, J., Schaller, M., Park, J. H., & Duncan, L. A. (2004). Evolved disease-avoidance mechanisms and contemporary xenophobic attitudes. *Group Processes & Intergroup Relations*, *7*(4), 333–353.

48. Navarrete, C. D., & Fessler, D. M. (2006). Disease avoidance and ethnocen-trism: the effects of disease vulnerability and disgust sensitivity on intergroup atti-tudes. *Evolution and Human Behavior*, *27*(4), 270–282.

49. Hodson, G., & Costello, K. (2007). Interpersonal disgust, ideological orientations, and dehumanization as predictors of intergroup attitudes. *Psychological Science*, *18*(8), 691–698.

50. Brenner, C. J., & Inbar, Y. (2014). Disgust sensitivity predicts political ideology and policy attitudes in the Netherlands. *European Journal of Social Psychology*, *45*(1), 27–38.

CHAPTER 12

1. Code of Hammurabi, Law 154, translated by L.W. King. Retrieved from the Avalon Project maintained by the Yale Law School's Lillian Goldman Law Library and accessible at http://avalon.law.yale.edu/ancient/hamframe.asp

2. Ibid., Law 157.

3. Sassoon, J. (2005). *Ancient Laws and Modern Problems: The Balance Between Justice and a Legal System*. Chicago: Intellect Ltd; Bryce, T. (2004). *Life and Society in the Hittite World*. Oxford: Oxford University Press.

4. See Laws 187, 188, 199, and 200, respectively. Roth, M. T., Hoffner, H. A., & Michalowski, P. (1995). *Law Collections from Mesopotamia and Asia Minor* (Vol. 6). Williston, VT: Society of Biblical Literature, pp. 236–237.

5. The Code of the Assura, I.20, translated by J. S. Arkenberg. Retrieved from the Internet Ancient History Sourcebook maintained by Fordham University and accessible at https://sourcebooks.fordham.edu/ancient/1075assyriancode.asp.

6. Bailey, D. S. (1975). *Homosexuality and the Western Christian Tradition*. Hamden, CT: Archon/Shoestring (original work published in 1955), pp. 64–70.

7. Brundage, J. A. (1987). *Law, Sex, and Christian Society in Medieval Europe*. Chicago: University of Chicago Press; McNeill, J. T., & Gamer, H. M. (Trans.) (1990). *Medieval Handbooks of Penance*. New York: Columbia University Press, pp. 179–215.

8. "The Penitential of Theodore." In McNeill, J. T., & Gamer, H. M. (Trans.) (1990). *Medieval Handbooks of Penance*. New York, Columbia University Press, p. 186.

9. Berkowitz, E. (2013). *Sex and Punishment: Four Thousand Years of Judging Desire*. Berkeley: Counterpoint; Bailey, D. S. (1975). *Homosexuality and the Western Christian Tradition* (original work published 1955). Hamden, CT: Archon/Shoestring.

10. An Act for the Punishment of the Vice of Buggery. 25 Henry VIII, Ch. 6 (1533–1534). In *Same-Sex Desire in the English Renaissance: A Sourcebook of Texts, 1470–1650*, edited by K. Borris. New York: Routledge, 2015; p. 82; Hyde, H. M. (1970). *The Love That Dared Not Speak Its Name: A Candid History of Homosexuality in Britain*. Boston: Little, Brown & Company.

11. Johnson, W. (1979). *The T'ang Code Volume I, General Principles*. Princeton, NJ: Princeton University Press, p. 17.

12. Bühler, G. (Ed.). (1886). *The Laws of Manu* (Vol. 25). Oxford: Clarendon Press, p. 69.

13. Ibid., pp. 318, 338, and 363.

14. Murrin, J. (1998) "Things Fearful to Name": Bestiality in Early America. *Pennsylvania History: A Journal of Mid-Atlantic Studies*, *65*, 8–43; see pp. 21–22.

15. Ibid., p. 25.

16. Shostak, M. (2000). *Nisa: The Life and Words of a !Kung Woman* (4th ed.). Cambridge, MA: Harvard University Press.

17. Berkowitz, E. (2013). *Sex and Punishment: Four Thousand Years of Judging Desire.* Berkeley: Counterpoint, p. 18.

18. Berkowitz, E. (2013). *Sex and Punishment: Four Thousand Years of Judging Desire.* Berkeley: Counterpoint, pp. 295 and 378.

19. Carroll, A. (2016, May). State-Sponsored Homophobia 2016: A World Survey of Sexual Orientation Laws: Criminalization, Protection and Recognition. International Lesbian, Gay, Bisexual, Trans and Intersex Association. Retrieved from http://ilga.org/downloads/02_ILGA_State_Sponsored_Homophobia_2016_ENG_WEB_150516.pdf; Bearak, M., & Cameron, D. (2016, June 16). Here are the 10 countries where homosexuality may be punished by death. *Washington Post.* Retrieved from https://www.washingtonpost.com/news/worldviews/wp/2016/06/13/here-are-the-10-countries-where-homosexuality-may-be-punished-by-death-2/?utm_term=.069c8ce66936.

20. Ochoa, T. T., & Jones, C. (1997). Defiling the dead: necrophilia and the law. *Whittier Law Review, 18,* 539–578; Troyer, J. (2008). Abuse of a corpse: a brief history and re-theorization of necrophilia laws in the USA. *Mortality, 13*(2), 132–152.

21. Kelly, R. L. (2013). *The Lifeways of Hunter-Gatherers: The Foraging Spectrum.* New York: Cambridge University Press; see chart on p. 194.

22. Waites, M. (2005). *The Age of Consent: Young People, Sexuality and Citizenship.* New York: Palgrave MacMillan.

23. Odem, M. E. (2000). *Delinquent Daughters: Protecting and Policing Adolescent Female Sexuality in the United States, 1885–1920.* Chapel Hill: University of North Carolina Press.

24. This is, at least, the most common purported justification. There are plenty of other reasons why people (especially men) might push back the age of consent, including a desire to keep children (especially girls) chaste until they reach the legal age of marriage. For purposes of our comparison, we'll stick with the purported justification for the age limits, which is whether they are old enough to voluntarily consent.

25. Note that this percentage may be skewed by the fact that many states prohibit sex with very young girls under separate statutes. You'll also notice that we're discussing this relationship as if men are always the adult and females always the underage participants; they aren't, of course, but they are *most* of the time—several studies indicate that upwards of 95 percent of all statutory-rape cases involve female victims with male offenders. See, for example, Snyder, H. N. S., & Troup-Leasure, K. (2005, August). Statutory rape known to law enforcement. *Juvenile Justice Bulletin.* U.S. Department of Justice, Office of Juvenile Justice and Delinquency Prevention. Retrieved from https://www.ncjrs.gov/pdffiles1/ojjdp/208803.pdf; Hines, D. A., & Finkelhor, D. (2007). Statutory sex crime relationships between juveniles and adults: a review of social scientific research. *Aggression and Violent Behavior, 12*(3), 300–314.

26. Texas Penal Code, §§ 21.02 et seq.

27. Haynes, A. M. (2014). The bestiality proscription: in search of a rationale. *Animal Law Review, 21,* 121.

28. Krishnaswamy, S., Subramaniam, K., Ramachandran, P., Indran, T., & Aziz, J. A. (2011). Delayed fathering and risk of mental disorders in adult offspring. *Early Human Development, 87*(3), 171–175.

29. Some have also suggested that children born of incest would have difficult social lives due to abnormal family structures. We are not saying that this is not a concern, but if it is, then why not extend this logic to prevent, for instance, drug users and alcoholics from marrying and having children? Children raised in households plagued by drugs and alcohol and other forms of abuse experience abnormal and unhealthy rearing environments. The fact that a child born of incest might have a more nuanced experience around the Thanksgiving dinner table could pale in comparison to other hazardous home environments.

30. *Locke v. State*, 501 S.W.2d. 826 (Tenn. Ct. App. 1973), p. 829 (Galbreath, J., dissenting).

31. And perhaps indicates his eagerness to strongly signal that he is of the morally correct (normal) camp. Judges, too, come equipped with the various psychological mechanisms we've been outlining, and it would be naïve to assume that they are immune to their effects.

32. *Israel v. Allen*, 577 P.2d 762 (Colo. 1978), p. 764.

33. See for example *Boyington v. State*, 45 Ala. App. 176 (1969); *Horn v. State*, 49 Ala. App. 489 (1973); *State v. McAllister*, 67 Or. 480 (1913).

34. *Bowers v. Hardwick*, 478 U.S. 186 (1986). For quotes in this paragraph, see pp. 188, 192, and 192, respectively.

35. Ibid., p. 196.

36. Ibid., p. 197 (Burger, J., concurring).

37. *Lawrence v. Texas*, 539 U.S. 558 (2003), pp. 560 and 572, respectively.

38. Ibid., pp. 588 and 599, respectively (Scalia, J., dissenting).

39. *United States v. Windsor*, 133 S.Ct. 2675 (2013).

40. *Obergefell v. Hodges*, 135 S. Ct. 2584 (2015).

41. To be fair, a few dissenting justices briefly discuss the interest of states in encouraging natural procreation within the unit that provides the best atmosphere for raising children (i.e., traditional marriage). And regardless of whether this is a strong policy argument, it is, at least, a policy argument.

42. Fischer, B. (host). (2014, August 21). *Focal Point* [radio program]. Tupelo, MS: American Family Radio.

43. Bryant, A. (1977) *The Anita Bryant Story: The Survival of Our Nation's Families and the Threat of Militant Homosexuality*. Ada, MI: Revell, p. 27.

44. Bever, L. (2016, June 15). Pastor refuses to mourn Orlando victims: "the tragedy is that more of them didn't die." *Washington Post*. Retrieved from https://www.washingtonpost.com/news/acts-of-faith/wp/2016/06/14/pastor-refuses-to-mourn-orlando-victims-the-tragedy-is-that-more-of-them-didnt-die/?utm_term=.12db3a1c8df5.

45. *State v. Start*, 65 Or. 178 (1913), p. 180.

46. *Bowers v. Hardwick*, 478 U.S. 186 (1986), p. 197 (Burger, J., concurring).

CHAPTER 13

1. Kass, L. R. (1997, June 2). The wisdom of repugnance. *The New Republic*, pp. 17–26.

2. Miller, W. I. (1997). *The Anatomy of Disgust*. Cambridge, MA: Harvard University Press, p. 202.

3. Kahan, D. M. (1998). The anatomy of disgust in criminal law (review of *The Anatomy of Disgust* by W. I. Miller). *Michigan Law Review, 96*, 1621.

4. Nussbaum, M. C. (1997, November 17). Foul play (review of *The Anatomy of Disgust* by W. I. Miller). *The New Republic*, 32–28; see p. 36.

5. Banishing disgust might not make the law blind, just anosmic. For Kahan's quotes, see Kahan, D. M. (1999). The progressive appropriation of disgust. In *The Passions of Law* (pp. 63–79), edited by S. A. Bandes. New York: New York University Press, pp. 63–79; see pp. 63 and 65 respectively.

6. Nussbaum, M. C. (1999). Secret sewers of vice. In *The Passions of Law*, edited by S. A. Bandes. New York: New York University Press, pp. 17–62; see p. 22.

7. Curtis, V. (2013) *Don't Look, Don't Touch: The Science Behind Revulsion*. Oxford, UK: Oxford University Press, p. 117.

8. Kelly, D., & Morar, N. (2014). Against the yuck factor: on the ideal role of disgust in society. *Utilitas, 26*(2), 153–177; see p. 153.

9. Hume, D. (1739). *A Treatise of Human Nature*. London: John Noon, p. 335.

10. *Lawrence v. Texas*, 539 U.S. 558 (2003), pp. 559, 571.

11. Robinson, P. H. (2013). *Intuitions of Justice and the Utility of Desert*. New York: Oxford University Press, p. 533.

12. Kelly, D., & Morar, N. (2014). Against the yuck factor: on the ideal role of disgust in society. *Utilitas, 26*(2), 153–177; see p. 174.

13. But courting also serves female interests to help ensure that a male is serious about investing, a proposition that may or may not end up being true, of course.

14. To make good on a promise made in the first chapter, this is why coming into contact with a lover's saliva while kissing them is acceptable, but why having them spit in your mouth seems repulsive. As a default rule, spit is a reliable vehicle of pathogens to be avoided. This default rule is simply downregulated in the face of a potential mate because a competing goal (mating) happens to carry potential benefits that merit the violation of the default rule (unless, of course, further evidence of pathogens is detected). This same type of default-rule suspension takes place in the caring of infants and the cleaning of their various bodily effluvia.

15. Chagnon, N. A. (2013). *Yanomamö* (Legacy 6th ed.). Belmont, CA: Wadsworth, p. 15.

16. And, of course, this is what clinical scientists are trying to do when treating conditions such as obsessive-compulsive disorder.

17. Marcus, G. (2009). *Kludge: The Haphazard Evolution of the Human Mind*. New York: Mariner; Olshansky, S. J., Carnes, B. A., & Butler, R. N. (2001). If humans were built to last. *Scientific American, 284*(3), 50–55.

18. Chapman, H. A., Kim, D. A., Susskind, J. M., & Anderson, A. K. (2009). In bad taste: evidence for the oral origins of moral disgust. *Science, 323*, 1222–1226; Eskine, K. J., Kacinik, N. A., & Prinz, J. J. (2011). A bad taste in the mouth: gustatory disgust influences moral judgment. *Psychological Science, 22*(3), 295–299; Cannon, P. R., Schnall, S., & White, M. (2011). Transgressions and expressions: affective facial muscle activity predicts moral judgments. *Journal of Personality and Social Psychology, 2*(3), 325–331.

19. Some recent analyses have called a particular subset of this research—those studies dealing with the "incidental" effect that bad smells or a dirty environment can have on moral judgments—into question. To read the back-and-forth between the different researchers, see first Landy, J., & Goodwin, G. P. (2015). Does incidental

disgust amplify moral judgment? A meta-analytic review of experimental evidence. *Perspectives on Psychological Sciences*, *10*, 518–536. Then Schnall, S., Haidt, J., Clore, G. L., & Jordan, A. H. (2015). Landy and Goodwin (2015) confirmed most of our findings then drew the wrong conclusions. *Perspectives on Psychological Science*, *10*(4), 537–538. And then Landy, J., & Goodwin, G. P. (2015). Our conclusions were tentative but appropriate: a reply to Schnall et al. (2015). *Perspectives on Psychological Science*, *10*, 539–540.

20. Lieberman, D., Tooby, J., & Cosmides, L. (2003). Does morality have a biological basis? An empirical test of the factors governing moral sentiments relating to incest. *Proceedings of the Royal Society B: Biological Sciences*, *270*(1517), 819–826.

21. Van Leeuwen, F., Park, J. H., Koenig, B. L., & Graham, J. (2012). Regional variation in pathogen prevalence predicts endorsement of group-focused moral concerns. *Evolution and Human Behavior*, *33*, 429–437.

22. Dare we say disgust is disgusting?

23. *Baskin v. Bogan*, 766 F. 3d 648 (2014), p. 669. See also Mill, J. S. (2002). *On Liberty*. Mineola, NY: Dover (original work published in 1869).

24. Holmes, Jr., O. W. (1897). The path of the law. *Harvard Law Review*, *10*, 457; see p. 469.

25. Jefferson, T. (1816, July 12). Letter to Samuel Kercheval. *Papers of Thomas Jefferson: Retirement Series*. (10:220–228).

Figures and boxes are indicated by an italic *f* and *b*, respectively, following the page number.